Heath Social Studies

Exploring Indiana

D.C. Heath and Company
Lexington, Massachusetts / Toronto

Program Authors

Senior Author *Clarence L. Ver Steeg,* Professor of History, Northwestern University, Evanston, Illinois; author of numerous history texts and articles

Bert Bower, Director of Teachers' Curriculum Institute and former teacher, Mountain View/Los Altos Union High School District, Mountain View, California

Charles F. Gritzner, Professor of Geography, South Dakota State University, Brookings, South Dakota; former Executive Director and President, National Council for Geographic Education

Evangeline Nicholas, Coordinator, Early Childhood Program, Chicago Public Schools

Jeff Passe, Assistant Professor of Education, University of North Carolina, Charlotte, North Carolina

Carol Ann Skinner, Author/consultant, Evanston, Illinois

Program Reviewers

Nancy Allen, Teacher, De Land Middle, De Land, Florida

Sharon J. Brady, Teacher, Country Primary, Weston Public Schools, Weston, Massachusetts

Sister Mary Dawson, I.H.M., Director of Curriculum and Instruction, Rockville Center Diocese, Rockville Center, New York

June B. Edwards, Social Studies Teacher, gifted students, J.G. Henig Elementary, Chesterfield County School District, Richmond, Virginia

Verona Grady, Teacher, Kings Highway Elementary, Coatesville, Pennsylvania

Carol Jones, Teacher, Lavaland Elementary, Albuquerque, New Mexico

Michael McSweeney, Social Studies Liaison Teacher, Federal Way School District, Federal Way, Washington

Mel Miller, Social Studies Consultant, Macomb Intermediate School District, Mount Clemens, Michigan

Anna Muriel Pitts, Teacher, Harper Elementary, Evansville-Vanderburgh School Corp., Evansville, Indiana

Edith Watt Ruscello, Teacher, Brookhaven Elementary, Morgantown, West Virginia

James Sellers, Principal, Price's Fork Elementary, Blacksburg, Virginia

Blanca Solitaire, Teacher, Clearwater Elementary, Brownsville, Texas

Marlane Tisdale, Teacher, Lakeside Elementary, Metro School District of Warren Township, Indianapolis, Indiana

Sharion W. Vandervort, Teacher, Forest Avenue Academics Magnet Elementary, Montgomery, Alabama

Joan Vanover, Teacher, Garrett Elementary, Augusta, Georgia

Consulting Reviewer

Virginia Mankin Lake, Teacher, gifted/talented specialist, Marion Community Schools, Marion, Indiana

Reading Specialist

Donna E. Alvermann, Professor of Reading Education and Fellow in the Institute for Behavioral Research, University of Georgia, Athens, Georgia

Developmental Specialist

Mark Schug, Professor of Curriculum and Instruction, University of Wisconsin at Milwaukee; Executive Director of Educational Programs of the Wisconsin Economic Education Council

Cover: Background "Flatboats on the Ohio River" from an old print. Photo "Indiana State Capital" by *Ed Kreminski/ Third Coast, Inc.* Cover design by *Ruby Shoes Studio.*

Supervising Editor *Lalia Nuzzolo*
Design Manager *Margaret-Ann Rice*
Series Designer *Pamela Daly*
Senior Production Coordinator *Maureen Bisso LaRiccia*
Editorial Development, Photo Research, and Production *Book Production Systems, Inc.*
Product Manager *Debbie R. Secrist*

Contents

Maps

Graphs, Charts, Diagrams, and Time Lines

Literature and Primary Sources

Social Studies Handbook

Geography Skill Finder

What Are Geography's Basic Tools?

KEY WORDS
geography   (jē äg′rə fē)
globe   (glōb)
map   (map)
legend   (lej′ənd)
symbol   (sim′bəl)
compass rose   (kum′pəs rōz′)
scale   (skāl)

What do you want to do when you grow up? Drive a truck? Buy and sell toys, radios, cars, or other things? Build roads? Raise crops? Plan buildings or whole towns? Teach people in other nations new ways of farming so that they can grow more food? Work for world peace? For all of these jobs and more, you need to know **geography.** Geography is the study of the earth's surface and how people use it.

Studying geography will be a little like traveling to new places. It will also give you a new understanding of the places you know and how they came to be the way they are.

Before you start your study of geography, you need some basic tools. Carpenters need saws and hammers. Cooks need pots and pans. Ball players need bats and gloves. Probably the most important tools for studying geography are **globes** and **maps.**

Globes   A globe is a model, just as a toy airplane is a model. A model airplane shows you where the wings are in relation to the tail. It shows how big the body is compared to the wings. In the same way, a globe shows you where the earth's land and water are. A globe shows what shapes the bodies of land and water have and how far apart they are. By looking at a globe, you can see the direction you need to go to get from one place to another.

Why is a globe the best model of the earth?

Maps Maps also show the earth, but they are not exact models the way globes are. You can see why this is true if you think of a globe as a hollow orange. Imagine trying to flatten your orange. What happens?

The drawing shows what the "skin" of a globe would look like if you could lay it flat. Not much use, is it? So mapmakers have to fill in the spaces to make maps readable. They have found many ways of doing this. Some maps show shapes correctly. Others show the right directions or distances. Still others show the right sizes. Flat maps can show some of these four things, but only a globe correctly shows all four at once.

DIAGRAM/MAP STUDY *When geographers flatten the globe to make a map, which parts of the earth change the most?*

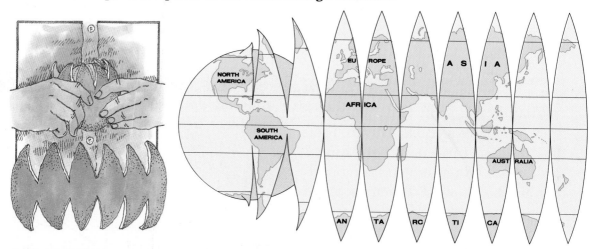

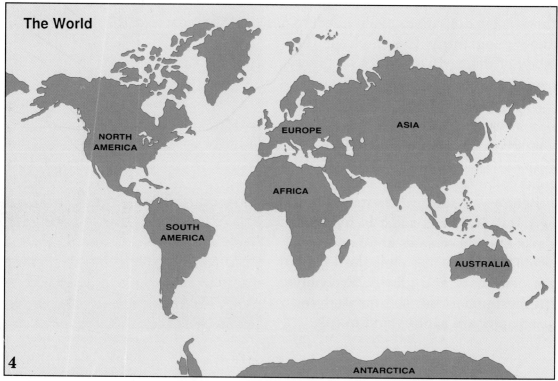

The World

NORTH AMERICA

EUROPE

ASIA

AFRICA

SOUTH AMERICA

AUSTRALIA

ANTARCTICA

4

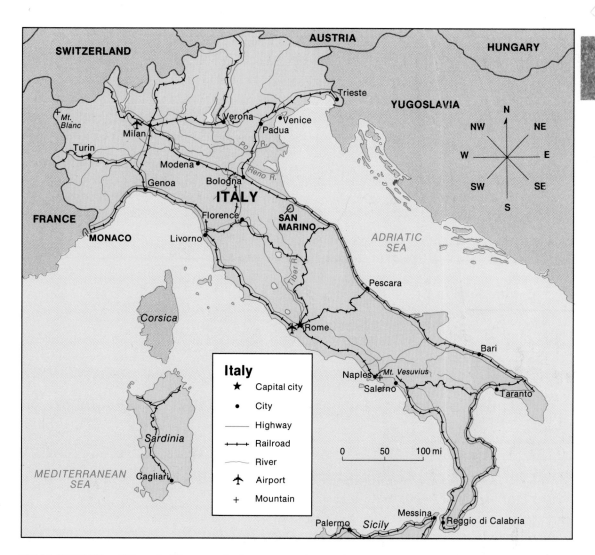

MAP STUDY   *What is the symbol for a highway? In what direction would you travel from Rome to Naples?*

Parts of a Map   In order to read a map, you need to know its basic parts. The first thing to look at is the title. It tells you what part of the earth the map shows. The next part of the map to look at is the key, or **legend.** The legend explains the **symbols** that are used on the map. A symbol is something that stands for a real object or idea. Look at the legend on the map above. What symbol is used for railroad?

Another important part of a map is the **compass rose.** The compass rose shows directions. A compass rose may show only north. Or it may show the four main directions: north, south, east, and west. Some compass roses show northeast, southeast, southwest, and northwest. These are the directions that come in between the main directions. Find the compass rose in the upper right on the map on this page.

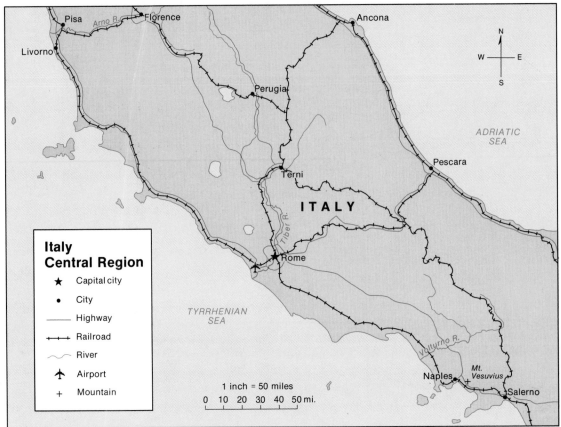

Italy
Central Region

★ Capital city
• City
—— Highway
+—+—+ Railroad
‿‿ River
✈ Airport
+ Mountain

1 inch = 50 miles
0 10 20 30 40 50 mi.

MAP STUDY   *What are two questions that the scale of this map might help you to answer?*

A very important part of a map is the **scale.** The scale shows the relationship between distance on the map and real distance on the earth.

Look at the scale on the map above. It shows that 1 inch stands for 50 miles. Find the distance in inches between Rome and Pescara on the map. It is about 2 inches, so these two places are almost 100 miles apart. Rome and Florence are almost 3 inches apart on the map, so they are about 150 miles apart on the earth. If you want to locate a place by telling someone how far away it is, you can use a map's scale.

Review

Define
geography, globe, map, legend, symbol, compass rose, scale

Comprehension
1. Which is a more exact model of the earth, a map or a globe?
2. What part of a map do you use to find where west is?
3. What part of a map would you use if you wanted to find distances between places?

Where Is It?

KEY WORDS

hemisphere   (hem′ə sfēr)
grid   (grid′)
latitude   (lat′ə tüd)
equator   (i kwāt′ər)
North Pole   (nôrth′pōl′)
South Pole   (south′pōl′)
longitude   (län′jə tüd)
prime meridian
    (prīm′mə rid′ē ən)

Now that you have some basic tools, you are ready to learn more about geography. Geography is a big subject. You can't learn everything there is to know about it all at once. Think of studying geography as eating an apple. When you eat an apple, you eat it one bite at a time. You don't try to put the whole thing in your mouth at once. In much the same way, geographers find it useful to divide their study of the earth by asking five main questions.

The first question geographers ask about a place is "What is its location?" or "Where is it?" People answer this question in many ways. They say, "It's 5 miles from Boston" or "It's between the park and the church" or "It's at 225 Main Street" or "It's north of the firehouse" or "It's on the corner."

Many Locations There are many ways you could tell where your hometown is. First, it is on the planet Earth. Earth is shaped like a ball, or sphere. This sphere can be divided into halves, or **hemispheres.**

The drawings below will provide you with another way of describing where your hometown is. They show two ways of dividing the earth into halves. The earth can be divided into Eastern and Western Hemispheres, as in the left-hand drawing. It can also be divided into Northern and Southern Hemispheres, as in the right-hand drawing. Your town is in the Northern Hemisphere. It is also in the Western Hemisphere. So far your town is in three places! Can you name two more places your town is located? (Hint: What country do you live in? What state?)

MAP STUDY   *Name one place in the Eastern Hemisphere. Name one place in the Northern Hemisphere.*

The Hemispheres

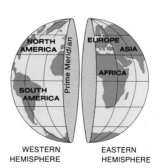

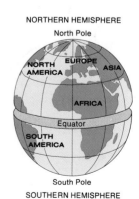

7

Road Maps People sometimes answer the question "Where is it?" by drawing a map. One kind of map used to show location is a road map. If you look at a road map, you will see that it has a **grid.** A grid is a set of lines that cross one another to form squares or boxes. Notice that the grid in the map below is labeled with numbers and letters. Find the letter B and point to it. Next find the number 5 and point to it, using a finger from your other hand. Now move your "B" finger straight across and your "5" finger straight down until your fingers meet. The box in which they meet is called B5.

If you know the box in which a city falls, it is much easier to find the city on the map. Most road maps have an index with the number and letter of the box in which cities and other places are located. On the map below, find the first five cities listed in the index by using the grid numbers and letters.

MAP STUDY *Use the index and the grid numbers and letters to locate Fort Smith and Texarkana.*

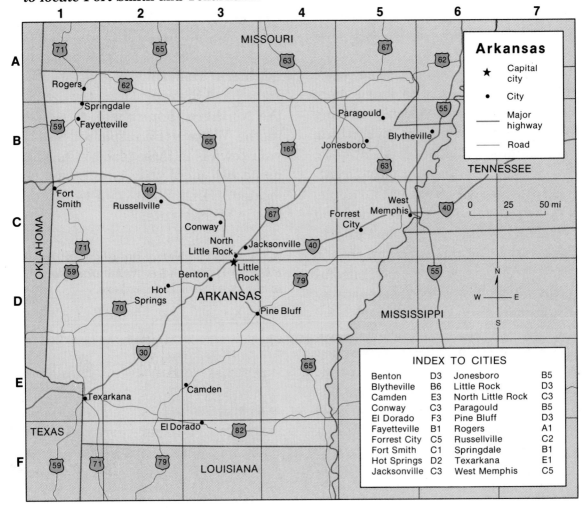

INDEX TO CITIES

City	Grid	City	Grid
Benton	D3	Jonesboro	B5
Blytheville	B6	Little Rock	D3
Camden	E3	North Little Rock	C3
Conway	C3	Paragould	B5
El Dorado	F3	Pine Bluff	D3
Fayetteville	B1	Rogers	A1
Forrest City	C5	Russellville	C2
Fort Smith	C1	Springdale	B1
Hot Springs	D2	Texarkana	E1
Jacksonville	C3	West Memphis	C5

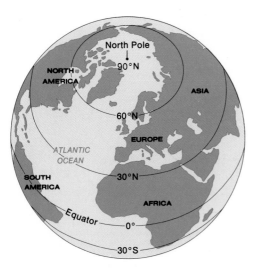

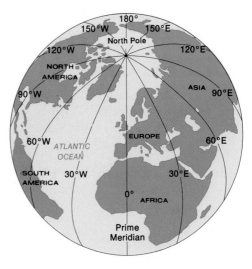

World Latitude   **World Longitude**

MAP STUDY *What is zero latitude? What latitude is the North Pole? Where do all the lines of longitude meet? Which line of longitude is opposite 0° on the other side of the globe?*

Latitude You can use another kind of grid to locate places anywhere on the earth. One part of this grid is made up of the lines that go around the globe from east to west. They are called lines of **latitude.** One line goes around the middle of the globe. That line is called the **equator.** It is numbered zero (0).

The equator is the starting point for latitude lines. The first line north of the equator is 1, the line after it is 2, and so on. The latitude lines south of the equator are numbered in the same way. The numbers get bigger the farther south they are.

Latitude lines measure how far north or south of the equator a place is. They measure in degrees. A small, raised circle after a number means "degrees." You read *10° N* as "ten degrees north." For *10° S,* you say "ten degrees south." The farthest north you can go is the **North Pole.** It is 90° N. The farthest south is the **South Pole.** It is 90° S.

Longitude The other lines on this kind of grid run from pole to pole. These are lines of **longitude.** Lines of longitude measure distance east and west.

The starting point for lines of longitude is the **prime meridian.** It is numbered 0°. The first line to the east of the prime meridian is 1° E, the next is 2°, and so on. The lines to the west of the prime meridian are numbered in the same way.

Halfway around the globe from the prime meridian is the line of longitude numbered 180°. Since the distance from the prime meridian to the 180° line is the same in both directions, the 180° line is not labeled west or east.

9

The World: Latitude and Longitude

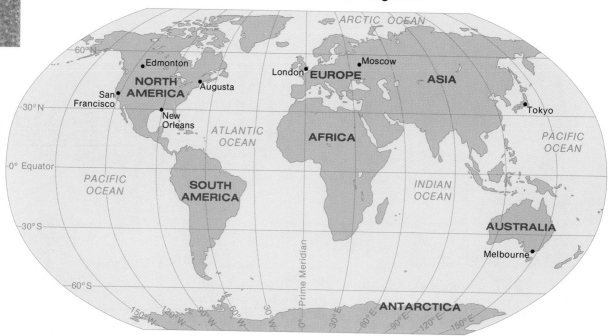

MAP STUDY *Can you guess roughly the latitude and longitude of the state in which you live?*

Locating Places on the Grid The two kinds of lines, latitude and longitude, together form a grid. Every place on the earth can be located using this grid. With this kind of grid, you don't describe location by using boxes, as on a road-map grid. Instead, you use the point at which two lines cross. For example, the city of New Orleans is located at the point where 30° N crosses 90° W.

If a place falls between the marked lines of latitude and longitude, you would use the closest lines to guess the location. For example, Augusta, Maine, on the map above is about halfway between the 30°N and 60°N lines, and a little closer to 60°W than 90°W. Its location is 44°N and 70°W.

Review

Define

hemisphere, grid, latitude, equator, North Pole, South Pole, longitude, prime meridian

Comprehension

1. What are three ways you could describe the location of a place?
2. Which kind of grid uses boxes to locate places, a road-map grid or a latitude-longitude grid?
3. How do lines of latitude and longitude help locate a place?
4. What is measured by degrees of latitude?
5. What is the highest possible number for a line of longitude?

10

What Does It Look Like?

KEY WORDS
aerial (ar′ē əl)
population (päp yə lā′shən)
relief (ri lēf′)
elevation (el ə vā′shən)
sea level (sē′lev′əl)

The second question geographers ask about a place is "What does it look like?" This question involves many other questions. Is it wet, or dry? Cold, or hot? Are there lakes? Rivers? Hills? Valleys? Grasslands? Forests? Are there a lot of people, or just a few? Where do they live? Are there farms? Shopping areas?

Getting Information Geographers have many ways of getting answers to those questions. They can walk around and look at an area and talk to people who live there. They can take photographs. Geographers also have special tools for measuring distance and height and for getting other kinds of information.

One way of getting information is to take **aerial** photographs of an area. An aerial photograph is one taken from the air, usually from an airplane. It shows many details about a landscape that help geographers draw maps. Geographers also

How would this aerial photo of the Mississippi help a mapmaker?

use electronic equipment to get information. Space satellites carrying such equipment record information about very large parts of the earth.

11

A. Population of Four Major Cities in the United States (in thousands), 1986

New York City	7,263
Los Angeles	3,259
Chicago	3,010
Houston	1,729

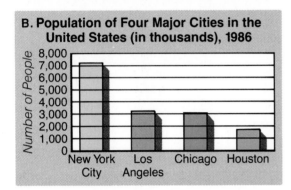

B. Population of Four Major Cities in the United States (in thousands), 1986

GRAPH STUDY *How does the bar graph help you compare the number of people in the cities listed in the table?*

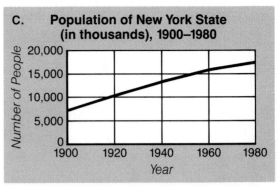

C. Population of New York State (in thousands), 1900–1980

GRAPH STUDY *How has New York's population changed?*

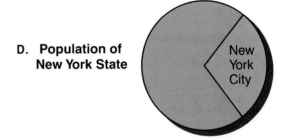

D. Population of New York State

GRAPH STUDY *Is the population of New York City more or less than one half of New York State's population?*

Tables and Graphs Once geographers have gathered information, they need a way of organizing and showing it. The way they choose depends on the kind of information. The best way to organize a lot of exact numbers is to put them in a table. The table above (A), for example, gives the **population,** or number of people, of four United States cities.

If you don't need to show what the exact population of each city is, a bar graph (B) may be the best way to give the information. Just a glance at a bar graph lets you compare the size of the populations of cities.

A line graph (C) is the best for showing changes over time. The line graph shows how the population of

New York State has changed since the year 1900. What was the population of New York in 1920? In 1950?

For showing parts of a whole, a circle graph (D) is the best tool. The circle graph shows the part of the population of New York State that lives in New York City. You can see that about a third of the state's population lives in New York City.

Relief or Elevation Maps Maps can help answer many questions about a place. A **relief** map uses lines, shading, and colors to show where the land rises and where it slopes down, where it is flat and where it is bumpy. A relief map also shows lakes and rivers.

12

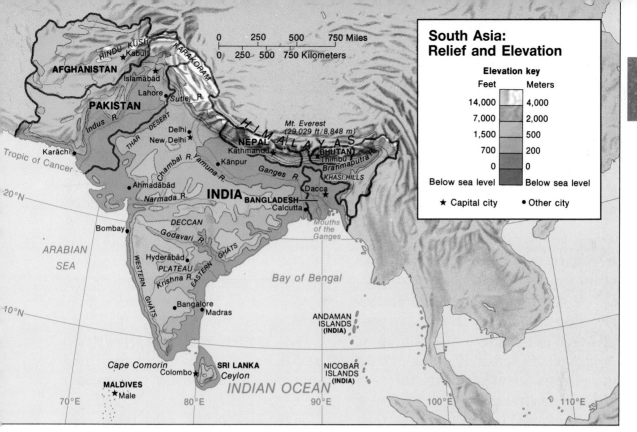

South Asia: Relief and Elevation

Elevation key

Feet		Meters
14,000		4,000
7,000		2,000
1,500		500
700		200
0		0
Below sea level		Below sea level

★ Capital city   • Other city

MAP STUDY *Where are the highest regions of India? Where do you find lowlands?*

A relief map can help you make decisions. If you wanted to build a road, a relief map would help you find where the road should go to avoid steep slopes. If a mountain could not be avoided, you might plan for a tunnel to go through it. You would also see where the road would need bridges to cross rivers.

Some relief maps, like the one above, also have a key that tells you what height the colors on the map stand for. This kind of map is called an **elevation** map because it shows elevation, or height above **sea level.** Sea level is the height of the surface of the ocean. What is the highest elevation on the map above? Where is it located?

Review

Define
aerial, population, relief, elevation, sea level

Comprehension
1. Name at least three ways geographers get information about what a place is like.
2. Which shows exact numbers better, a table or a graph?
3. Which is the best graph for showing change over time?
4. Which is the best graph for showing parts of a whole?
5. Name three things you could find out by looking at a relief map.

13

How Have People Used or Changed It?

The third question geographers ask about a place is "How have people used or changed it?" Different groups of people use the land and its **natural resources** in many different ways. A natural resource is anything that people use that is found on or in the earth.

What resources have these people in Cameroon used to build their huts?

Using the Land What people do with land and resources depends on several things. The first is the kind of land and resources available. Other things that affect people's use of the land are people's decisions about the way they wish to live, the kinds of tools and knowledge they have, and their beliefs.

With modern tools and knowledge, people can do just about anything anywhere on the earth. That doesn't mean that they do so, however. Although you could grow crops (in greenhouses) at the South Pole, it would be very costly. You could build a steel mill thousands of miles from the nearest iron mine, but you probably wouldn't because of the time and money it would take to get the iron to your mill. Chances are you would buy steel and steel products rather than trying to make them in a mill of your own.

People's beliefs also affect what they do with land and resources. For example, a country may be ideal for raising pigs. It may have materials for building shelters for the pigs. The corn and other crops that pigs eat would grow well in this land. However, the people of this country may believe that pork (pig meat) is unclean. Their religion forbids eating pork. People in this country would not raise pigs.

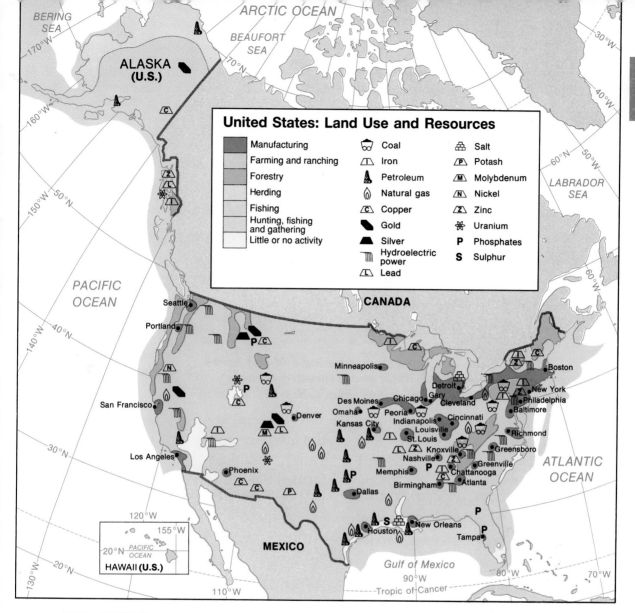

United States: Land Use and Resources

- Manufacturing
- Farming and ranching
- Forestry
- Herding
- Fishing
- Hunting, fishing and gathering
- Little or no activity

- Coal
- Iron
- Petroleum
- Natural gas
- Copper
- Gold
- Silver
- Hydroelectric power
- Lead

- Salt
- Potash
- Molybdenum
- Nickel
- Zinc
- Uranium
- Phosphates
- Sulphur

MAP STUDY *Where is the land used for hunting, fishing, and gathering? What is the main resource near Houston?*

Changing the Land Most of the ways that people use the land and its resources cause many other changes. Suppose people decide to build a dam on a river. The lake that forms behind it will store drinking water and water for crops. In the dam will be machines that use moving water to make electricity. The water and electricity are badly needed.

Before they build the dam, these people will have to think about many other changes that may take place. For example, land that people own will be flooded. People downriver from the dam will get less water. They may be very unhappy about that. Also, fish may travel up the river to get to a breeding ground. The dam will block their way. People who

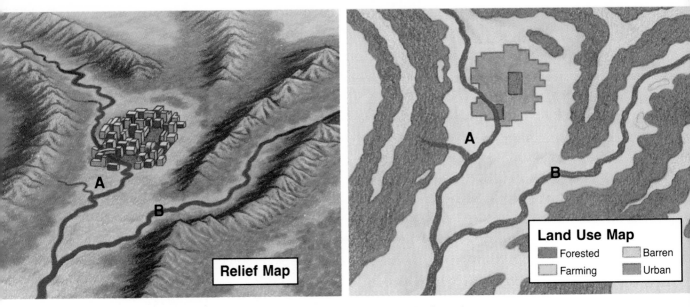

Relief Map

Land Use Map
Forested
Farming
Barren
Urban

MAP STUDY *Do these two maps show farming and city areas in places of high or low relief? What about forested areas? Why would Valley A have a city rather than Valley B?*

fish for a living will have fewer fish to catch unless fish ladders are built around the dam.

There is yet another problem. The lake that forms behind the dam may cover up homes or even a whole town. People will have to choose between water and electricity on the one hand and their homes or town on the other.

Comparing Maps When people make decisions that will change the land, they need to get information from different kinds of maps. For instance, look at the two maps above. If you were asked what would be the best place to build a dam, how would these maps help you decide? First look at the relief map to see where there is a fairly steep river valley. There are two, A and B. Now check the land use map to see what, in each valley, would be flooded by the lake formed behind the dam. Which place will you choose, A or B?

Review

Define

natural resource

Comprehension

1. People A live in a land that has plenty of water and plants. Many animals live in the forests. These people do not eat the meat of animal X. Give a possible reason why they would not.
2. Why should people learn a lot about the land before they make changes in it?

How Is It Connected to Other Places?

KEY WORDS
transportation   (trans pėr tā′shən)
communication
     (kə myü nə kā′ shən)
seaport   (sē′pōrt)

The fourth question geographers ask about a place is "How is it connected to other places?" You already know how some places are connected. For example, you may have come to school on a bus this morning. Or maybe you called your friend on the telephone last night. You may have read a newspaper story about an event that took place in another town last weekend. If you did any of these things, you know about connections between places.

As you may have guessed, places are connected by **transportation** and by **communication.** Transportation is the moving of people and goods from place to place. Communication is the passing of information and ideas from person to person.

Transportation   People have been traveling for thousands of years. They have made paths and roads between villages and towns. In ships and boats, people have explored rivers and oceans, trying to find the best

One early means of communication was the Pony Express. Swift riders raced across the country carrying mail.

water routes between places. People have built airplanes that fly across oceans and continents.

Communication   People have also found many ways of passing ideas and information from person to person and place to place. Ancient people drew pictures on the walls of their caves. People also memorized stories and legends and information that everyone needed to know. This knowledge was passed from parent to child orally, which means by speaking. Later peoples developed systems of writing, which they used to record information. At first, they wrote on rocks and clay tablets. Later they used paper. Today books, magazines, newspapers, computers, radios, and televisions are all used as means of communication.

Depending on Connections People depend on transportation and communication in many ways. Let's suppose you have some fish sticks for lunch. The fish was caught in the ocean and carried on the fishing boat to a **seaport.** A seaport is a place where oceangoing ships are loaded and unloaded.

From the seaport, the fish was taken to a food-processing plant. There the fish was made into fish sticks. Then the fish sticks were sent by truck to warehouses all over the country. From the warehouses, the fish sticks were carried on trucks to grocery stores. Finally someone in your family drove to the store, bought the fish sticks, and served them for your lunch.

Getting fish sticks to your lunch table took three kinds of transportation—fishing boat, truck, and car. If your fish came from another coun-

MAP STUDY *If you wished to deliver a lot of corn from Minneapolis to New Orleans, what would be the easiest route?*

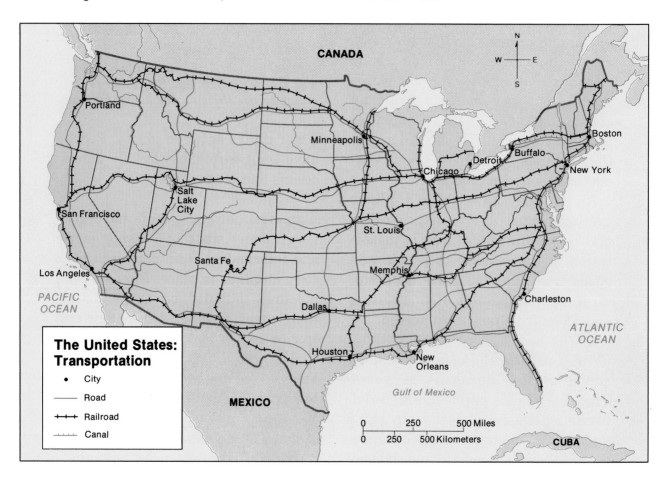

the fish are caught.

the fish are trucked to a food processing plant and then trucked to a grocery store.

FROZEN FISH

the fish sticks are displayed for the shoppers.

the fish sticks are brought home and heated for your lunch.

DIAGRAM STUDY *How many steps does this drawing show are needed to get the fish sticks to your plate?*

try, such as Japan, you could add another means of transportation—the plane needed to fly the fish to the United States.

As the fish made its journey, communication was needed too. Perhaps the fishing boat captain radioed or called the food-processing plant to sell the fish. The food-processing plant had to order the cartons. The grocery store manager had to order the fish sticks from the warehouse.

You can see that many links are needed to get the fish sticks for your lunch. For the food, clothing, and other things you need, you depend on many people and businesses. Most of them are far away, but they are linked to your town by transportation and communication.

The map on page 18 shows some of the major highways, railroads, and waterways in the United States. Use it to figure out a possible route to get wheat from a farm near St. Louis to a flour mill in Minneapolis to a bakery in your state.

Review

Define
transportation, communication, seaport

Comprehension
1. Name three different means of transportation.
2. Name at least three different ways of communicating.
3. Name at least four links in the communication and transportation chain that brought the cotton in your clothing from a farm in Texas to you.

How Can Places Be Grouped?

KEY WORDS
region (rē′jən)
climate (klī′mət)

The fifth question geographers ask is "How can places be grouped?" Sometimes people divide a subject into small parts to study it. That can be especially helpful when you are interested in lots of details or when you have a very large subject. At other times, people are more interested in an overall picture. In that case, it makes sense to group people or places together.

Regions Geographers group places into **regions.** A region is an area of the world that is different from the areas around it, but whose parts are in some way alike.

There are many kinds of regions. A part of the world that has lots of hills and mountains may be called a mountain region. Areas that share the same **climate** can form a region. Climate is the kind of weather a place usually has.

Places can be grouped by the language people speak, by the kind of government they have, by religion, or by many other things. For example, Switzerland has several regions, based on language.

MAP STUDY *How many languages are spoken in Switzerland? Which two languages have the largest regions?*

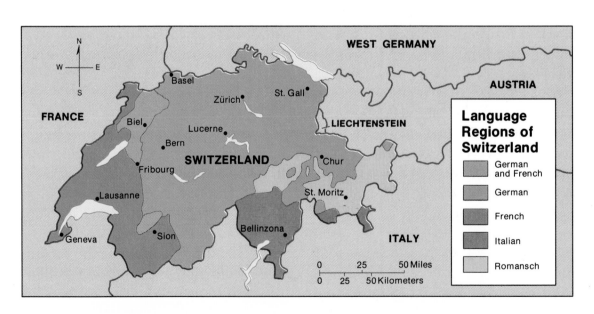

20

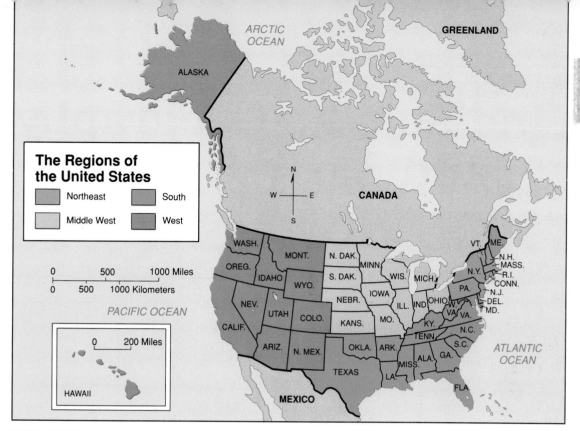

The Regions of the United States

- Northeast
- South
- Middle West
- West

0   500   1000 Miles
0   500   1000 Kilometers

PACIFIC OCEAN

0   200 Miles

HAWAII

ARCTIC OCEAN

ALASKA

GREENLAND

CANADA

WASH. MONT. N. DAK. MINN. VT. ME. N.H. MASS.
OREG. IDAHO S. DAK. WIS. MICH. N.Y. R.I. CONN.
WYO. NEBR. IOWA PA. N.J.
NEV. UTAH COLO. ILL. IND. OHIO W. VA. VA. DEL. MD.
CALIF. KANS. MO. KY. N.C.
ARIZ. N. MEX. OKLA. ARK. TENN. S.C.
TEXAS MISS. ALA. GA.
LA. FLA.

MEXICO

ATLANTIC OCEAN

MAP STUDY *In which region do you live?*

United States Regions The United States has four main regions—the Northeast, the South, the Middle West, and the West. Find those regions on the map above.

What makes these areas regions? Location is one thing that determines region. All of the states in each region are in the same part of the country. Some of these states are alike in their histories, climate, landforms, or animal or plant life. The people in the region may have a common background or earn their living in many of the same ways.

Find your state on the map above. In which region is it located? How many other states are there in this region? As you read this book, ask yourself: What do these states have

in common? How might your region be different from the other regions in the country? How might it relate to other parts of the world?

Review

Define

region, climate

Comprehension

1. Name two ways that places can be grouped into regions.
2. What four areas, or regions, are found in the United States?
3. What makes each of these four areas a region?
4. Which region is largest in size?

Indiana: Its Geography and Early History

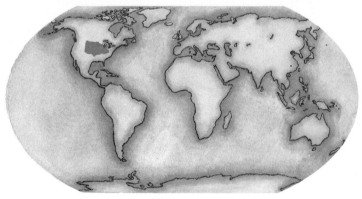

▲ *A typical farm in Illinois*

River traffic in Detroit, Michigan ▶

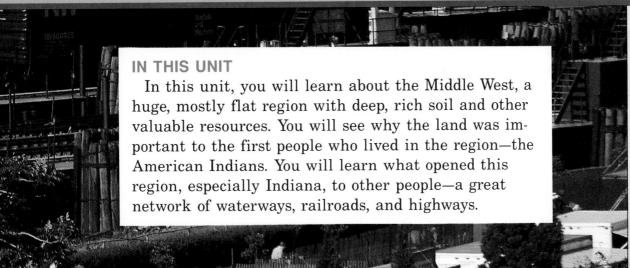

IN THIS UNIT

In this unit, you will learn about the Middle West, a huge, mostly flat region with deep, rich soil and other valuable resources. You will see why the land was important to the first people who lived in the region—the American Indians. You will learn what opened this region, especially Indiana, to other people—a great network of waterways, railroads, and highways.

Geography of the Middle West

KEY WORD

plain (plān')

Between the Applachian Mountains in the East and the Rocky Mountains in the West lies a region of 12 states known as the Middle West. Along the northern border, formed by Canada and the Great Lakes, are North Dakota, Minnesota, Wisconsin, Michigan, and Ohio. The other states are Iowa, Nebraska, South Dakota, Kansas, Missouri, Illinois, and Indiana.

Land and Water

Miles and miles of **plains** are the main physical feature of the Middle West. A plain is land that is mostly flat. Within the broad stretch of plains lie two main areas—the Central Plains and the Great Plains.

The Central and Great Plains

The Central Plains begin to the west of the Appalachians at an elevation of about 500 feet (150 meters). As the plains extend westward, the elevation of land rises to about 2,000 feet (600 meters).

The higher, drier Great Plains lie west of the Central Plains. The great Plains begin where the Central

Plains end—along the eastern edge of the Dakotas, Nebraska, and Kansas. The Great Plains increase in elevation to nearly 5,000 feet (1,500 meters) as they reach toward the Rocky Mountains. The change is so gentle that the land looks flat.

Hills and Low Mountains

Although much of the Middle West stretches out in endless plains, in the north and east are areas of varied relief. For instance, on the dairy farms of Michigan, Wisconsin, and Minnesota, cows graze on gently rolling hills and valleys. In the northern part of these states, where

MAP STUDY *With which river does the Platte River connect? What mountains are located in the northwestern part of the Middle West?*

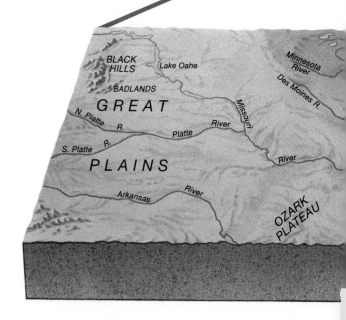

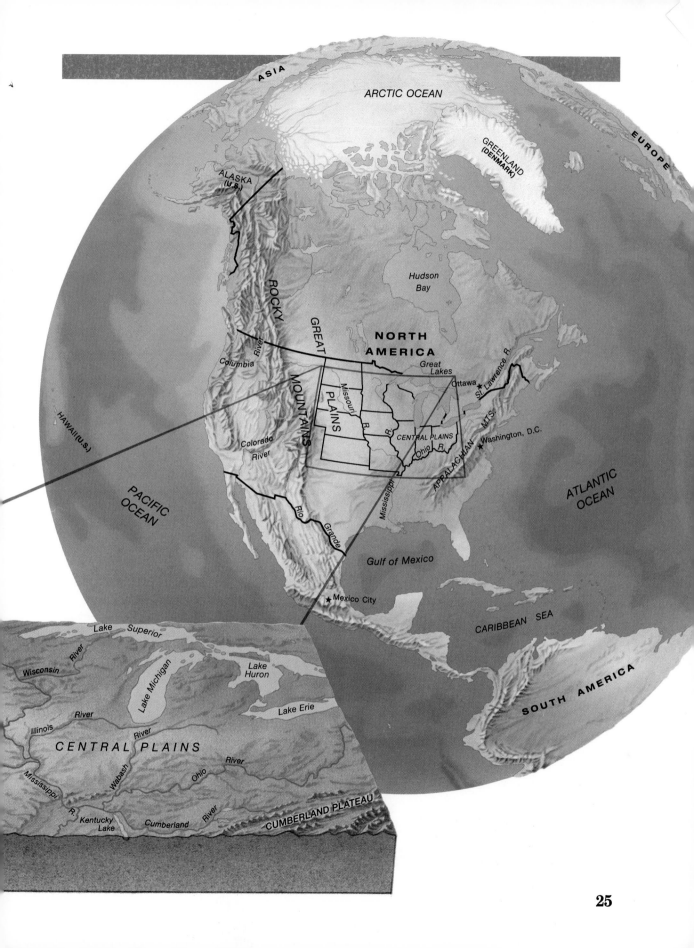

ASIA

ARCTIC OCEAN

GREENLAND
(DENMARK)

EUROPE

ALASKA
(U.S.)

Hudson
Bay

ROCKY

GREAT

NORTH
AMERICA

Great
Lakes

St. Lawrence R.

Ottawa ★

Columbia River

MOUNTAINS

PLAINS

Missouri R.

R.

CENTRAL PLAINS

APPALACHIAN MTS.

Washington, D.C. ★

HAWAII (U.S.)

Colorado
River

Ohio R.

ATLANTIC
OCEAN

PACIFIC
OCEAN

Mississippi

Rio Grande

Gulf of Mexico

★ Mexico City

CARIBBEAN   SEA

SOUTH AMERICA

Lake   Superior

River

Wisconsin

Lake Michigan

Lake
Huron

Lake Erie

Illinois

River

River

CENTRAL PLAINS

Wabash River

Ohio   River

Mississippi

R.

Kentucky
Lake

Cumberland   River

CUMBERLAND PLATEAU

little farming is possible, rich mineral areas of iron ore and copper are mined on low mountain ranges.

Farther west, in the Black Hills of South Dakota, are low mountains with an elevation of about 7,000 feet (2,000 meters). Here, Harney Peak— the highest peak in the United States east of the Rocky Mountains —rises above the plains.

The Badlands in the Dakotas and Nebraska is another area of high relief. Rain, wind, and sand have worn the land into steep hills, deep gullies, and odd-looking forms.

Farms are found throughout the Middle West. On what land feature is this rich farmland in Illinois located?

Lovely ice castles are built every winter in St. Paul, Minnesota. What climate makes building ice castles possible?

Great Lakes and Long Rivers No other region in the United States can match the freshwater resources of the Middle West. The Middle West is dotted with thousands of lakes. Michigan, Wisconsin, and Minnesota together have about 30,000 crystal clear lakes. Six Middle West states border the largest lakes in the country—the Great Lakes. These five lakes separate the United States from Canada.

Water from the Great Lakes could cover the United States—except Alaska and Hawaii—to a depth of 10 feet (3 meters). Lake Superior, the

Much of the Central Plains (left) is covered with tall, thick grasses that blanket the rolling hills. The Great Plains (right) is flatter with much shorter grass.

deepest of the lakes, is the largest freshwater lake in the world. More than 150 rivers empty into it.

The greatest river in the nation—the Mississippi—starts as a small, clear stream in northern Minnesota. It flows all the way south to the Gulf of Mexico. Along the way, many other rivers and streams empty into the Mississippi. From the east, the broad Ohio River joins the Mississippi at the southern tip of Illinois. From the west, the wide Missouri empties into the Mississippi near St. Louis, Missouri.

These great river systems served as natural highways for the Indians and then the settlers who came into the region. Before long the rivers became crowded with boats that carried grain, coal, and steel.

Indians used the land differently from the settlers who came to settle the area. As you will read, before long the two groups found it very difficult to share the Middle West.

Focus Review

Define

plain

Comprehension

1. What natural features form the boundaries of the Middle West?
2. What is the main physical feature of the Middle West?

Critical Thinking

3. How did the rivers of the Middle West help the region to develop?

CHAPTER 1

The Changing Middle West

As Vine Deloria, Jr., left the courtroom, reporters swarmed around him. They had watched as he spoke for the rights of Indians. Deloria, a lawyer, was a known spokesperson for Indians, and the reporters knew he would answer their questions.

Vine Deloria, Jr., was born in Pine Ridge, South Dakota, on land that had been set aside just for Indians. As an Indian, Deloria experienced the hardships that many Indians have faced in the United States. While growing up, he came to believe that Indians deserved better lives. Deloria went to law school to learn how to help his people. As a lawyer and a writer, he has worked hard to improve conditions for Indians. He has made people remember the history of his region and his country.

Like many people who live in the Middle West, Vine Deloria has noticed many changes in the region during his lifetime. He is concerned about some of the changes and happy about others. As you read this chapter, you will learn how the Middle West has grown and changed—and how the region fits into the world today.

LESSON 1 The First People of the Middle West

The Indians were the first people to live in the Middle West. How has life changed for them over the years?

KEY WORDS
extinct (ik stinkt')
reservation (rez'ėr vā'shən)
heritage (her'ət ij)

Let us begin the study of the Middle West by looking at the very first people to live in the region—the Indians. It is important to remember that Indians were living in the Middle West thousands of years before anyone else. Their lives have changed a great deal since they came to the region.

The Earliest Times

Thousands of years ago, groups of Indians made their homes along the shores of the Great Lakes and the major rivers of the Middle West— such as the Mississippi, the Missouri, and the Ohio. Other Indians lived on the plains farther west.

Big Game Hunters These very early Indians did not live in villages. They traveled around in search of food. They are known as Big Game Hunters because they survived by hunting huge animals that are now

extinct. Animals become extinct when they no longer are found on earth. Two animals that the Big Game Hunters hunted were the mammoth and the mastodon. These animals were bigger than elephants.

Long after the mammoth and mastodon became extinct, Indians still hunted with spears and bows and arrows. The horse, brought to America by the Spanish, made the Plains Indians feared hunters.

Developing Villages Over several thousand years, the Indians gradually developed a new way of life. They began to farm in addition to hunting. This new way of life meant the Indians did not have to move around constantly. They could grow their food instead of having to go and look for it.

The Indians lived together in large family groups. Family members of all ages often lived together in one house or in several small houses grouped together.

A group of families, called a clan, would settle in a certain area and stay there most of the year. They built houses, planted crops, and hunted for small game found in their area.

Arrival of Europeans

The Indians continued to develop a more settled, comfortable way of life. When the first Europeans arrived in the Middle West, they found Indian villages that had been settled for hundreds of years.

Disappearing Lands At first, the Indians benefited from the presence of the Europeans. By trading with the Europeans, the Indians gained many useful items such as horses. However, over time, the Indians suffered as the Europeans took over more and more of their land. Soon the Indians found it hard to find food or land for farming. Their way of life was being threatened.

An Indian village was well organized and busy. Everyone had a job to do. What types of jobs do you see the Indians in this picture doing?

Soon the Indians and the Europeans fought for control of the land. Often the Indians could not match the Europeans' military strength. With each defeat, the Indians were forced to give up more of their land.

Removal of the Indians As the Europeans settled the land and founded a new country, they decided they wanted all of the Indians' land. The government leaders sent the Indians to live together on areas of land called **reservations.** These areas were set aside for the Indians but were run by the government.

Reservation life was hard for the Indians. They were used to their own way of life, and it had been taken away from them. The Indians were not allowed to practice many of their traditions, and the poor living conditions caused many to suffer.

Changing Indian Life

Today many Indians are leaving the reservations. Some have moved to Middle Western cities and taken jobs as nurses, librarians, teachers, and road workers. Some, like Vine Deloria, are working to improve the lives of their people.

The government also has helped the Indians. Money has gone to improve the reservations, to help Indians find jobs and receive college educations, and to help keep alive the rich **heritage** of the Indians. Heritage is a people's history and traditions that are passed from parent to child.

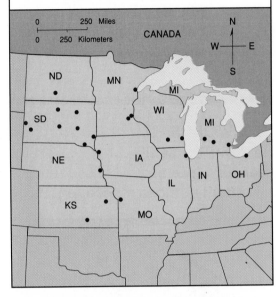

Locations of Middle Western Cities with Large Indian Populations

MAP STUDY *Today many cities in the Middle West have large Indian populations. Which state has the most centers of Indian population?*

Lesson Review

Comprehension

1. How did the Big Game Hunters survive in early times?
2. Why were Indians eventually able to settle in villages?
3. Why were Indians sent to live on reservations?
4. How does government today help the Indians?

Critical Thinking

5. What changes did the Indians experience when the Europeans arrived in the Middle West?
6. How are Indians' lives still changing today?

LESSON 2 Settling the Middle West

Middle Westerners make up more than a fourth of the national population. What brought so many people to the region?

KEY WORDS
descent (di sent′)
pioneer (pī′ə nir′)
nationality (nash′ə nal′ət ē)

The variety of people in an area affect its development. As you study the Middle West, you will find that its history is tied closely to the region's unique blend of people.

If you ask several Middle Westerners about the people from whom they are **descended**, you will not hear the same story twice. A person's descent is his or her family beginnings. Some Middle Westerners whom you talk to might be descended from the Indians, the first people to live in the Middle West. Some might be from families who have lived in the Middle West since the 1800's. They might be descended from people born in any one of a number of European countries. Other Middle Westerners might have moved recently to the region from another region or from a foreign country.

The Middle West is made up of a variety of people from many different backgrounds. In this lesson, you will learn how all these different

people came to live in the region. You will learn where they came from and why they chose to settle in the Middle West.

MAP STUDY *Settlers from the East had a difficult time reaching the Middle West. What geographical feature stood in their way?*

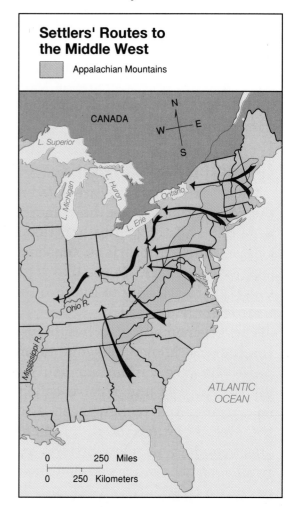

Settlers' Routes to the Middle West

Appalachian Mountains

Some pioneers were able to use a geographical feature—the Ohio River—to help them make the journey to the frontier. They loaded as many of their possessions as they could on the small boats.

The First European Settlers

In the 1800's, white settlers moved to the Middle West to live. They began the difficult task of building homes and setting up farms.

Settlers' Routes The early European settlers in the Middle West were known as **pioneers**. Pioneers are the first members of a particular group to settle a region.

Many of the earliest pioneers came over the Appalachian Mountains onto the Central Plains. Some traveled down the Ohio River on boats and settled in what is now southern Ohio, Indiana, and Illinois.

Settlers from New England traveled through New York to the Great Lakes. People just arriving from Europe also took this route.

One City's Development Some of the settlers, especially those of German descent, helped settle the city of Milwaukee, Wisconsin. These early German settlers included people with skills in crafts—such as bakers and carpenters—as well as farmers.

Today the German heritage can be seen throughout Milwaukee. Many houses in the city look as if they were carried over from Germany. There are German singing groups and dances and German churches, clubs, businesses, restaurants, and festivals.

People from Poland and other nations in Europe also came to Milwaukee. By the early 1900's, Milwaukee had the greatest number of foreign-born people of any city in the United States of America.

Today, to celebrate the various **nationalities**—or countries of descent—of Milwaukee's citizens, the Milwaukee Public Museum houses the European Village. Here visitors can see displays for each country. In a park in the city, each nationality can hold a festival to celebrate its traditions.

Other Towns and Cities Milwaukee is only one example of growth in the Middle West. Throughout the region, towns, cities, and the beautiful countryside attracted settlers from other countries.

Because the geography and climate of the Middle West reminded people of their homelands, many settlers from northern Europe made the region their home. Dense forests attracted German settlers, while broad, open fields and snowy winters attracted Scandinavians—people from Norway, Sweden, and Denmark. The grasslands of the Great Plains in the Dakotas became the new home for pioneers from Denmark, Germany, Norway, and Russia.

Towns and cities also swelled with new citizens from different countries. For example, people now living in Sheyboygan, Wisconsin, trace their roots to Holland, while people in Fond du Lac trace their roots to Switzerland. People in Superior look back to Finland and people in Racine to Denmark. In Kenosha,

Ethnic festivals occur every summer weekend in Milwaukee. Costumes differ by region or country. Why do people enjoy getting together for celebrations like the one shown?

Carl B. Stokes has served as mayor of Cleveland and as a judge in the city. He was the first black mayor of a major United States city.

Lithuanians remember their home country. People in Oshkosh trace their background to Russia.

Settlers from the South

In the 1920's, people from other regions of the country—especially black people from the South—moved to the Middle West. Newspapers owned by black people—like the *Chicago Daily Defender*—told of good jobs in the Middle West. In about 30 years, almost 5 million black people from the South moved to Middle Western cities.

The Urban League Many of the new arrivals from the South had limited skills. They had to take the lowliest factory jobs. These people needed help finding new homes and better jobs.

One of the most important groups to help the newcomers was the Urban League. By 1920, the League operated in cities such as Youngstown and Cleveland in Ohio, Detroit in Michigan, and Chicago in Illinois. Members of the League helped new arrivals learn where to shop and how to find homes and good jobs.

A Major Force By the 1980's, black people made up one half the population of many cities. Black people are important today in the work force of every city in the Middle West. Cities such as Detroit, Cleveland, and Chicago have elected black mayors.

Lesson Review

Comprehension

1. How did the pioneers reach the Middle West? Name three different routes they took.
2. Why might Milwaukee be thought of as a German city?
3. Why did many black people move from the South to the Middle West in the 1920's?
4. Why was the Urban League so important to people arriving in the Middle West from the South?

Critical Thinking

5. What features of the Middle West attracted northern Europeans to the region?
6. Why are groups such as the Urban League important to communities?

Taking Notes

When you read books or listen to a speaker, you might find that taking notes will help you remember what you have read or heard. Notes are short phrases about important facts. They do not have to be complete sentences. Often your notes will answer:

Who or *what* is important?
What happened?
When did it happen?
Where did it happen?
Why did it happen?

You can take notes to help you remember facts from your book. Read the following paragraph from Lesson 2 and then read the three sample notes below.

Some of the settlers, especially those of German descent, helped settle the city of Milwaukee, Wisconsin. These early German settlers included people with skills in crafts—such as bakers and carpenters—as well as farmers.

Read questions 1-3 about the paragraph above. Answer the questions by referring to the sample notes.

1. What group helped settle the city of Milwaukee?
2. What crafts did the settlers bring with them?
3. What jobs did the German settlers have in Milwaukee?

Project

Notes also can help you write a report. By taking good notes and organizing them, you will find research easier. Read three paragraphs about the Middle West in an encyclopedia or other source like a travel book. Take notes on these paragraphs. Then write a paragraph of your own using your notes.

German settlers — settled the city of Milwaukee

Work — bakers, carpenters, farmers

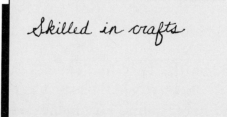

Skilled in crafts

LESSON 3 The Middle West Today

Nearness to water routes and abundant resources led to the growth of the Middle West. How did this growth connect the region to the rest of the world?

KEY WORDS
interdependence
(int´ėr di pen´dəns)
stockyard (stäk´yärd´)
grain elevator (grān´el´ə vāt´ėr)
megalopolis (meg´ə läp´ə ləs)
competition (kom´pə tish´ən)

The Middle West today is known for its huge cities. Many of these cities owe their growth, in part, to their locations along waterways.

The region also is known for its part in global **interdependence**. This interdependence means that countries around the world are affected by one another's changes.

Giant Cities

Let us take a look at just three of the large cities in the Middle West—Chicago, Minneapolis, and St. Paul. How did these cities develop, and what are they like today?

Chicago The largest—and perhaps most famous—of the Middle Western cities is Chicago. Potawatomi (pot ə wot´ ə mē) Indians were probably the first to set up a village at Chicago's location, on the river they

called the Checagou (chē chä´ kō). In 1779, a black trader named Jean Baptist Point du Sable (pwan´ dü säblə´) began a small trading post nearby on Lake Michigan.

A canal, the city's location on Lake Michigan, and the growth of railroads turned Chicago into a transportation center. In the 1860's, Chicago became the receiving center for cattle, hogs, and sheep sent north by prairie farmers. The Chicago **stockyards**, where livestock are kept before they are slaughtered, stretched for miles.

For what is the pioneer Jean Baptist Point du Sable famous?

Over the next hundred years, huge **grain elevators**, buildings for storing and unloading grain, were set up in Chicago. The city became a grain processing and shipping center for the nation and the world.

In 1871, Chicago was nearly destroyed by a great fire. Many of the wooden buildings in the city were destroyed as the fire raged for 24 hours. In spite of their losses, the people of Chicago quickly rebuilt the city. By the 1890's, Chicago was the second largest city in the nation.

Today slightly more than 3 million people live in Chicago, making it the third largest city in the United States. Moreover, Chicago is at the center of a **megalopolis**, or thickly populated area including many cities, of about 7.5 million people. The population includes people from

What means of transportation might be used to send products from the Middle West to other countries?

Middle West Farm Exports

Soybeans

Corn

Wheat

FLOUR

every part of the world. More than 100 different neighborhoods are found in the city.

Business still booms in Chicago today. Today Chicago's factories produce more machines and more steel than those of any other city in the world. In addition, Chicago is the nation's biggest transportation center.

Twin Cities — Minneapolis-St. Paul The cities of St. Paul and Minneapolis, Minnesota, are located about 400 miles (640 kilometers) northwest of Chicago on the Mississippi River. St. Paul, on the north bank of the Mississippi, was settled first. Settlers liked the area because of its broad fields for farming and its hardwood forests for lumbering.

In 1849, the village that would become Minneapolis was set up near the Falls of St. Anthony. This was as far as boats in the mid-1800's could go with their passengers and goods. The settlers were able to use waterpower to help them produce flour and wood products.

By the late 1800's, Minneapolis had become the state's leading lumbering center. Flour also became an important product of the city. By 1930, great flour producing companies helped Minneapolis lead the world in flour production.

To help distribute the products of the region, a resident of St. Paul — James Jerome Hill — worked to make the city a transportation center. He brought railroads to the area and built a shipping company.

What river divides the Twin Cities (above)? The Minnesota Twins baseball players rejoice at winning the World Series (right).

The growth of Minneapolis-St. Paul continues. St. Paul is the capital of the state, and Minneapolis is the state's largest city. Together, the two cities account for half the people who live in Minnesota cities. Farm equipment, corn, soybeans, wheat, flour, and lumber all make their way from the Twin City area to the rest of the country and the world.

Middle West Global Connections

The way people live and work in the United States always is changing. Some of these changes come about because people in the United States find new ways to do things. Other changes take place because of events in foreign countries. Even though the United States is the richest, most powerful country in the world, its people have to respond to changes around the globe. Because of its importance in farming and producing goods, the Middle West must keep up with global changes.

World Trade In the first half of the 1900's, the United States was one of the only countries making factory products. Since then, however, companies in foreign countries have learned how to make products like those in the United States. As a result, world **competition** has increased. Competition happens when two or more persons or groups are trying to do the same thing.

For example, a company called Caterpillar in Peoria, Illinois, makes bulldozers and other heavy equipment. Although it is among the largest companies in the United

39

These Caterpillars were made in Japan and shipped to the Middle West.

States, Caterpillar faces fierce competition from Komatsu (kō mät′ zü), a Japanese company that makes the same products.

Because Komatsu has been very successful, Caterpillar has had to make some changes. Not all of the changes have been good for Middle Westerners. To cut costs, the company closed about one third of its factories, putting 36,000 workers out of work.

At the same time, Caterpillar looked for ways to reduce the prices of its products, making them cheaper than Komatsu products. This was a good change brought about by competition. Customers could buy the products for less money.

In many ways, the Middle West has been strengthened by global competition. Middle Western companies have had to improve the ways they make goods and do business. One sign of the new strength of the Middle West is that nations overseas have begun to buy more goods made in the region. In Taiwan, for example, many car buyers prefer the automobiles made in Detroit to those made in Taiwan.

Connections through Heritage

You have learned how many Middle Westerners have brought their heritage from other countries. Their traditions, foods, and celebrations have enriched the Middle West.

Many Middle Westerners stay in touch with people still living in Europe. For example, Middle Westerners who still have family in Poland have watched carefully the changes in their homeland. In the past, the government of Poland did not allow its people much freedom. The Polish people also had very few basic goods. Polish Americans aided relatives and friends in Poland by sending money and goods such as soap, clothing, and food. They also helped keep alive the idea of a freer Poland.

Today people in Poland finally have been allowed more freedom by the Polish government. When this change occurred, some Polish Americans returned to their homeland. Others were joyful to be able to communicate with long lost relatives and friends. For all, it was a time to renew connections between the United States and one of the old homelands of Europe. Middle Westerners from other countries—such as Lithuania, Latvia, and Hungary—feel the same kind of connection to events in their homelands.

Middle Westerners also rejoice in their heritage by having festivals. Milwaukee has a yearly event called the Milwaukee World Festivals. The festivals include an Afro Fest, Polish Fest, Irish Fest, Mexican Fiesta, German Fest, and still another festival called Indian Summer.

Many other Middle Western cities have similar festivals. In Topeka, Kansas, for instance, the Cinco de Mayo (sing kō də mī′ ō), or Fifth of May celebration, honors the heritage of the city's large Mexican population.

Ethnic festivals remind Americans of their global links. They are a way of reaching out to homelands in a time of change. They prove that no matter what else changes, people's honor for their traditions remains the same.

These children, dressed in Dutch costumes, are celebrating the Tulip Festival in Missouri.

Lesson Review

Comprehension

1. Why did Chicago become a transportation center?
2. Why did pioneers choose to settle in St. Paul?
3. Why has world competition become important to businesses of the Middle West?

Critical Thinking

4. Name two things for which Chicago is known today. Do the same for Minneapolis-St. Paul.
5. How do the ethnic backgrounds of Middle Westerners add to the region's global interdependence?

CHAPTER 1 REVIEW

Words to Know

Use a complete sentence to answer each question.

1. When do animals become *extinct*?
2. What is *heritage*?
3. What is a person's *descent*?
4. What is global *interdependence*?
5. For what is a *grain elevator* used?
6. What is a *megalopolis*?
7. When does *competition* occur?

Main Ideas

1. Describe the life of the early Big Game Hunters that lived in the Middle West.
2. What made it possible for the Indians to begin settling villages in the forests of the Middle West?
3. How did the taking of Indian lands by Europeans hurt the Indians' way of life?
4. Why was reservation life hard for the Indians?
5. Why were the first European settlers in the Middle West known as pioneers?
6. What does the city of Milwaukee do to celebrate the many nationalities of its citizens?
7. Why did settlers from northern Europe choose to make the Middle West their home?
8. Why was the Urban League important to black people?
9. How did Chicago's location affect its settlement?
10. Why did Chicago have so many stockyards by the 1860's?
11. What disaster happened in Chicago in 1871?
12. What natural resources were settlers in the Minneapolis area able to use?
13. How did James Jerome Hill contribute to the growth of St. Paul?
14. How has global competition strengthened the Middle West?
15. How do festivals help people preserve their heritage?

Critical Thinking

1. Imagine that the Indians of the Middle West never had met the European settlers. The Indians probably still would have experienced changes—but much more slowly. Think about the kinds of changes the Indians might have experienced if they had been left alone. Make a list of your ideas. Consider ways the Indians could have improved their way of life. Think about inventions or events that would have made it possible for the Indians to settle down in bigger groups.
2. Chicago has grown into a huge megalopolis with little open land. Yet the city depends upon the products of farms—which need open stretches of land. Explain why a region needs both big cities and open country.

Writing for Understanding

1. Imagine that you are Vine Deloria, Jr. You have been asked to give a short speech at an elementary school located on an Indian reservation. You want to tell the children about the importance of remembering their Indian heritage. As you write the speech, keep in mind that you will be speaking to children. Use words that they will understand. Make your speech no more than one page long.

2. Find out more about a northern European group that settled in the Middle West—for example, the Swiss in Fond du Lac or the Danish in Racine. Go to the library to learn facts about their traditions and how they are carried on in America. Write a short report about the group you choose. Tell when they came to America, where they settled, and how they preserve their native customs.

Applying Skills

Use the notes below about Kansas to answer the questions.

1. What kinds of farm products are grown in Kansas?
2. What is the main landform found in Kansas?
3. Did the population of Kansas go up or down in the 1980's?

Plains state — mostly flat

Main crop = wheat

Largest city = Wichita

Hard times in 1980's — population rose only a little

CHAPTER 2

Indiana Geography

A famous writer from Indiana named Theodore Dreiser once took a trip from New York back to his home state. He traveled with a friend, also a Hoosier. During their travels, they tried to think of what made Indiana unique, or different from other states. This is what Dreiser's friend said: *You should go sometime to a Speedway race at Indianapolis. . . .There, just when the first real summer days begin to take on that wonderful light, and a kind of [glowing] silence over things suggests growing corn and ripening wheat and quails whistling in the meadows over by the woods, you will find a [gathering] of people from all over this country and from other countries. . . which make you feel that this is the center of things.*

Even though Indiana is not in the center of the United States, Dreiser's friend felt the state was "the center of things." What, do you think, did he mean by this?

LESSON 1   Describing Indiana

In many ways, Indiana is a hub, or center of activity, in the United States. Why might Indiana have become a hub?

KEY WORDS

temperate   (tem′pə rət)
precipitation   (pri sip′ə tā′shən)
tornado   (tôr nād′ō)
forest   (fôr′əst)
deciduous   (di sij′ə wəs)
aquatic   (ə kwät′ik)

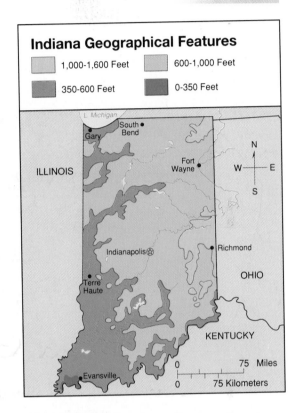

Indiana Geographical Features

1,000-1,600 Feet	600-1,000 Feet
350-600 Feet	0-350 Feet

L. Michigan — South Bend, Gary, Fort Wayne, ILLINOIS, Indianapolis, Richmond, OHIO, Terre Haute, KENTUCKY, Evansville

N W E S

0 — 75 Miles
0 — 75 Kilometers

MAP STUDY *Look at the map key to see the different ranges of elevation. In what elevation range does land around most Indiana rivers fall?*

The state of Indiana covers 36,291 square miles (93,990 square kilometers). You might think this is a large area, but actually Indiana is not a very large state. In fact, except for Hawaii, Indiana is the smallest state west of the Appalachian Mountains. Indiana does, however, have a large population—5,550,000 people.

A Seaport with No Ocean

If you wanted to walk from the Atlantic shore of the United States all the way to Indiana, you would have to walk about 700 miles (1,126 kilometers). Even with all those miles between the Atlantic Ocean and Indiana, the state has seaports where ships can come and go. How is that possible?

Lake Ports On the map of Indiana (above), look at the northwest corner. This part of the state borders Lake Michigan. Docked at the port of Burns Harbor, near Gary, are ships from other Great Lakes states, like Minnesota, and from Canada. Ships from Burns Harbor can journey all the way to the Atlantic Ocean. The ships travel through Lake Michigan, Lake Huron, Lake Erie, Lake Ontario, and then out through the St. Lawrence Seaway.

45

River Ports Indiana also has river ports. Look at the southern border of the state. This border is created by the Ohio River, an important shipping route to the Mississippi River. The Mississippi flows to the Gulf of Mexico. From there, ships can take products made in Indiana to places all over the world.

These lake and river ports are important to Indiana because of the state's location within its region. Look again at the map (page 45). Note how Indiana is bordered by Ohio to the east, Michigan to the north, Kentucky to the south, and Illinois to the west. Products flow from these states into Indiana and from Indiana into these other states. Indiana's central location makes the state an important hub within its region. So you see, although Indiana is about 700 miles (1,126 kilometers) from the nearest ocean, the state is important in shipping.

Climate

Indiana has what is called a **temperate** climate. In a temperate climate, temperatures change within a wide range, but usually the weather is not terribly cold or extremely hot. Because of its climate, Indiana receives plenty of rain.

The port of Burns Harbor is just one of Indiana's busy lake ports. Many of the ships using the port are huge. These ships can travel thousands of miles—all the way from Indiana to South America. On what lake are Indiana's ports located?

Climate Variations Although all of Indiana is temperate, the climate varies in different parts of Indiana. In the south, the average temperatures are generally warmer than in the north. In January, southern temperatures average about 35 degrees (2°C), but in the north, temperatures average 25 degrees (-4°C). In July, the south is warmer again, with an average temperature of 78 degrees (26°C) compared to 73 degrees (23°C) for the north.

The state of Indiana receives about 42 inches (107 centimeters) of **precipitation** every year. Precipitation is moisture that falls in the form of rain, snow, or sleet. The southern part of the state receives more rain than other parts because it is closer to the wet air masses coming north from the Gulf of Mexico.

Dangerous Weather Sometimes Indiana's weather can be dangerous. When rain falls, a low pressure system, or a part of the atmosphere that is heavier than normal, squeezes rain out of clouds. When the pressure of the atmosphere is very low, severe thunderstorms may develop. Sometimes these thunderstorms produce **tornadoes**, which are storms with whirling winds and funnel-shaped clouds. These storms can produce winds of up to 300 miles (480 kilometers) per hour. Luckily, modern weather forecasting can help us predict when tornadoes might occur so that people can protect themselves.

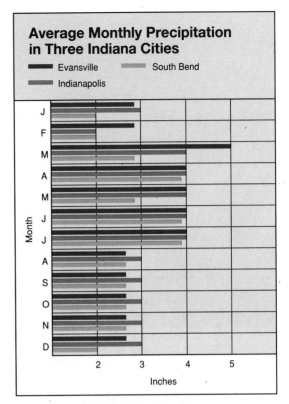

Average Monthly Precipitation in Three Indiana Cities

CHART STUDY *South Bend is in northern Indiana, Indianapolis in central Indiana, and Evansville in southern Indiana. Does precipitation vary much throughout the state?*

Environments

Because of Indiana's temperate climate, many different kinds of plants and animals can be found in the state. Imagine for a moment that you wanted to see every plant and animal that lives in Indiana. What might you see along the way? As you traveled the state, you would probably notice that Indiana has many different environments, just as it has many climates. An environment is all the living and nonliving things that make up a place. Each environment provides a different type of home for animals.

Indiana forests would be good places to look for the state bird—the cardinal. The bright red males are easy to find.

Forests If you wanted to see birds, squirrels, deer, or rabbits in Indiana, you probably would go to a **forest**, or a tree-covered area. All of these animals are plentiful in the wooded areas of the state. If you look carefully, you might see Indiana's state bird, the cardinal. The males are a deep red with black markings around their faces. The females are a rusty color.

Once Indiana was covered almost totally by thick forests. Now forests cover about four million acres of Indiana, much of them in the south.

The most common types of trees in Indiana include maple, hickory, beech, oak, sassafras, and locust. In the spring, the white and pink flowers of dogwood trees explode into a fantastic display of beauty. In the fall, the trees put on a beautiful display of color as their leaves change from green to red, gold, and orange. This color change and the falling leaves mean that most of Indiana's trees are **deciduous**. In other words, the trees lose their leaves in fall.

The Hoosier National Forest in Perry, Crawford, and Orange counties and the Brown County State Park are famous for the scenery these forests provide. In all, Indiana has 12 state forests.

Sand Dunes, Water, and Plains A special environment is found along the shores of Lake Michigan at Indiana Dunes National Lakeshore. Here, large sand dunes are piled up along the lake. These dunes contain some forms of life that cannot be found anywhere else in the state. Some special kinds of plants struggle to sink roots into the dunes. Shore birds make nests around the dunes. Unfortunately, this special environment is threatened by pollution from nearby industries. Laws have been written to cut down pollution there and protect the area.

Visitors to Indiana Dunes National Lakeshore can enjoy water sports or explore to find unique plant and animal life.

Indiana is fortunate to have a plentiful water supply. Not only does the state border Lake Michigan, but Indiana also has many smaller lakes and streams. In fact, there are more than 1,000 lakes in the state. These waters are home to several kinds of fish like bass, bluegill, carp, and catfish. These **aquatic** environments also host waterfowl, like ducks, and aquatic plants. In an aquatic environment, plants and animals live in water.

Some animals and plants have adapted to life on the open plains. Indiana's plains once were covered with trees, but farmers have cleared most of these areas. Game birds such as quail and pheasant make their homes in these open plains.

Lesson Review

Comprehension

1. How can products be shipped from Indiana to South America?
2. What kind of climate does Indiana have?
3. Why do many kinds of plants and animals live in Indiana?
4. Why are Indiana forests beautiful in the fall?
5. Why are the dunes of Indiana protected by laws?

Critical Thinking

6. How did Indiana's location turn the state into a shipping hub?
7. What outdoor activities can be enjoyed in Indiana?

Making an Outline

An outline is a written plan used to organize ideas. An author of a book makes an outline before beginning to write so that the book is well organized and includes all the important ideas. The author can follow the outline as a sort of road map showing him or her where the writing should go.

Making an outline as you read helps you see how a book is organized and what the important ideas are. An outline also helps you when you are studying. Reviewing ideas in outline form is a fast way to help you recall what you have read.

You easily can make an outline of any lesson in this book. Your outline would follow the titles and headings in the book. Look at the outline on this page. It is the last part of an outline for Chapter 1 of this book—the part outlining Lesson 3. Roman numeral III is the title for Lesson 3 of Chapter 1; the capital letters are the main headings; and the Arabic numerals are the subheadings. The small letters give the details.

Notice too the way the parts of the outline are set up. Capital letters line up with one another as do Arabic numerals and small letters. Lessons 1 and 2 are included at the beginning of the outline as Roman numerals I and II. They line up with Roman numeral III.

III. The Middle West Today
  A. Giant Cities
    1. Chicago
      a. settled first by Potawatomi Indians
      b. began as trading post in 1779
      c. became a transportation center by 1860's
      d. third largest city
    2. Twin Cities—Minneapolis-St. Paul
      a. located on Mississippi River about 400 miles northwest of Chicago
      b. Minneapolis became lumbering and flour center by 1930
      c. St. Paul started as transportation center for products of area
      d. Twin Cities have half the population of Minnesota today
  B. Middle West Global Connections
    1. World Trade
      a. competition with foreign companies
      b. strengthens the region
    2. Connections through Heritage
      a. stay in touch with homelands
      b. have festivals

On this page is an outline of Lesson 1 of Chapter 2. The second part of the outline has not been filled in. Copy the outline on a separate sheet of paper and fill it in with information from Lesson 1.

I. Describing Indiana
  A. A Seaport with No Ocean
    1. Lake Ports
      a. Burns Harbor
      b. ships can travel all the way to Atlantic Ocean
    2. River Ports
      a. found along the southern border
      b. Ohio River leads to Mississippi River
      c. ships can travel to ports throughout the world
  B. Climate
    1. Climate Variations
      a. temperate climate
      b. warmer in the south
      c. more rain in the south
    2. Dangerous Weather
      a. severe thunderstorms
      b. tornadoes
  C. Environments
    1. _____
      a. _____
      b. _____
      c. _____
    2. _____
      a. _____
      b. _____
      c. _____

Answer the questions below based on the outline you have completed. Refer only to the outline. Do not use your book.

1. What are the three main topics of the lesson?
2. How are the main lesson topics identified on the outline?
3. Where in Indiana are the state's river ports located?
4. How would you describe Indiana's climate?
5. What types of dangerous weather might people in Indiana experience?
6. What sorts of environments does Indiana have?
7. Give two details about one Indiana environment.
8. How are the details of the lesson labeled on the outline?
9. Why is using the outline to review the lesson easier than going back through the book?

Project

Make an outline for the next lesson in this book. Use the outline on this page as a model. Write the title of the lesson and the first heading. Then choose one important fact from each paragraph under the heading and list it in your outline. Do this until you have outlined the whole lesson. Save the outline. It will help you as you read the lesson. The outline also will help you as you study for a test on the lesson.

Save the Dunes Council

Tom Serynek grew up in Gary, Indiana. He remembers how nice it was when he was a boy to walk along the sand dunes on the shore of Lake Michigan. He also remembers the stories his mother told him of what the dunes were like when she was a young girl.

When Mr. Serynek became a fourth-grade teacher, he told his students these stories. He told them about the dunes and what they used to look like years ago. He also told them he was worried about the dunes.

Others besides Mr. Serynek were afraid for the dunes. Pollution and buildings were destroying many dune areas. One group of people was working to perserve the dunes. Mr. Serynek joined the group which was called the Save the Dunes Council. After a few years, in 1989, he became president of the group.

Citizens living in the area of northwest Indiana formed the council in 1952, many years before Mr. Serynek joined the group. These people wanted to preserve the special environment of the dunes that had been part of the area since glaciers left Indiana. The council knew that hundreds of birds and special kinds of plants lived in the dunes.

The council asked government leaders to help them save the dunes. Many years passed before anything was done. Finally a senator from Illinois—named Paul Douglas—introduced a law that in 1966 made part of the dunes area a national park.

The Indiana sand dunes are home to many interesting and rare plants and animals. Part of the money in the Save the Dunes Council budget goes to researching these life forms.

Tom Serynek has enjoyed the Indiana sand dunes throughout his life. Now he works hard to protect them.

The council's work was not finished, however. The park was very small. Before long, many unprotected areas were scheduled to be leveled for new buildings. Also, some industries were dumping harmful waste into Lake Michigan. These wastes damaged the dunes and affected the wildlife that lived there.

Mr. Serynek and other members of the council went to Washington, D.C., to talk to government officials. Through their efforts, the park was expanded in 1976, 1980, and again in 1986.

The Save the Dunes Council has a small budget. Only two people are paid for their work. The rest of the 1,200 members are volunteers. They work hard to preserve and expand the park because they see value in the dunes.

The council members understand that the dunes were formed over thousands of years. They want to keep the dunes as a home for the many species of birds that live there.

So that others can benefit from what they know, the council leads walks along the dunes. Along the way, walkers learn information about the dunes.

The council also works to help solve problems. Members suggest ways for industries to do their work without harming the environment. They ask new businesses to move to buildings in other areas instead of building along the dunes. In this way, new jobs can be created, but no dunes will be destroyed.

The efforts of the Save the Dunes Council have preserved an important natural resource. Now Mr. Serynek can lead his class from Jacques Marquette School on walks through the dunes. His students can enjoy the sights Mr. Serynek and his mother saw when they were children.

Citizenship and You

1. Think of a place in your community —an old building, a park, or a natural environment—that you hope future children will be able to enjoy. Find out whom you could write to and express your hope for saving this place. Then write a letter to that person.
2. Make a list of ways you can protect the environment every day.

LESSON 2 **Regions of Indiana**

Indiana has three main regions. How might the region you live in affect your life?

KEY WORDS

glacier (glā′shėr)
moraine (mə rān′)
fertile (fėrt′əl)
transport (trans′pôrt)
industry (in′dəs trē)
quarry (kwôr′ē)
tributary (trib′yə ter′ē)

Indiana lies the farthest east of all the plains states. Starting about 200 years ago, people began to clear forests to build homes and plant crops. Before that, Indiana made a kind of border between the heavily wooded, rolling hills regions to the east and the very flat plains to the west. For example, the highest point in Indiana, 1,257 feet (383 meters), is located just north of Richmond on the Ohio border. The lowest point in the state, 320 feet (98 meters), is located in the southwest corner where the Wabash River flows into the Ohio River. This means that Indiana has a very gradual upward slope to the east.

How Glaciers Carved Indiana

The way Indiana looks now is due to events that happened thousands of years ago. Huge **glaciers**, or slow moving rivers of ice, covered parts of Indiana three different times.

The first glacier, called the Illinoian, covered almost the whole state. Only the extreme southern part of the state was not covered. The second glacier, the Early Wisconsin, stopped about where Columbus, Indiana, is today. The third glacier, the Late Wisconsin, traveled through Indiana about 14,000 years ago. The ice ended then about where Kokomo was established.

MAP STUDY *What type of geographical feature helps to divide the Fertile Central Plains region from the Uplands and Lowlands region?*

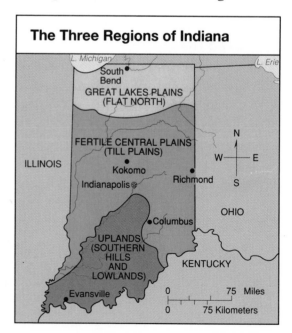

The Three Regions of Indiana

Rivers of Ice These rivers of ice worked like giant plows as they moved from the north to the south. As the glaciers spread, they picked up the top layers of soil and mountain-sized rocks and pushed them toward Indiana.

The glaciers also gouged, or dug, the earth in their paths and made deep depressions, or dips. In other words, the glaciers that flowed through Indiana completely changed the land.

Slowly, the temperature of the earth began to warm. The rivers of ice melted into water. The water filled the depressions in the earth and made lakes. Also, as the glaciers melted, the soil and the rocks stopped moving and came to rest wherever they happened to be when the melting began.

Moraines When the glaciers returned for the third time, they brought more sand and gravel. When they melted, the glaciers left this material in big piles and ridges that we now call **moraines**. There are many moraines in the northern part of the state.

The map on page 45 shows the surface features of Indiana. Which part of the state was affected most by

(Below) Large glaciers like this one— which still can be seen in Banff National Park in southwestern Canada—carried rocks and soil with them as they moved through Indiana. The rubble from glaciers is found in many Indiana areas (right).

Glaciers often left behind different layers of soil. You can see these layers in some of Indiana (left). Fortunately, some of the soil left behind is fertile and good for farming.

glaciers? If you guessed the north, you were right. Notice how many small lakes can be found in the northern half of the state. Now look at the Great Lakes. These lakes also were formed by glaciers. The first water in these lakes was nothing more than melted ice.

The Three Regions

The glaciers created three distinct regions in Indiana. In the north, the glaciers formed the Flat North or Great Lakes Plains. The middle of the state became the Fertile Central Plains, sometimes called the Till Plains. In the south, the glaciers formed the Uplands, or Southern Hills, and the Lowlands.

Fortunately for the farmers of Indiana, the glaciers left behind some very **fertile** soil in the middle of the state. Fertile soil is good for growing crops. The soil in the southern half is not quite as fertile, but the land can be farmed.

Northern Region The Flat North, or Great Lakes Plains, was not used for large farms. Instead, large cities grew in this region. Small vegetable farms developed around these cities. These farms are called truck farms because trucks are used to **transport**, or carry, the vegetables directly to marketplaces.

Because of the glacier's second visit to the north, the soil on the Great Lakes Plains is not as fertile as in the central plains. The sandy, rocky moraines are not suited for large farms. Still, the truck farms are an important source of many foods for Hoosiers.

Northern Cities Gary, Hammond, South Bend, Elkhart, and Fort Wayne are located in the northern region. Workers in these cities produce much of the manufactured, or machine-made, products of Indiana. Many industries are found in these cities. An **industry** is a manufacturing or business activity.

Gary was founded in 1906 for the purpose of making steel. The city is located between the great iron mines of the Mesabi Range in Minnesota and the coal fields of southern Indiana and Kentucky. Iron and coal are necessary to make steel, so steel companies decided to meet halfway in Gary. Plus, Gary's location on Lake Michigan means that the finished steel can be shipped. Gary and Hammond, Indiana's other important steel town, also are close to the rail center of Chicago, Illinois, so that products can be sent by rail.

South Bend is both an industrial center and the home of Notre Dame (nō' tėr dām'), a well-known university in the United States. Most people around the country think of

Flutes are made in the Armstrong factory in Elkhart.

Why did steel companies choose Gary as a location for steel manufacturing?

Notre Dame when they think of South Bend. Sports fans especially know about the university's football players, the Fighting Irish. The largest industry in South Bend, however, is auto manufacturing. This industry makes the city part of a long tradition of automaking in Indiana.

Elkhart's largest industry may be the most interesting of all the industries found in northern Indiana. Workers in this city make musical instruments—trombones, trumpets, tubas, and saxophones.

Fort Wayne is a famous toolmaking center. Its forges, or metalmaking workshops, create tools used by other industries. Fort Wayne is especially known for making diamond tools used in cutting. Some of these tools are used to cut and remove large building stones from the ground.

Central Region The Fertile Central Plains are where most of Indiana's large farms are found. This region sometimes is called the Till Plains because of the fertile soil the glaciers left behind. Because this region is especially flat, farmers can plant large fields of corn, the area's most important crop. Other crops include wheat, soybeans, and hay. Some farmers raise animals like pigs, turkeys, and dairy cows.

Central Cities Indianapolis, the state capital, is the largest city in the central region. If Indiana is a hub for the country, then Indianapolis is the center of the hub. Interstate highways 70, 74, 65, and 69 all lead to Indianapolis, as do several important rail lines.

Indianapolis was modeled after a beautiful city in France called Versailles (vėr sī'), and after Washington, D.C., the nation's capital. Both

CHART STUDY *You can see from this plat, or chart of a piece of land, that Indianapolis was designed like a wagon wheel. Where are the government buildings located?*

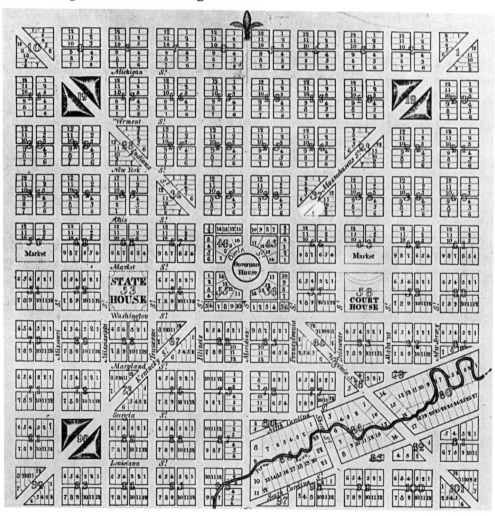

of these cities were designed like giant wagon wheels with most roads leading to the center. The main industries in Indianapolis are shipping, packing, and banking. The city's role as a transportation hub has made it the largest city in the state. By 1989, about 720,000 people lived in Indianapolis.

Anderson and Terre Haute (ter' rə hōt) are other important Till Plains cities. Terre Haute, located on the Wabash River, lies near most of the state's coal and oil deposits. Anderson is just a short distance northeast of Indianapolis. If you ride a school bus to school, there is a good chance your bus was made in Anderson.

Southern Region Because the glaciers did not reach most of the southernmost part of Indiana, this area, called the Uplands, still has some hills. If you wanted to explore caves, you probably would go here.

Some people in the Uplands still live in log cabins tucked into the hills. Artists and craftspeople have come to the Uplands for the quiet peacefulness of village life. Some of the villages have names like Gnaw Bone, Oolitic, and Stoney Lonesome.

This southern region has an important natural resource—limestone. Limestone is one of the best building stones in the world. If you have a large courthouse or city hall in your town, it probably was built with limestone from this region.

The southern region also has farms. The Wabash River flows along the western border. The branches of the White River flow right through the western part of the southern region. This part of the southern region is the Lowlands.

The Wabash and White rivers carry fertile soil from other parts of the state. Over the years, this soil has collected in the Lowlands near the southwestern corner of Indiana. This land is very good for farming.

A device called a channeling machine cuts through limestone at quarries. The cutting must be done carefully to avoid cracking the blocks.

Southern Cities Bloomington, Vincennes (vin senz'), Evansville, and New Albany are the major cities in the southern region. Bloomington is the home of Indiana University. The city is also the center of the state's limestone industry. The stone is **quarried**, or dug out, south of Bloomington.

Vincennes, Evansville, and New Albany are all river towns. At first, they were important shipping ports, but then railroads began to replace river barges. These cities played important roles in Indiana's history.

Highways of Water

Indiana is lucky to have so many rivers. In the past, these rivers carried Indians, pioneers, European immigrants, and traders. The rivers helped the development of Indiana, and they still are important transportation routes for some goods like farm products.

Remember that the land of Indiana slopes down toward the southwest. Water flows from higher to lower elevations, so much of the state's water drains toward the southwest. In other words, most Indiana rivers flow from the east toward the south and southwest.

The Great Wabash The most important river in Indiana is the Wabash. This river, which starts in western Ohio, was once a release valve, or spillway, for an ancient lake called Lake Maumee (mô'mē). This lake covered much of Ohio and parts of Indiana. Lake Erie is what remains of Lake Maumee.

Wabash is an Indian name. The name means "water over white stones." When the French came to Indiana, they spelled this Indian name "Oubache."

The Wabash River is important because it is 529 miles (851 kilometers) long and runs across the Till

The Wabash River is an important transportation route through Indiana. The river also offers Hoosiers beauty and the chance for water sports.

Plains region. The river then turns south to form the border between Illinois and Indiana. The Wabash River was used to explore the state and to move products from the east to the west and then to the south. The French used the river as a route between the Canadian city of Quebec (kwi bek′) and what is now the state of Louisiana.

Along its route, the river is fed by several **tributaries**. A tributary is a small river or stream that flows into another river. The most important tributaries are the Tippecanoe (tip′ ē kə nü′) River in the north and the east and west branches of the White River in the south.

Three Rivers The Wabash flows into the Ohio River near Mount Vernon. The Ohio River forms the southern border of Indiana. The river is formed by two other rivers, the Monongahela (mə nän′gə hē′ lə) and the Allegheny, that meet at Pittsburgh, Pennsylvania.

Not far from where the Wabash joins the Ohio, the Ohio flows into the Mississippi at Cairo, Illinois. From the time of the earliest explorations, these rivers were how most people traveled over long distances. The Wabash, the Ohio, and the Mississippi all helped Indiana become what it is today.

Other rivers that flow through Indiana include the Kankakee River in the northwest corner of the state and the Eel River, a tributary of the White River in the south.

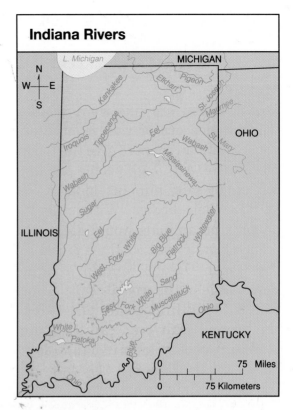

Indiana Rivers

MAP STUDY *In what direction do most Indiana rivers flow? Why?*

Lesson Review

Comprehension

1. Name three things that glaciers left behind in Indiana.
2. What are the three distinct regions of Indiana?
3. Why is the Wabash River important to Indiana?

Critical Thinking

4. If you were deciding which Indiana region to live in, what features would you look at as you compared the three regions?
5. Name two reasons for the growth of many Indiana cities.

People and the Environment

If you are like some people who eat popcorn or raw vegetables, you use salt on them to give the foods more taste. Although people can eat too much salt, humans must have salt in their bodies. Without salt, people and animals would die.

Fortunately, salt easily is found in the world. Oceans contain a large percentage of the world's salt. Some salt is found in deposits just below the ground. Salt even can be found sticking out of rocks or in handfuls of sandy earth. How did the salt get into rocks and dry earth?

Most of the time, the salt you see on dry land has been there for millions of years. At one time, an ocean covered what is now Indiana. Over thousands of years, when the ocean waters evaporated, salt was left behind on land. When rain came or small rivers were formed, the salt was carried by water. Sometimes it was dumped in one place and became part of the soil or rocks that formed there.

When the first pioneers left the eastern part of the United States for the areas of present-day Ohio, Kentucky, and Indiana, they brought cattle with them. The cattle were important for their survival. Cattle, at times, need salt in their diets. How, do you think, could the pioneers provide salt for the cattle?

Because the pioneers could not bring large amounts of salt with them, they had to rely on salt that occurred naturally. When they found a salt deposit, they brought their cattle to that place. The cattle then could lick the salt when they needed it. These places became known as salt licks. They often were open for everyone to use. Sometimes towns grew up around salt licks—especially when they were located in convenient places.

MAP STUDY *Why, do you think, were more places in southern Indiana named for salt than in northern Indiana?*

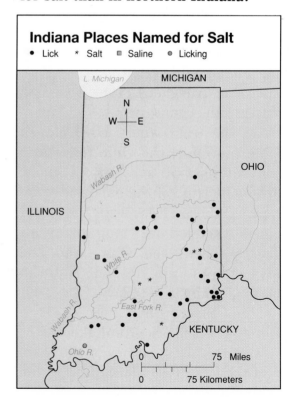

Indiana Places Named for Salt

• Lick * Salt ▪ Saline ● Licking

Cattle need salt in their diets. Today, on many farms, you can see cattle licking salt blocks left in the fields by farmers. Why did the pioneers have to depend on natural salt deposits?

People often gave the salt licks names—almost always using words that meant "salt" or "lick." The word *mahoning* also was used in the names of salt licks. It was an Indian word meaning "lick at." The map on page 62 shows where there were places in Indiana named after salt licks. For example, one Indiana town is called French Lick.

Today farmers easily can put blocks of salt out for their animals to lick. They no longer depend on natural salt deposits. Still, some Hoosiers remember the interesting story behind their towns' salty names.

Comprehension

1. Where is salt found?
2. What are two ways salt deposits can be formed?
3. Why was it so important for the pioneers to find salt deposits?
4. What does *mahoning* mean?

Critical Thinking

5. Why might many of the salt licks that the early pioneers found be located close to rivers?
6. What places in Indiana do you know that have *salt, saline, lick, licking,* or *mahoning* in their names? Make a list.

Words to Know

Number your paper from 1 to 6. Write the word that fills in each blank next to each number.

temperate   precipitation
tornado   forest
deciduous   aquatic

Because Indiana is located between the tropics and has hot and cold temperatures, its climate is called **1.** ___. In this kind of climate, **2.** ___ may fall in the form of rain, snow, or sleet. Sometimes the weather can be violent such as when a **3.** ___ strikes.

The ample rainfall permits ponds and lakes to support many kinds of **4.** ___ life. Indiana's climate also allows many kinds of trees to grow. Most of the trees are of the **5.** ___ variety. At one time, most of the state was one big **6.** ___ of trees.

Main Ideas

1. Name an important Indiana port on Lake Michigan.
2. On what river are Indiana's southern river ports located?
3. What kind of climate does Indiana have?
4. How does Indiana's climate change from north to south?
5. What region of Indiana is known for its rock quarries?
6. Name three different environments in Indiana.
7. What is special about the sand dunes in Indiana?
8. Why is Indiana described as having a plentiful water supply?
9. What is a glacier?
10. What good thing did glaciers leave behind in Indiana?
11. What is a moraine?
12. Name Indiana's three regions, and name two important cities in each region.
13. Why was Gary founded?
14. In what region of Indiana are the most farms found?
15. List three important facts about the southern region of Indiana.
16. Why is the Wabash River important to Indiana?

Critical Thinking

1. Indiana is a diverse state. That means Hoosiers have different kinds of jobs and live in different kinds of places. Some Hoosiers work in factories; others work on farms. Some Hoosiers live in cities and others in small villages. How do you think the state's geography made these differences possible?
2. The way Indiana appears today is due mostly to how the glaciers affected the land. How did glaciers change Indiana?
3. Indiana has several major rivers and many streams running through it. These waterways are important. They provide water for

towns and farms, for example. How did Indiana's waterways help the state to develop in the past and in the present?

Writing for Understanding

1. Imagine that you are in charge of attracting businesses to come to Indiana to set up new factories. Your job is to make business people think that moving to Indiana will help their businesses grow. You also need to explain the good qualities for the workers who might have to move to Indiana. Write a speech you might give to a group of business people. Your purpose is to make them want to come to Indiana. Remember to close the speech very strongly.

2. In the beginning of this chapter, you read what a friend of Theodore Dreiser said about his home state. Choose one thing you like in Indiana, such as a bird, a tree, a river, the people, or a forest. Write a paragraph that explains how you feel about the thing you have chosen and how it makes you feel about Indiana. Pretend that someone living in another state will read your writing. Try to make it very descriptive.

Applying Skills

Study the outline (right) and answer the questions.

1. Which line in the outline is a title of a lesson?
2. Which symbol comes before more important information—a capital letter or an Arabic numeral?
3. How would you know by looking at the outline what the main ideas are in this lesson?
4. Which lines include details about the lesson?
5. On a separate sheet of paper, complete the outline.

I. Regions of Indiana
   A. How Glaciers Carved Indiana
      1. Rivers of ice
         a. worked like giant plows
         b. made deep depressions
         c. melted into water and formed lakes
      2. Moraines
         a. made of sand and gravel
         b. glaciers left piles in northern part of state
   B. The Three Regions
      1._____
         a. _____
         b. _____
      2._____
         a. _____
         b. _____
      3._____

CHAPTER 3

How American Indians Lived in Indiana

Have you ever wondered who the first people were to live in Indiana? How did they get here? How did they live? This is what a famous Shawnee Indian named Tenskwatawa (tens'kwä täw'ə)—The Prophet—once told an early settler about how Indians were created.

"Now," said the Great Spirit, "I can hear and I will give you ears to hear even small noises. I can speak and I will give you tongues so you can talk to each other. I will also give you teeth like mine so you can chew food. You will eat corn, beans, cucumbers, squash, melons, elk, deer, buffalo, turkey, and raccoon. You will have 12 kinds of vegetables and 12 kinds of meat. Remember who made you and do not say that anyone else made you. You will live to 200 years, then your head will become white and you will die. When you become old. . .tell your children all that I have told you."

LESSON 1 Indiana's First Inhabitants

Scientists can tell us many things about ancient peoples by studying the places where they lived. What might the things that people leave behind tell us about them?

KEY WORDS
archaeologist (är kē äl'ə jist)
ancestor (an'ses tėr)

Many centuries ago, before history was written down, some parts of the earth that now are not connected were connected. Look at the map. Locate Alaska, Siberia, and the small sea called the Bering Sea. As you can see, at one time, a strip of land, called a land bridge, connected Alaska with the Asian continent.

Ancient Peoples

Scientists are not sure exactly when the first people crossed this land bridge from Asia to North America. Some scientists think that the people came to North America at about the same time the last glacier was moving through Indiana, nearly 16,000 years ago. Some people think that the bridge itself actually was part of a glacier.

Scientists who study ancient peoples are called **archaeologists**. Most archaeologists agree that the people who crossed over this bridge thousands of years ago are the **ancestors** of the American Indians.

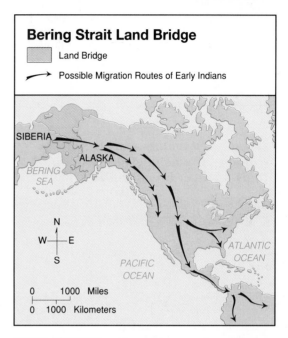

Bering Strait Land Bridge

☐ Land Bridge

➤ Possible Migration Routes of Early Indians

SIBERIA
ALASKA
BERING SEA
PACIFIC OCEAN
ATLANTIC OCEAN

0 1000 Miles
0 1000 Kilometers

MAP STUDY *Siberia is in the northeast corner of the Union of Soviet Socialist Republics (USSR). How close is Alaska to the USSR?*

Ancestors are people in a family who lived in the past.

These first peoples to arrive in North America took several routes southward. Some stayed in Alaska. We call them Eskimos. Some journeyed all the way to South America. These people include the Inca of Peru and the Amazonian people of Brazil. Some people, like the Aztec, went to Central America. The rest settled in different parts of North America from the Atlantic to the Pacific oceans.

First Peoples Several large groups of Indians arrived in what is now Indiana. Some of these groups settled in the area. Other groups, however, moved on.

Most archaeologists think the first Indians to come into Indiana arrived about 10,000 years ago. Then, perhaps about 4,000 years later, the Shell Mound Indians arrived. They left behind the shells of shellfish in large mounds.

In the shell mounds left behind by Indians, archaeologists have found tools made of bones and shells.

The Mound Builders Then, about 2,000 years ago, other groups of Indians settled in the Indiana area. They are called Mound Builders because they constructed large earthen burial mounds.

The Mound Builders lived along the rivers in what is now Ohio, Kentucky, and Indiana. They fished and gathered shellfish, berries, and roots. The Mound Builders hunted small game such as deer and raccoons. They used these animals for meat and clothing. The Mound Builders also grew crops like corn in the fertile soil along the rivers.

The Mound Builders were probably several different groups. Scientists have put these Indians into three groups: the Adena, the Hopewell, and the Mississippians. The scientists think the Adena were the first to arrive after the Shell Mound Indians and that the Hopewell and Mississippians followed.

Because of archaeological digs, archaeologists know some things about these people, even though the Indians lived here thousands of years ago. A dig is a place where archaeologists have found the remains of a people. Archaeologists have discovered, for example, that the Adena used chipped rocks to make knives and axes.

In other digs, archaeologists have found evidence that the Hopewell traded with Indian groups who lived long distances away. The scientists also have found proof that the Hopewell made jewelry and pottery.

Scientists can tell many things about ancient people from the digs. Not only do the scientists find things that belong to the people, but they also can tell how the people lived. For example, scientists know that the Mississippians were more settled than the Adena and the Hopewell. The Mississippians farmed more, and they knew how to grow more kinds of crops.

Mound Builder Sites Because the Mississippians were a settled group of people, they sometimes built large towns. The Angel Mounds, near Evansville, is a Mississippian site.

Archaeologists think that as many as 3,000 Indians lived in the Angel Mounds area. The Mississippians even planned their town around a central meeting ground and built important buildings that might have been temples or other meeting places.

Woodland Indians

The Mound Builder civilization declined about 1,000 years ago. Then new Indian groups called tribes developed. Some of these tribes may have descended from the Mound Builders. Others may have come from the north, south, or east. These tribes included the Miami, the Delaware, the Potawatomi, the Wyandot, the Kickapoo, and the Shawnee. Small bands of other Indian groups, like the Iroquois, also could be found in Indiana during this period of time. We now refer to all of these Indian groups as Woodland Indians.

Archaeological digs at the Angel Mounds have uncovered—among many other things—bits of pottery made by the Indians.

More than 40 Indian groups lived in the area called the Eastern Woodlands. This area spread over all of the United States east of the Mississippi River.

Problems with the Iroquois Some of the Woodland Indians were driven out of the eastern part of North America by the Iroquois Nation. The Iroquois were really six different groups centered in New York. They controlled much of the area along the Atlantic.

The Iroquois were fierce fighters. They often attacked smaller groups of Indians to get control of fur trapping areas or land that was good for

69

planting crops. As the Iroquois spread west, they pushed the groups ahead of them. Some, like the Delaware, arrived in the area of Indiana.

When the Iroquois arrived in Indiana during the 1600's, they wanted to control the land. The Miami, however, fought back. The Iroquois were not able to push the Miami any farther west, as they had done with other Woodland Indians.

Where Woodland Indians Lived

The Miami Indians were the largest tribe in Indiana. Their area ranged from eastern Illinois, through most of Indiana, and into western Ohio.

Many Shawnee also lived in this area. Their territory overlapped with the Miami. The Shawnee were the most powerful tribe from the valley of the Ohio River to the Appalachian Mountains.

The Wyandot lived near the shores of Lake Erie. The Potawatomi lived along the shores of Lake Michigan. These tribes were included in a group of Indians called The Great Lakes Indians. The groups included the Ojibwa (ō jib′ wā′) and the Ottawa in Michigan and the Winnebago and the Fox in Minnesota.

Many of these tribes traveled long distances. Their home territory was flexible. The Shawnee, for example, traveled all the way to the Wabash from central Ohio, where most of the tribe lived. Each tribe had a territory it considered home, but most tribes did not feel they owned any particular area.

Woodland Indian Territories

MAP STUDY *This map shows only approximate territories. Why is it impossible to give exact locations of the Woodland Indians' homes?*

Lesson Review

Comprehension

1. According to archaeologists, how and when did the first people come to North America?
2. What kind of life-style did the Mound Builders have?
3. How did the Iroquois Nation treat other Indians?

Critical Thinking

4. What facts about the Mound Builders have archaeologists learned from digs?
5. Why were most Indian groups not concerned about letting other Indians live in their territories?

LESSON 2 **Indians' Way of Life**

Hundreds of years ago, Indians had no guns, no tractors, and few tame animals. How did the Indians live without these things?

KEY WORDS
flint (flint′)
silt (silt′)

By the time the first English settlers set foot on North America, between one and two million Indians lived here. No one can be sure exactly how many Indians lived in Indiana because they moved from place to place. Yet some scientists think as many as 30,000 Indians once lived in the area that makes up the present state of Indiana.

Indian Beliefs

Beliefs among the various groups of Indians living in Indiana varied somewhat, but most of the Indians believed in similar things. For example, they believed that the Great Spirit made the first man an Indian. Some legends say this first man was imperfect, so the Great Spirit made another man. This time the Indian was perfect. Then, according to the legends, the Great Spirit made a perfect woman.

After creating man and woman, the Great Spirit opened the door to the skies and told the Indians that

Indian beliefs and culture—including traditions such as dances celebrating special events—still are being passed down to Indian children today.

they should leave the place of the Great Spirit and live on the earth. The Great Spirit promised them that the earth belonged to them and that it always would provide for their needs.

The Indians believed that since the Great Spirit had made them and put them on the earth, he was finished with them. The Indians also thought the Great Spirit had created other spirits that sometimes interfered in the lives of Indians.

The Indians believed spirits could be inside plants, animals, or people. The Indians believed they had to please these spirits in order to have good hunting and personal happiness.

The Great Spirit's Storehouse

Indians treated the earth with great care. They looked upon it as the storehouse of the Great Spirit. They believed the earth could be wounded. The Indians also thought that if they made the Great Spirit angry, they might be punished by severe weather or a shortage of food.

Belongings from the Storehouse

The Indians believed that everything they needed came from the storehouse of the Great Spirit. They depended on the earth's bounty for their daily needs.

Indian clothing was made of soft deerskin. To stay warm in winter, the Indians wore the furs of animals such as beaver and raccoon. Often they decorated their bodies with paints made from crushed berries or plants.

Indians used beads only after they had contact with European settlers. The beads were sewn on clothing to make many different patterns. The moccasins (above) and pants (below) are examples of Indian clothing. The type of clothing worn by Indians often was determined by the climate and by materials available to different groups.

Indians' possessions—including canoes and weapons—were made from what nature offered. Why were possessions mostly limited to useful items?

When the Indians traveled on the rivers and lakes around what is now Indiana, they used canoes made of birch trees. They first made frames from small branches. Then they sewed pieces of birch bark together using root fibers. Finally they stretched the bark over the frame, sealing it with tar.

The Indians' other belongings also came from the earth. They made musical instruments like drums from wood and hides. They carved flutes out of tree branches, and the seeds in dried gourds became rhythm instruments. In addition, the Indians used parts of the earth to help them hunt for and prepare their food. They worked on rounded stones to mash berries or grain. They also made spear points from **flint**, a hard rock that could be chipped away until a sharp edge was formed.

Indian Possessions

Most Indians did not believe that gathering possessions was necessary since everything they needed could be found from the earth. In addition, most Indians wandered from place to place. They knew that permanent possessions would slow them down when they traveled.

Most tribes in the area now known as Indiana grew some crops, but farming did not give the Indians all of their food. Instead, they gathered much of their food.

Berries, roots, and wild fruits all were found in the forest. The Indians hunted animals with bows and arrows and with spears. They also chased animals into traps and speared fish in the rivers and streams.

This type of Indian home is called a wigwam. The Miami Indians wove cattails into mats to cover their wigwams.

Farms In the spring, most tribes planted crops like corn and squash near riverbeds. These were good places for planting because the rivers overflowed and laid down a layer of fertile **silt**, or fine soil, along the river banks. Sometimes these farming areas would support a village of several hundred Indians for years. Then the Indians moved to another place. At other times, the Indians stayed only for a season.

Homes The homes the Indians built in these farming villages were simple. Usually they were made of poles cut from trees. The poles were arranged to make a dome-shaped frame, then the frame was covered with tree bark. Finally a hole was cut in the roof to let out smoke from the household fire.

When the fall harvest came, Indians often left the area where they grew crops to return to the forest. Even if they returned to a farming village many times, the Indians did not consider the village to be their only home. Because of this way of life, the Indians needed large areas of land. In contrast, the settlers who came to the Indiana area lived in permanent villages or towns. Even the early settlers stayed on the same land all the time. They did not gather their food; they grew it. The settlers tamed animals and raised them on farms. These differences between Indians and settlers in time would cause conflict between the two cultures.

Indian Culture

In a time of war or other crisis, an Indian tribe or village would look to a chief for instruction. The great Miami leader Little Turtle was one such chief.

As settlers began coming to the Indiana area, conflicts occurred between the two groups. When the conflicts became common, the need for a powerful, wise Indian leader increased. In time, the advice of a leader or chief was greatly needed.

Entertainment Like all people, the Indians did not work at all times. After they had taken care of their

Lacrosse, similar to ice hockey and soccer, was called bagataway *by the Indians. A game could last two to three days. Why did the Indians refer to it as "The Little Brother of War"?*

needs, such as gathering food and making clothing, they had time for play. The Indians mostly liked physical contests. They also liked to dance, to play music, and to put on dramas. Sometimes the events were religious, but they were also just for the Indians' enjoyment.

The Indians invented a game that is now called lacrosse. They played this game with great enthusiasm. In fact, the game could be quite dangerous. Sometimes players were seriously injured. The Indians called lacrosse "The Little Brother of War."

Battles Some Indians, such as the Shawnee, were more warlike than other tribes. Before the settlers arrived, however, all the groups fought battles among themselves.

The battles, or wars, were fought with clubs, bows and arrows, and spears. Sometimes the battles were violent, but they often seemed like another sporting event. Not many men were killed in these wars. Usually the wars were fought to control hunting grounds or to defend the honor of the village or tribe. Warriors felt it was important to fight in order to prove their bravery, so at times small wars were fought for that reason alone.

Most battles did not last long; some lasted only one day. Because Indians did not gather and store great amounts of food, hunting often was important to them. When the warriors were fighting, they could not hunt, and a long battle could cause the groups to go hungry.

moose

woodchuck

skunk

opossum

Therefore, the Indians could not afford to spend much time fighting. For a similar reason, most battles were fought in early fall. During the fall weeks, the harvest was in and food was more plentiful than at any other time of year.

Language Even though the Indians in the area now known as Indiana may have had similar ways of living, they could not always communicate with one another. Researchers have divided Indian languages into several different families. Most of the Indian groups living in Indiana spoke languages that belonged to the Algonquian (al gän′kē un) language family.

The Miami, Delaware, Kickapoo, and Shawnee are all classified as Algonquians. However, this does not mean that each tribe could understand the others or that the tribes themselves knew of this language family. In fact, the Shawnee warred less with Indians of other language groups than with the Miami.

At one time, the Algonquian language family was made up of 40 to 50 different languages. Today the names of many North American animals come from Algonquian origins. Since the Algonquian had no written language, how were the names passed on?

Lesson Review

Comprehension

1. Why were the Indians careful with nature?
2. Why did most Indians have no possessions or permanent homes?
3. Why were there few battles among the Indians?

Critical Thinking

4. Make a list of things the Indians got from nature. Now list anything the Indians really needed that they could not get from the earth's bounty. What conclusion can you draw by comparing the lists?
5. How might life have been different for the Indians if they all had spoken the same language?

Using a Card Catalog

A card catalog can be a key to finding things in your library. The card catalog is like a chest of small drawers full of index cards. These cards are the alphabetical catalog, or list, of all books in the library.

Every card catalog has three kinds of cards. One is a subject card. If you wanted to know about corn, for instance, you would look under the letter *C* for the subject *Corn*. Each card under the heading *Corn* is a subject card and lists a book on corn.

Another kind of card is an author card. An author card is filed under the author's last name.

The third kind of card is a title card. Title cards are filed under the first word of a book's title.

Study the sample cards below from a card catalog and answer the following questions.

1. Which type of card is each sample?
2. If you wanted to find information in the library on a certain subject or a particular book, how would the card catalog help you?

Project

Choose one of your favorite books. Make three cards for the book—an author card, a title card, and a subject card.

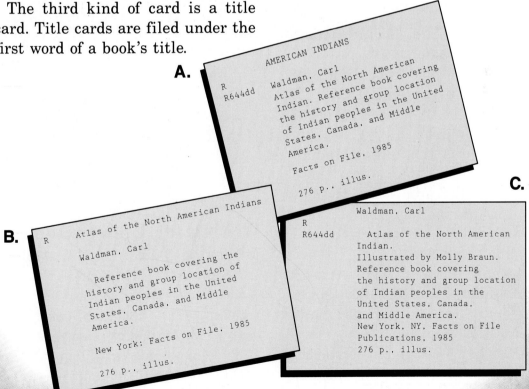

A.

AMERICAN INDIANS

R
R644dd

Waldman, Carl
Atlas of the North American
Indian. Reference book covering
the history and group location
of Indian peoples in the United
States, Canada, and Middle
America.
Facts on File, 1985
276 p., illus.

B.

R   Atlas of the North American Indians

Waldman, Carl

Reference book covering the
history and group location of
Indian peoples in the United
States, Canada, and Middle
America.

New York: Facts on File, 1985

276 p., illus.

C.

Waldman, Carl

R
R644dd   Atlas of the North American
Indian.
Illustrated by Molly Braun.
Reference book covering
the history and group location
of Indian peoples in the
United States, Canada,
and Middle America.
New York, NY, Facts on File
Publications, 1985
276 p., illus.

CHAPTER 3 REVIEW

Words to Know

Number your paper from 1 to 4. Next to each number, write the word that fits the definition.

archaeologist   flint
silt   ancestor

1. A scientist who studies the remains of ancient peoples
2. A person in a family who lived in the past
3. A hard rock
4. Fine soil that often is found along waterways

Main Ideas

1. When did the first people arrive in Indiana?
2. How did the Shell Mound Indians get their name?
3. Where can you see evidence of Indiana's first people today?
4. How did the Iroquois affect other Indian groups?
5. Which was the largest Indian group in Indiana? Name three other Indian groups that lived in or around Indiana.
6. Why did the Indians treat the earth carefully?
7. Name four ways the Indians used the storehouse of the Great Spirit.
8. Where did the Indians plant crops? Why?
9. Describe a Woodland Indian home.
10. Describe what the Indians did for entertainment.

11. Why were wars usually fought between Indian groups?

Critical Thinking

1. Different peoples have been living in Indiana for 10,000 years. The first people came from Asia and traveled thousands of miles before arriving in Indiana. They passed through many other places with different environments. Why, do you think, did they stop in Indiana and settle there?
2. Imagine that your class is taken to a land that looks much like Indiana did 300 years ago. The only other people living on this land are six classes from other schools. These classes are your neighbors, but much land lies between the different groups. Now imagine that you depend only on the land for your food and shelter. Do you think you would stay in your own area, or do you think you might wander to where the other classes live? Why?

Writing for Understanding

1. Imagine that you are placed in the middle of the wilderness. You do not know where you are, but you do know that nobody is looking for you. You will have to live in the wilderness as best you can. Write three paragraphs about what you would do. Include information

about what you would eat, how you would protect yourself against animals and weather, and how you would have fun. You might want to begin your writing by explaining what you would do first, then second, and so on in order of importance.

2. The Woodland Indians made up several stories about how they came to be and how the world was created. These were their myths. There are many myths in the world. For example, people in Northern Europe had myths about creatures that lived in swamps. Make up your own myths. For example, Why does it snow or rain? Why do some dogs have spots? For each item you discuss, include explanations for why the thing was needed and why it looks the way it does. Then tell how it was created.

Applying Skills

Study the cards below and answer the questions.

1. Which is the subject card?
2. Who is the author of the book on the subject card?
3. What is the name of the book on the title card?
4. Under what letter in the library's card catalog would the author card be listed?
5. How would you know where to find these books in the library?

INDIANS, AMERICAN

914   Baldwin, Gordon C.
         How Indians Really
Lived.

New York: Putnam, 1967
96 p., illus.

914.2   The Mound Builders
         Scheele, William E.

New York: World, 1960
96 p., illus.

         Glubok, Shirley

623   The Art of the
         Woodland Indians.

         New York: Macmillan,
         1978
         112 p., illus.

Settlers in Indiana

Imagine you are moving to a place about which you know very little. You don't know about the land or the rivers and streams or even if the weather is pleasant most of the time. You feel a bit frightened about what you might find in this new place. You do know that no friends are waiting there to greet you. You know that no stores have been built where you can buy your food and clothing. You also know that the trip you have to take to get to this place is very long and very difficult.

In the 1500's and 1600's, people from other countries came to such an unknown place. These people came for many reasons. To them, the land was the New World. The people felt the New World was full of opportunities. We now know this place as the United States of America.

This world was *not* new to the Indians. For the people who came to the New World, the land did, in time, offer opportunities for freedom and independence. The Indians, however, were not able to share these opportunities.

LESSON 1 The Arrival of the French and English

Think about the Indians who lived on Indiana land before anyone else arrived. How might the new settlers, who were used to a different way of life, use the land?

KEY WORDS
raw material (rô'mə tir'ē əl)
portage (pōrt'ij)
settlement (set'əl mənt)
confederation (kən fed'ə rā'shən)
surveyor (sėr vā'ėr)

The Indians who lived in what is now Indiana had their own beliefs and ways of doing things. They had lived on the land for centuries and had no reason to believe anything would change. Events thousands of miles away from Indiana, however, would change forever the way of life of the Indians.

French Control of Indiana

During the 1400's, nations in Europe began exploring the world. European ships sailed farther away from land than ever before. Each European country wanted to discover and claim more and more foreign land. The leaders of these countries thought that the nation that controlled the most land could become the most powerful country in Europe. The leaders also hoped to find wealth in the new lands.

Columbus actually thought he was going to find a sea route to Asia when he sailed across the Atlantic Ocean.

At that time, France and England competed with each other for power. After Christopher Columbus sailed to the Americas in 1492, England and France, among others, sent their ships to explore and claim some of the New World for themselves.

The English claimed lands along the east coast of what is now the United States. The French explored what is now southern Canada and also the coastline of the Gulf of

81

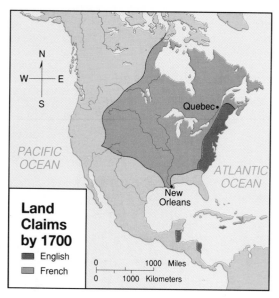

Land
Claims
by 1700
■ English
■ French

0   1000   Miles
0   1000   Kilometers

MAP STUDY   *Which country had claimed the most land?*

Mexico. The French explorers trapped animals for fur. Sometimes they gave gifts of weapons, jewelry, and tools to the Indians in return for Indian furs. The furs then were sold to make clothes in France. The English wanted to be part of this new business.

Two French Capitals   By 1608, a group of French explorers had settled at Quebec in what is now Canada. The settled area of Quebec was the capital of New France, an area that included present-day Indiana.

French explorers also claimed land as far south as New Orleans (Louisiana.) They made New Orleans into a capital where leaders could oversee the southern French territory.

By looking at the map above, you can see that New Orleans and Quebec were separated by a large area of land. In the 1600's, traveling

a long distance such as this was both difficult and dangerous. French leaders, however, wanted to find a way to travel between their two capitals. They also wanted to know what kind of land could be found along the way.

One section of this unknown land the French explorers wanted to learn about was the area we call Indiana. They wanted to know what **raw materials** could be found there. Raw materials were important because they could be used to make products necessary for daily life. If raw materials were available, the French would want to begin developing the land. They felt it was important to claim the land and its raw materials for France before the English settlers claimed the area for their country.

La Salle's Exploration of Indiana
To learn more about the land, the French leaders knew they would have to choose an explorer who had

Robert de La Salle is remembered for being the first European to follow the Mississippi River to its mouth.

82

The French explorers traveled in Indian canoes. Often they had to carry the canoes from river to river (above). Along the way, they traded furs with the Indians (right).

experience living and traveling in a wilderness area. They turned to Robert de La Salle, who was a French military officer living in present-day Canada. The leaders asked La Salle to find a good way to travel from Quebec to New Orleans. They also wanted him to explore the area that is now Indiana.

In 1679, La Salle and 29 men became the first recorded white people to enter Indiana. They stayed near the present site of South Bend and then continued their journey on the Kankakee River.

When the explorers moved from river to river to find a route south, they had to carry their canoes and supplies across the land to the next river. This kind of travel is called **portage**. You can imagine how difficult a long portage could be. La Salle and his party picked the shortest land routes possible and stayed on the rivers as much as they could.

The First French Trading Posts

After La Salle's visit to Indiana, the Indians' way of life was changed. By 1713, French people, mostly fur traders, had moved into the area. A trading post called Post Ouiatenon (wē at′ ə non) was built in 1717. This site is near present-day Lafayette. In 1722, the French built a fort called Saint Phillipe de Miami at Kekionga. A large, settled group of Miami Indians lived there. The site now is called Fort Wayne. The third French population center was at Post Vincennes on the Wabash River. It was founded in 1732.

Why, do you think, did the French group their shacks and surround them by a wall?

Only a few hundred French people lived at these three outposts. The French tried to get along with the Indians. The two sides traded for furs. The Indians usually felt they could trust the French.

French Settlement Life The French settlers lived in simple shacks made of stakes covered with bark. The shacks had no windows or floors. The French grouped the shacks together in a **settlement**. A settlement is the first small community that settlers build when they come to a new area. The French settlements were surrounded by walls made of wood. Outside these walls, the settlers cleared small plots of land where they grew vegetables. They hunted for other food or bought it from the Indians.

The French introduced new things to Indian life. To encourage the Indians to trap more animals for fur, the French traded their guns for the Indians' furs.

Perhaps the worst thing the French introduced to the Indians was the disease called smallpox. Over many years, the French had built up protection in their bodies to help them fight off the disease. The Indians, however, were not able to fight smallpox. They often died of the disease.

Declaration of War

While France developed its territories, English leaders watched the French jealously. The fur trade had brought great wealth to the French treasury, and the English king wanted some of that wealth for his own treasury.

In 1756, England declared war on France. Because most Indians sided with France and fought against the English, this war was called the French and Indian War by the English who lived in America. The Iroquois, however, fought on the side of the English.

One famous American who was still an English subject, or citizen, also fought for England. His name was George Washington. His fame grew after he proved himself to be a good fighter in this war.

In Europe, the war is remembered as the Seven Years' War because it took seven years for England to win it. In a peace treaty signed in 1763, the French gave up their land in North America to the English.

Pontiac's Attack   After the English victory, the Indians were concerned. They feared many settlers would come into the new English land. The Indians also did not like the way the English traded. The English fur traders, for example, did not pay as much as the French traders had paid.

One Indian, an Ottawa named Pontiac, decided to fight the English. To make the Indians stronger, Pontiac formed a **confederation**, or united group, that included the Potawatomi, Chippewa, and Ottawa. Pontiac led such a successful campaign against the English that nearly all the English forts fell to the Indians. Only Detroit and Fort Pitt were able to withstand Pontiac's attacks.

One English leader, Sir Jeffrey Amherst, suggested that the way to fight Pontiac and other Indians was to send them blankets that had been infected with smallpox. Amherst thought this would kill the Indians and end the trouble. The English decided on another plan.

The Proclamation of 1763   To calm the Indians, the English made the Proclamation of 1763. This order said that no English subjects could settle on lands west of the Appalachian Mountains.

Pontiac spoke out against all the hardships Indians had to face because of the English.

Although Pontiac's uprising lasted two more years, the Proclamation did help the Indians accept English rule. The Indians thought they would be able to continue their lives as they always had and that nothing would change. They were wrong.

Jeffrey Amherst was a military leader before being named head of North American English holdings in 1760.

Surveying still is an important job as land continues to be developed.

English subjects living in America did not like the Proclamation of 1763. These people thought the proclamation would prevent them from buying and selling land in the new territories.

Some land companies already had staked out claims in Ohio and Indiana. Before the land companies could claim the land, it had to be measured by a **surveyor**. A surveyor is someone who uses certain instruments to make exact measurements of land. One land company was represented by a young surveyor named George Rogers Clark. He worked for some wealthy Virginians, including Washington, who wanted to claim large parts of Ohio.

A survey expedition that included Clark had to fight the Shawnee in Ohio. Hundreds of men were lost on both sides. Peace was made, but within a few years that peace was broken. The Indians were pushed farther west, beyond Ohio.

Lesson Review

Comprehension

1. Why did European leaders want to discover foreign land?
2. What was Robert de La Salle's mission in 1679?
3. Why did England and France go to war against each other?
4. Why were the Indians concerned about the English?

Critical Thinking

5. Once the European settlers claimed land in the New World, for what purposes did they use it?
6. Why might it have been important to measure out exact land claims?

Reading a Time Line

Time lines are one way to organize information visually. They can help you place historical events in their proper order. The time line on this page shows events in Indiana history from prehistoric times to the coming of Europeans.

One advantage of using a time line to organize history is to help you see how much time passed between events. In a sense, this is like a scale on a map that helps you determine distances. Just as a map scale might say that one inch equals 100 miles, a time line also uses the length of a line to show the passage of years.

On the time line below, one inch stands for 5,333 years. If you wanted to make a time line that would cover fewer years, you might make one inch stand for 500 years.

Note that the break in the time line—between 100 B.C. and A.D. 1584 —is used to represent many years. If the time line had shown all of those years to scale, it would not have fit on the page.

Use the time line to answer the questions below.

1. How many inches are there between the coming of the last glaciers to Indiana and the beginning of the Mound Builders' Construction?
2. How many years passed between the arrival of the Shell Mound Indians and the start of the Mound Builders' construction?
3. How did you find the answer to Question 2?
4. How long did it take the French—represented by Robert de La Salle—to meet the Indians in Indiana after the English met the Indians in Virginia?

Project

Use the important events of your life to create a time line. Start with your birthday and end with today. Your line could include when you started school or when you learned to swim or ride a bike.

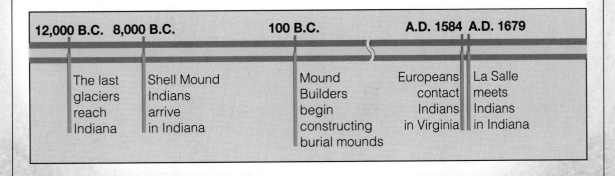

12,000 B.C.	8,000 B.C.	100 B.C.	A.D. 1584	A.D. 1679
The last glaciers reach Indiana	Shell Mound Indians arrive in Indiana	Mound Builders begin constructing burial mounds	Europeans contact Indians in Virginia	La Salle meets Indians in Indiana

LESSON 2 Indiana and the War for Independence

The War for Independence began in 1775. In 1775, Indiana was still mostly unpopulated by settlers. What role did this area play in the War for Independence?

KEY WORDS
colony (kol′ə nē)
colonist (kol′ə nəst)
surrender (sə ren′dėr)

Many people wanted to move west beyond the boundaries set up by the Proclamation of 1763. Most of the people were living in the **colonies** along the east coast. A colony is a settlement or group of settlements far from the country that rules it. Some **colonists**, or people who lived in the colonies, felt there were opportunities in the west. People without much land saw the west as their chance to get more land. Other people saw the west as a chance to profit by claiming and then selling the land to newcomers.

The War for Independence

Before the Americans could continue their push westward, they became involved in a war against England—the War for Independence. For almost 200 years before this war, the colonies and the unsettled areas to the west were controlled by

In the Declaration of Independence, the American colonists declared why they wanted to be separate, or independent, from the English. What reasons might they have given?

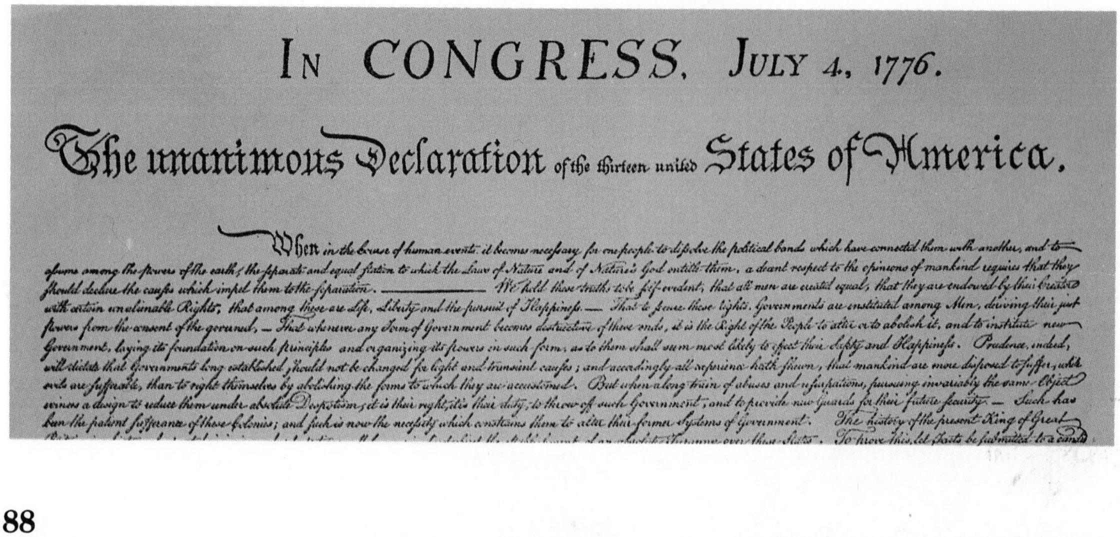

IN CONGRESS, JULY 4, 1776.

The unanimous Declaration of the thirteen united States of America,

When in the Course of human events, it becomes necessary for one people to dissolve the political bands which have connected them with another, and to assume among the powers of the earth, the separate and equal station to which the Laws of Nature and of Nature's God entitle them, a decent respect to the opinions of mankind requires that they should declare the causes which impel them to the separation. —— We hold these truths to be self-evident, that all men are created equal, that they are endowed by their Creator with certain unalienable Rights, that among these are Life, Liberty and the pursuit of Happiness. — That to secure these rights, Governments are instituted among Men, deriving their just powers from the consent of the governed, — That whenever any Form of Government becomes destructive of these ends, it is the Right of the People to alter or to abolish it, and to institute new Government, laying its foundation on such principles and organizing its powers in such form, as to them shall seem most likely to effect their Safety and Happiness. Prudence, indeed, will dictate that Governments long established should not be changed for light and transient causes; and accordingly all experience hath shewn, that mankind are more disposed to suffer, while evils are sufferable, than to right themselves by abolishing the forms to which they are accustomed. But when a long train of abuses and usurpations, pursuing invariably the same Object evinces a design to reduce them under absolute Despotism, it is their right, it is their duty, to throw off such Government, and to provide new Guards for their future security. — Such has been the patient sufferance of these Colonies; and such is now the necessity which constrains them to alter their former Systems of Government. The history of the present King of Great

England. By the late 1700's, however, the colonists began to feel that they wanted to be a separate country. The colonists did not agree with the way English leaders ruled the colonies. The disagreements led to the War for Independence in 1775.

For the settlers in western areas such as Indiana, the war was not as much a part of daily life as it was for the eastern colonists. Instead, the western settlers had to worry about Indian attacks.

The English knew that the Indians were attacking the settlers. For this reason, the English thought the Indians would fight for England. Some Indians did decide to fight on the English side. Other Indians chose to wait to see what would happen.

George Rogers Clark One man had a plan that he thought would protect settlers from Indian attacks while also taking the Indiana area away from English control. George Rogers Clark, the surveyor you read about in the last lesson, knew that the English had built their own forts in the wilderness area. He wanted to capture these forts.

Clark asked the governor of Virginia, Patrick Henry, for men and supplies to attack the forts. Patrick Henry agreed with Clark that the wilderness forts increased the English and the Indian threat. Patrick Henry asked Clark to capture three forts—Fort Sackville at Vincennes, Fort Kaskaskia, and the fort at Detroit.

Patrick Henry became famous when he gave a speech on why the colonists should separate from the English.

Clark's First Successes Clark set out with 175 soldiers. He went to Kaskaskia first. On July 4, 1778, Clark and the soldiers surrounded the fort. Many of the soldiers defending Kaskaskia were French people who had joined with the English. The French, however, were not completely loyal to the English. When they saw the Americans, the French gave up without a fight.

Next Clark marched to Vincennes and took Fort Sackville, again without much fighting. He left an aide, Captain Helm, in charge of Fort Sackville. Clark himself returned to Kaskaskia.

Fight for the Forts

The English governor at Detroit, Henry Hamilton, was upset by the American victories. He was determined to recapture Fort Sackville and Kaskaskia.

Clark's march to Vincennes was very hard on the men. Why did the soldiers attempt such a difficult march?

Hamilton's Plan Hamilton, dressed in Indian clothing and prepared for war, held a meeting with the Miami and the Potawatomi. Hamilton convinced the Indians to join him in the march to Vincennes to fight the "Long Knives," as the Indians called the Americans because of the swords the soldiers carried.

The governor, leading an army of 500 English soldiers and Indian warriors, left Detroit and marched to Vincennes. At Fort Sackville, Clark's aide Captain Helm was low on supplies and had only a few soldiers with him. He had little choice but to give up the fort to the English on December 17, 1778.

After recapturing Fort Sackville, Hamilton decided to let the Indians who fought with him leave the fort for the winter. He reasoned that there would be no more fighting until spring.

Clark's Daring Move At Kaskaskia, Clark heard that Hamilton had only 80 men with him at Vincennes. Clark decided to take a daring gamble. He wrote of his plan to Patrick Henry.

"...we must Either quit [leave] the C[o]untry or attack Mr. Hamilton ...Great Things have been affected [done] by a few Men well Conducted."

Clark took his force of about 175 soldiers, including some French soldiers from Kaskaskia, and set out for Vincennes. The march was extremely difficult. Although it was the middle of winter, some of the snow and ice had melted, and the land was like a swamp. At times, the men had to wade in waist-deep water for many miles. Food supplies were low, and the men were exhausted when they reached Vincennes 16 days and 200 miles (322 kilometers) later.

American Victories

When Clark and his soldiers were in sight of Fort Sackville, Clark spread out his forces and gave a flag to each small group. This made the English think Clark had more soldiers than he did. Once the shooting started, the Americans proved to be more accurate than the English. Hamilton was afraid he was greatly outnumbered. After seeing many of his soldiers fall, the English governor of the fort agreed to **surrender**, or give up, on February 25, 1779.

With his victory, Clark renamed the fort after Patrick Henry and claimed Indiana for Virginia. Indiana was under American control for the first time.

End of War Clark's campaign was not a complete success as he never managed to capture Detroit. Nevertheless, American victories in the east at Saratoga and Yorktown won the War for Independence in 1781. The Treaty of Paris in 1783 recognized the United States of America as a separate country.

Forts were important to the French, the English, and the Americans. When Captain Helm (inset) had to surrender Ft. Sackville, it was considered a great loss.

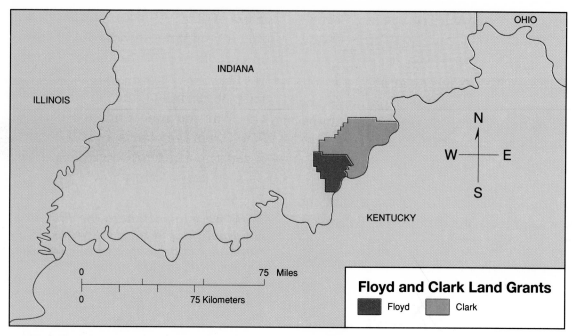

MAP STUDY   *In what part of Indiana are Floyd and Clark counties located?*

At first, the Indians in Indiana did not think the end of the war would have much effect on them. They remembered that neither the French nor the English allowed many settlers in the area. The Indians thought the Americans would do the same thing. Later the Indians would see that they had guessed wrong.

American Villages in Indiana

After the War for Independence, George Rogers Clark and some of the soldiers who fought with him were given large land grants by the new United States government. They received 150,000 acres in what are now Clark and Floyd counties. These people established the first American villages in this area. The doors to Indiana were open. Settlers soon moved in.

Lesson Review

Comprehension

1. What events led to the War for Independence?
2. What did George Rogers Clark set out to do in 1778?
3. Tell about two important battles that occurred at Fort Sackville.
4. What event brought Indiana under American control?
5. How was George Rogers Clark rewarded for his victories in the War for Independence?

Critical Thinking

6. Why were the forts in the Indiana area considered important in the War for Independence?
7. What role did the Indians play in the War for Independence?

CHAPTER 4 REVIEW

Words to Know

Write a sentence that shows the meaning of each word.

1. raw material
2. portage
3. confederation
4. surveyor
5. colony
6. surrender
7. settlement
8. colonist

Main Ideas

1. Which European nation controlled Indiana first?
2. What two cities served as the French capitals in newly settled North America?
3. Who was Robert de la Salle?
4. Where was the first trading post in French Indiana?
5. What disease did the French introduce to the Indians?
6. Describe how the first French settlers obtained food and shelter.
7. How did the English gain control of the French lands in North America by 1763?
8. Who was Pontiac and what group of fighters did he organize?
9. How did the Proclamation of 1763 protect Indian life on the Plains?
10. Who was George Rogers Clark?
11. What two forts did Clark capture at the beginning of the War for Independence?
12. Which fort did Clark capture twice? How did he do it?
13. Was Clark's campaign a complete success? Why or why not?

Critical Thinking

1. In the 1500's and 1600's, countries in Europe set out to claim new lands. A rivalry always had existed among the European nations to see who could be the most powerful, build the best navy, or have the most money. Many wars were fought, and land changed hands often along the borders of the European countries. When the Americas were discovered, these rivalries became based upon the new lands. Why, do you think, were the Americas so important to the European nations?

2. In the French and Indian War, the Indians fought on the side of the French because the Indians did not like the way they had been treated by the English. Later the Indians fought against the English again. In the War for Independence, however, the Indians sided with the English against the American colonists. Why, do you think, did the Indians fight against the colonists?

Writing for Understanding

1. Pretend that you are Pontiac and that you are traveling from one Indian group to another asking for help. You want to convince the groups to join your cause. Write a speech you could give before these other Indians that would make

them want to join you. Your speech must accomplish several things. First, you must explain why there is a problem. Second, you must tell your audience what they can do to help solve the problem. Third, you must convince them that your solution will work.

2. Pretend that you are a soldier in Clark's army. You are marching to Vincennes to recapture Fort Sackville. Write several diary entries spaced a few days apart. Describe what you are going through. Tell how you feel about what you are doing. Are you afraid? Are you happy? Are you thinking about your family? Are you wondering what will happen when you meet the enemy? Be sure to include details about what you are wearing and eating and what your daily life is like.

Remember that with each entry you should be closer and closer to your destination.

Applying Skills

Use the time line below to help you answer the questions.

1. In what year did England agree to recognize the United States?
2. How many years passed from the beginning of the War for Independence to the end of it?
3. How many years passed from the arrival of La Salle in Indiana to the beginning of the War for Independence?
4. How many wars were fought between 1679 and 1783?
5. How many years passed between Queen Anne's War and King George's War?

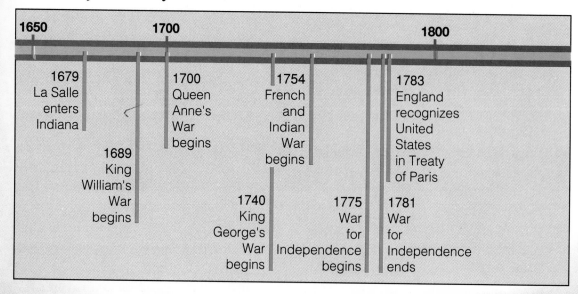

1650   1700   1800

1679
La Salle
enters
Indiana

1689
King
William's
War
begins

1700
Queen
Anne's
War
begins

1740
King
George's
War
begins

1754
French
and
Indian
War
begins

1775
War
for
Independence
begins

1783
England
recognizes
United
States
in Treaty
of Paris

1781
War
for
Independence
ends

UNIT 1 REVIEW AND STUDY GUIDE

Key People/Places	Key Terms	Key Ideas
The Changing Middle West (pages 28-43) Point du Sable, Hill ___ Middle Western states, Central and Great Plains, Great Lakes, Milwaukee, Chicago, Minneapolis, St. Paul, Appalachian Mountains, *Rivers*—Mississippi, Missouri, Ohio	extinct, reservation, heritage, descent, pioneer, nationality, interdependence, stockyard, grain elevator, megalopolis, competition	■ Life changed greatly for Indians of the Middle West after European settlers arrived. ■ People who settled the Middle West came from many different nationalities. ■ The Middle West is known for its large cities, its diverse population, and the role it plays in global interdependence.
Indiana Geography (pages 44-65) Northern, Central, and Southern regions; Burns Harbor, St. Lawrence Seaway; Indiana rivers	temperate, precipitation, tornado, forest, deciduous, aquatic, glacier, moraine, fertile, transport, industry, quarry, tributary	■ Indiana's location and waterways make it a center of transportation and trade. ■ Indiana has three distinct regions: the Northern, Central, and Southern regions.
How American Indians Lived in Indiana (pages 66-79) *Indian Groups*—Mound Builders, Woodland, Algonquian	archaeologist, ancestor, flint, silt	■ Archaeologists can tell who first came to Indiana and how these people lived. ■ Indians did not settle in any one place and had great respect for the earth.
Settlers in Indiana (pages 80-94) de La Salle, Washington, Pontiac, Clark, Hamilton ___ Quebec, New France, New Orleans, South Bend, Fort Sackville	raw material, portage, settlement, confederation, surveyor, colony, colonist, surrender	■ People from France and England settled in the New World and changed the Indians' ways of life forever. ■ Control of forts in the Indiana area played a key role in the colonists winning the War for Independence.

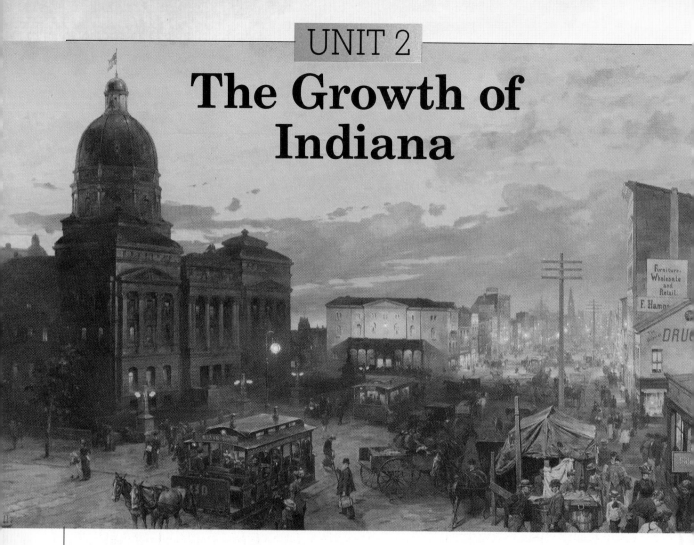

UNIT 2

The Growth of Indiana

1750   1800   1900

1787
Government
set up
for Northwest
Territory

1816
Indiana
made
19th
state

1830
National
Road
reaches
Indiana

1906
Steel
Company
starts
building
Gary

1920
51 percent
of Hoosiers
live
in cities

▲ Washington Street at Dusk, *by Theodore Groll*

detail of Treaty of Greenville, 1795 ▶

IN THIS UNIT

In this unit, you will learn about the history of
Indiana from the time right after the War for
Independence until the end of World War II. You will
find out how Indiana became the nineteenth state. You
will read about the growth of the Indiana area during
the years leading up to statehood, and you will meet
some important Hoosiers who worked hard to solve
problems and make progress. You also will find out
about the different groups who helped the state to grow
and prosper.

Planning for the New United States

KEY WORDS
noble   (nō′bəl)
capital (kap′ə təl)

Thomas Jefferson was an important person in the early years of the United States. He is known as one of the founders of the country. Two of the many things for which he is remembered are writing the Declaration of Independence and serving as the third President of the United States.

Owning Land in the United States

Jefferson and some of the other founders thought a great deal about what they would like to see happen to the land of the United States. They looked to other countries to find out how other governments had developed their land.

For example, the founders knew that in some European countries most people did not own much land. Instead, it was owned by kings or **nobles**, who were the wealthiest and most important citizens of the country. These people hired others to work on their land. Sometimes the nobles rented small amounts of land to farmers.

Jefferson and the other leaders identified problems in this system. If only kings and nobles own land, people cannot control their own lives. If people do not own their land, a king or noble can remove them from the land at any time.

In addition, the founders saw that farmers who rented small plots of land did not have as good a chance as landowners had to increase the amount of money they earned. Their children never could own the farms on which they worked. All the wealth of the country belonged to just a few people who owned land.

Thomas Jefferson was a person of many talents. Besides serving in government, he was an inventor, an architect, and the founder of the University of Virginia.

Thomas Jefferson hoped for a nation made up of farms and small cities. Why did he think this was the best way for the United States to develop?

Jefferson's Plan Jefferson wanted Americans to be able to own their own land. He imagined a country where most people would own small farms. Some of the food they grew would be used by the farm families. The rest of the food would be sold in markets. In time, a few people would live in cities. These city dwellers would make products the farmers would need such as dishes, shoes, and wagon wheels.

In this way, Jefferson felt that each person could control his or her own life. Farmers could grow what they wanted. They could pass their land on to their children. If they were able, they could buy more land to make more money. Likewise, people who chose not to farm could find useful and profitable jobs in cities.

Indiana Land Indiana was formed in part because of the desire for family-owned farmland. The leaders of the new United States made laws that divided Indiana into small sections. Even settlers who had little money could move to Indiana and buy these sections.

The land that was divided, however, already was being used by Indians. The Indians did not want the land to be cleared for farms. Although the Indians did not feel that they owned the land, they felt closely connected to it. Settlers did not understand the Indians' ways and they felt they could use the land more wisely than the Indians. As you might guess, soon there were conflicts between settlers and Indians. After several wars between

99

the Indians and the new Americans, the Indians were defeated and forced to move out of Indiana.

After the Indians were gone, many people began their own farms. Thousands of new pioneers moved into Indiana, especially after it became a state. These people came from other places in the United States where land was more expensive.

Changes in Land Use

In just a few years, villages sprang up in Indiana and throughout the country. A new state **capital** was built at Indianapolis. A capital is a city where the government of a state or country is found. People from other countries moved to the United States and Indiana to work. They lived in the new towns and cities.

From Farms to Cities By the late 1800's, farm life began to change rapidly. New inventions changed the way farmers worked, allowing them to farm more land. Farms could be much bigger. Fewer people than before were needed to work the land.

New inventions also helped factories to become bigger and to make new products. More people were needed to work in these factories. This meant that cities grew and that some land previously used for

Battles between settlers and Indians lasted well into the 1800's. This famous battle occurred in Indiana on November 7, 1811. Why did the settlers and Indians fight?

The invention of the automobile led to rapid development of the United States. Many of the most popular automobiles—like this 1932 Auburn Speedster—were made in Indiana.

farming was developed for cities. Many people left farming to work in manufacturing jobs in the cities.

The Need for Roads One invention in particular changed the country and Indiana. The automobile meant that people could live farther away from where they worked. Roads had to be built. The cities grew even faster and took up even more land that used to be farms. Finally, by 1920, more people lived in the cities than lived on farms.

More than 200 years after the nation's founders discussed how to use the new country's land, the United States does not look much like they imagined. Many things can happen in 200 years. The country of farms has become a place of great activity, of roads that stretch from coast to coast, and of cities with millions of residents. However, Jefferson and the other founders of this nation probably would be pleased to see how the people of the United States actually do control their own lives in the late 1900's.

Focus Review

Define
noble, capital

Comprehension
1. What happened when only nobles and kings owned land in Europe?
2. Why did cities begin overtaking farmland in the 1800's?

Critical Thinking
3. What would Jefferson like about the United States today?

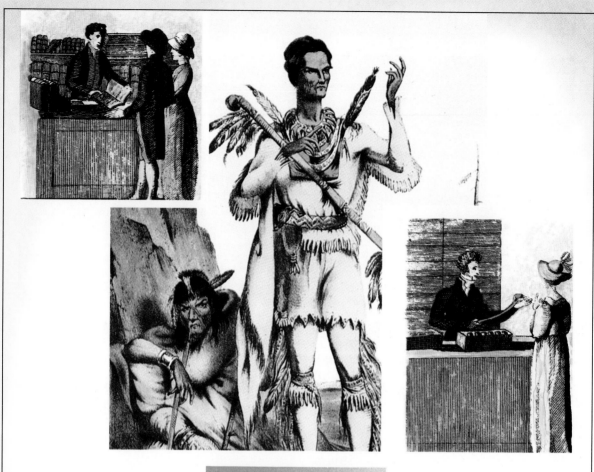

CHAPTER 5

New Laws for New Lands

As more and more people came farther west into the new United States, the Indians' way of life was replaced by a new way. This is what the great Miami chief Little Turtle said about the new way of life.

Here I am deaf and cannot speak. When I walk through the streets, I see every person in his shop doing something. One makes shoes, another hats, a third sells cloth and everyone lives by this work. I say to myself, which of these can you do? Not one. I can make a bow or an arrow, catch fish, kill game, and go to war, but none of these is of any use here. I would be like a piece of furniture, useless to my people, useless to whites and useless to myself.

LESSON 1 The Northwest Territory

When the Americans won the War for Independence, the United States of America was born. What problems did this new country have to face?

KEY WORDS

Northwest Territory (nôrth west′ ter′ə tōr′ē)
ordinance (ôrd′ən ənts)
township (toun′ship′)
legislature (lej′ə slā′chėr)
delegate (del′i gət)

After the Americans won the War for Independence, they had a great celebration. A new country had been created. Right after the war, however, the new government went to work. Leaders like George Washington had to find a way to govern the country and all the new western land won from the English.

A New Plan

After winning the war, the new United States government controlled all the land that had been claimed by the English. In 1787, the area that was surrounded by the Great Lakes, the Ohio River, and the Mississippi River was called the **Northwest Territory**. This area included present-day Ohio, Indiana, Illinois, Wisconsin, Michigan, and parts of Minnesota. Mostly members of Indian groups lived in this area.

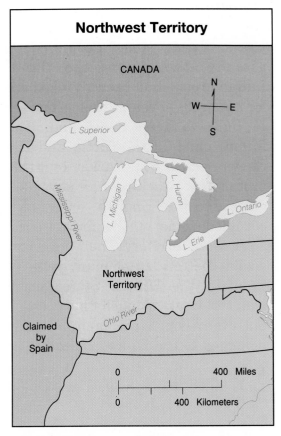

MAP STUDY *Compare this map of the Northwest Territory with the map of the United States (p. 260). How many present-day states were part of the territory?*

Dividing Land Many people from the East wanted to move into this new territory, however. Most of these people had little money, and they saw the Northwest Territory as a place where they could own their own land and start their own farms.

103

Other people, called land speculators, also wanted the new area to be opened up for settlement. They wanted to buy the land at cheap prices and then sell it later to newcomers for more money.

Roadblocks Several problems stood in the way of the speculators' plans. First, some people were already living on the land. Indian groups had been living there for hundreds of years. They promised to fight to keep their land. The Miami chief Little Turtle and the Shawnee chief Blue Jacket kept this promise by attacking new settlers.

Second, the English army still occupied some of the forts in the Northwest Territory. Their main fort was at Detroit. After many years of fighting, the United States army was too weak to push the English out even though the land officially belonged to the United States.

Little Turtle was born near present-day Fort Wayne, Indiana.

A third problem was deciding how the newcomers would be able to buy the land. The new United States government officially owned all the new territory. The leaders didn't know how to sell the lands in such a way that everyone could benefit.

Yet another problem was the fact that United States leaders were not sure how to govern the territory. Should the new area be a state? Who should make laws for the Northwest? Who would control the area?

The Ordinances of 1785 and 1787

The United States government thought of some good solutions to their problems with the Northwest Territory. First the states of New York, Massachusetts, Connecticut, and Virginia gave up their claims in the Northwest. Then the government passed the **Ordinance** of 1785. This special law established how the land was to be sold.

The Grid System Under this law, the whole territory was to be mapped out as a giant rectangle. Imaginary lines were drawn across and up and down inside the rectangle. This made a grid of squares. Each square represented a six-mile (15 square kilometers) area of land called a **township**. The townships were further divided into 36 one-mile (2.5 square kilometers) squares. These small squares were called sections. Each one was made up of 640 acres and was sold for 640 dollars.

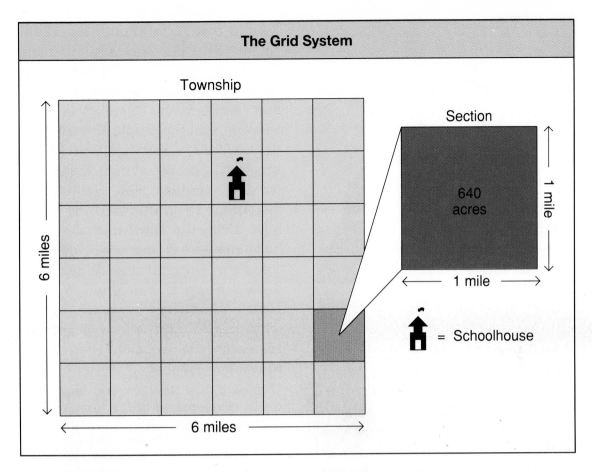

The Grid System

Township

6 miles (vertical)

6 miles (horizontal)

Section

640 acres

1 mile (vertical)

1 mile (horizontal)

🏠 = Schoolhouse

CHART STUDY *The grid system divided the Northwest Territory into townships. What fact lets you know that education was important to the people who wrote the Ordinance of 1785?*

One section in each township was set aside as land where a school would be built.

When the Ordinance of 1785 was passed, more and more settlers came into the Northwest Territory. At first, most people settled in southern Ohio and Indiana.

The United States government still could not solve one problem—how to govern the new territory. The settlers wanted to know how they could become a part of the United States. Some settlers were concerned about how they would be governed.

Ordinance of 1787 To help calm the settlers' fears, another law was passed. The Ordinance of 1787 set up a government for the territory. The ordinance also planned for the way parts of the territory would, in time, become states.

First the law formed one government for the whole territory. This government was headed by one person and included a secretary and a small court system. All these government workers were appointed by the United States government rather than being chosen by the people.

Arthur St. Clair was born in Scotland in 1736. He owned more land west of the Allegheny Mountains than any other settler.

During this time, only white men could vote. When the territory had 5,000 men who each owned at least 50 acres of land, these men could elect a **legislature** for the territory. A legislature is a group of people who are elected by citizens to make and pass laws.

The legislature for the Northwest Territory could elect one man to go to the United States government as a **delegate**, a person who is chosen to speak for others. The new delegate, however, could not vote.

Second, the law stated that the territory could, in time, be divided into states. At least three, but no more than five, new states were to be made out of the Northwest Territory. When any one area of the territory had 60,000 people living in it, the people could ask for their area to be admitted to the union as a state.

The First Governor In 1788, Arthur St. Clair was appointed the first governor of the Northwest Territory. He was unpopular with the new settlers. St. Clair was very wealthy, and the people of the Northwest felt he ruled the area like a king. Still, people did not let this or word of conflicts with the Indians discourage them from settling there.

By 1798, the Northwest Territory had enough voting men to form its own legislature. When the legislature met, it selected William Henry Harrison, a young soldier who had fought the Indians, to represent the area in the United States government.

William Henry Harrison was important to the development of the Northwest Territory. He later became the ninth President of the United States, but he died after only one month in office.

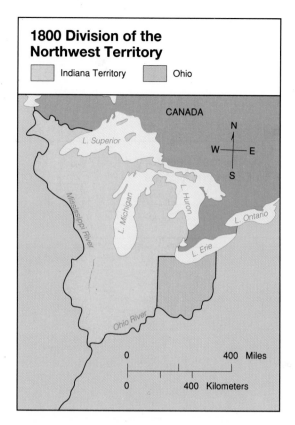

1800 Division of the Northwest Territory

Indiana Territory   Ohio

CANADA

L. Superior

L. Michigan

L. Huron

L. Ontario

L. Erie

Mississippi River

Ohio River

N
W — E
S

0   400 Miles

0   400 Kilometers

MAP STUDY   *What geographical features formed natural borders for the newly formed Indiana Territory?*

The Road to Statehood Harrison did well in government. He helped to write a new law that made it easier to buy land in the Northwest Territory. He also worked to pass laws dividing the whole area into two territories.

The part of the territory that would become Ohio had developed more quickly than the other areas. People came to Ohio more easily because that part of the territory was closer to the East where the established states were. Also, many of the Indians had left Ohio, so the settlers could move about the area more freely.

By 1800, the Ohio area had almost enough people for statehood. The legislature divided the Northwest Territory into two parts. One part was renamed Indiana Territory. In 1803, the other part, Ohio, was admitted as the seventeenth state to join the United States.

Indiana Territory In 1800, the same year the Northwest Territory was divided, William Henry Harrison became governor of the new Indiana Territory. He moved to the new capital at Vincennes and built a big house called Grouseland. Over the years, he would host some very important people at Grouseland.

Lesson Review

Comprehension

1. Why did people want to live in the Northwest Territory?
2. Why was the Ordinance of 1785 necessary?
3. What governing system did the Ordinance of 1787 set up?
4. Why was Ohio settled more quickly than the other areas in the territory?

Critical Thinking

5. Name three problems the United States government faced concerning the Northwest Territory.
6. How did the goals of the land speculators differ from those of the United States government?

Comparing Maps of Different Scale

The scale on a map is an important tool. It shows the relationship between distance on the map and real distance on the earth. By using a ruler and the map scale, you can tell the actual distances between the places on the map.

Look at the two maps on this page. Both maps show the Northwest Territory, but each one is drawn to a different scale. Use the maps to answer the questions.

1. Measure the scale lines of the two maps with a ruler. How are the scales of the two maps different?
2. Look at the map on the top. How many inches is it from Marietta, Ohio, to Vincennes?
3. Is the measurement the same on the map at the bottom?
4. Which map shows the larger area?
5. What is the relationship between real distance and distance as it is shown on a map?
6. How is the scale on a map useful?

Project

Draw two maps of your classroom using two different scales. Show the entire room in one map. Then focus on a specific part of the room for the other map. The maps should have several common features in order to show that they are indeed drawn to different scales.

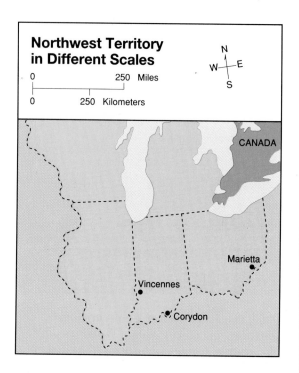

Northwest Territory in Different Scales

0 — 250 Miles
0 — 250 Kilometers

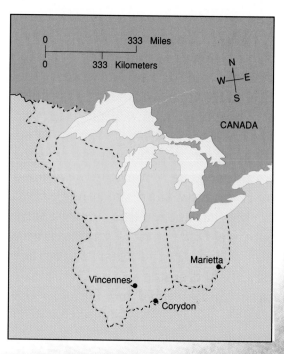

0 — 333 Miles
0 — 333 Kilometers

LESSON 2 The Indian Wars

The Indians and the settlers could not live together on the same land. How did the two groups work out their differences?

KEY WORDS
council (koun′səl)
treaty (trēt′ē)
ally (al′ī)
siege (sēj)

The Indians did not like the settlers coming into the Northwest Territory. They knew that when settlers moved into a new place they often cut down trees and built fences through Indian hunting grounds. Each group—the settlers and the Indians—knew how they wanted to live on the land. Before long, the two groups knew that they both could not live in the same area.

The First Indian Wars

The French and the English had not had much trouble with the Indians who lived in the area that became Indiana Territory because few white settlers had moved there. After the War for Independence, however, more settlers came into the area. The Indians fought back.

MAP STUDY *The Miami Indians in Indiana lived in the area shown. Why might they have chosen this spot?*

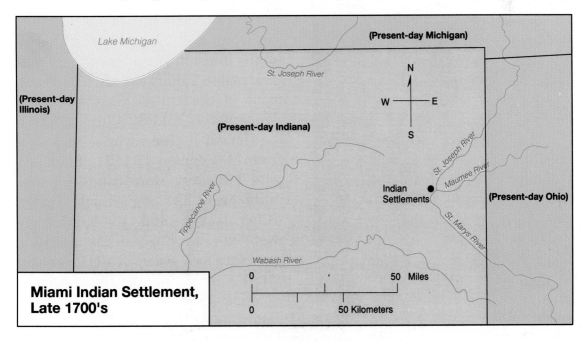

(Present-day Michigan)

Lake Michigan

(Present-day Illinois)

St. Joseph River

(Present-day Indiana)

N
W—E
S

St. Joseph River
Maumee River

Indian Settlements

(Present-day Ohio)

Tippecanoe River

St. Marys River

Wabash River

Miami Indian Settlement, Late 1700's

0   50 Miles

0   50 Kilometers

Two Powerful Chiefs Two Indian leaders, Little Turtle of the Miami and Blue Jacket of the Shawnee, led Indian warriors in the fighting. The Miami lived mostly in the northern part of Indiana. They had a group of villages, called Kekionga, near the spot where the Maumee, St. Joseph, and St. Mary's rivers meet. The Shawnee lived mostly in central Ohio, but as more settlers moved there, the Shawnee began to move west.

Little Turtle and Blue Jacket had great success in fighting the newcomers. Their raiding parties destroyed new settlements, and many people began to fear the Indians. For a time, the two chiefs and their warriors were able to keep many settlers from going to the Northwest Territory.

George Rogers Clark's attempt to defeat the Indians failed when many of his soldiers refused to fight.

Some groups of settlers began to fight the Indians. In 1786, George Rogers Clark tried to defeat Little Turtle, but the chief beat Clark in battle. The next year, General Josiah Harmar also tried to overcome the Indians, but he, too, was beaten.

More Defeats In 1790, Harmar gathered a large force of the people living in the territory. These men were farmers and hunters, not professional soldiers. Harmar and his new soldiers marched toward Kekionga. They burned a few small villages, but Little Turtle had been warned. When the time was right, Little Turtle struck back. His warriors killed 183 soldiers. Just a few Indians were killed. This Indian victory convinced other Indians that they could fight back. They believed they could defeat the soldiers they called Long Knives after the long swords attached to their guns.

The territory's governor, Arthur St. Clair, decided to go after the Indians himself. He gathered together more than 2,000 soldiers. The President of the United States, George Washington, told St. Clair to watch out for an Indian surprise attack.

On November 4, 1791, St. Clair and his army were camped a few miles from Kekionga. Little Turtle, Blue Jacket, and 1,000 warriors were close by. Early in the morning, the warriors swooped down on St. Clair's army. Some of the surprised soldiers tried to run away. Three hours later, the battle was over. St.

General Anthony Wayne's skills as a soldier were highly respected by the Indians.

Clair's army had lost 647 men. The Indians had lost 150 men, but they still controlled Indiana.

A Tough General The new United States government was angry. It wanted control of the Northwest Territory. The government raised a new army and chose General Anthony Wayne as commander.

General Wayne worked hard to train his soldiers. He wanted to avoid the mistakes made by St. Clair and Harmar. In 1793, Wayne moved his troops to a spot near Cincinnati and prepared them to face the Indians in battle.

At first, the United States government tried to talk peace. A **council**, or meeting, was held near Detroit. The United States sent three representatives. The Indians sent representatives from 16 groups.

The Indians wanted to claim all the land north of the Ohio River. The United States representatives said their country owned the land, but they offered to pay the Indians for it. The Indians refused.

Fallen Timbers Wayne set out from Cincinnati to attack the Indians. As he traveled north through Ohio, Wayne was careful. He did not want to be taken by surprise. Indian scouts kept track of his movements. They called Wayne *Sukachgook,* or "Black Snake," for his smart tactics. They also called him "he who never sleeps" because he was alert and had his soldiers keep watch at night.

The Indians tried to find a way to trap Wayne. They waited to attack the general from behind a grove of trees that had been blown down during a tornado.

Wayne's huge army was too well trained to be surprised by the Indians. On the morning of August 20, 1794, Wayne attacked. The Battle of Fallen Timbers lasted one hour. The Indians were forced to retreat to the shores of Lake Erie.

A Peace Treaty Wayne went on to Kekionga and built a fort. He named the fort after himself—Fort Wayne. Wayne and his soldiers stayed there for the winter.

The next spring the Indians wanted peace. Many Miami returned to Kekionga and built villages near Fort Wayne. Soon more than 1,000 Indian leaders and warriors gathered at Wayne's headquarters in Greenville, Ohio, to talk about a **treaty**. A treaty is an agreement between two or more groups.

The Battle of Fallen Timbers lasted only one hour. Wayne's army forced the Indians to flee to Lake Erie.

Wayne offered the Indians payments of money. In return, the Indians gave up almost all of Ohio and a small part of Indiana. Wayne promised that settlers would not be allowed to pass the new boundary line. The Indians promised to keep the peace. Little Turtle, the last to sign the treaty, said he would be the last to break it.

Tecumseh

One young Shawnee warrior was not at Greenville. His name was Tecumseh (tə kum′ sə), and he did not like the Treaty of Greenville.

A few Indians soon began to agree with Tecumseh. At different times, Tecumseh spoke to settlers in Ohio and Indiana. ·He convinced them that he would not make trouble if they stayed on their side of the Greenville boundary line. Many settlers who heard Tecumseh speak respected him. They thought he was a great man. Still, some settlers continued to move west of the Greenville boundary.

The Indian Federation Tecumseh thought the only way to protect the remaining land was to join with other tribes. He wanted to form a group, or federation, of Indians even bigger than the one between Blue Jacket and Little Turtle.

Tecumseh gathered more followers. Tecumseh's brother, called *Tenskwatawa*, or "The Prophet," gained many religious followers. The two brothers made a new village called Prophetstown on the Tippecanoe River in northern Indiana. Hundreds of Indians came to this new place.

No Peace Governor Harrison watched these developments nervously. He knew that Tecumseh was angry about a new treaty, called the Treaty of Fort Wayne. In it, more Indians had agreed to sell their land west of the Greenville line. Tecumseh said these Indians had no right to sell land that belonged to all Indians. He demanded that the new treaty be destroyed.

Harrison asked Tecumseh to come to Vincennes in the summer of 1810 to talk to him about these matters. Tecumseh came to Grouseland, but

Tecumseh (right) and Harrison never agreed about land. How does the picture (below) show their lack of trust in each other?

the two men could not agree. Tecumseh went home, and Harrison prepared for battle.

The next year Tecumseh and Harrison tried again to reach an agreement, but they were unsuccessful. Tecumseh headed south to talk to more Indians. Harrison went north to attack Prophetstown.

The Battle of Tippecanoe Tecumseh had told his brother not to fight the Long Knives while he was away, but The Prophet did not follow Tecumseh's advice. On November 7, 1811, the Indians attacked Harrison's troops. The fighting lasted two hours. There was no clear winner. Because Harrison burned Prophetstown after the battle, the Indians retreated from the Tippecanoe.

In the spring, the Indians returned to rebuild their villages, but they were not as strong. The battle had convinced some tribes not to join Tecumseh's Indian federation.

Decline of the Indian Federation
In 1812, a war broke out between the United States and England. During the War of 1812, Tecumseh and his followers joined with the English against the United States. The Indians became **allies,** or partners, of the English. At first, the Miami tried to stay out of the fighting, but they, too, became involved in the war.

Governor Harrison needed a victory. American soldiers had lost some early battles in the War of 1812 and their spirits were low. In addition, the Miami were holding

On December 18, 1812, Lieutenant Colonel John B. Campbell led his troops in battle against the Miami Indians along the Mississinewa River. The battle is re-enacted each year.

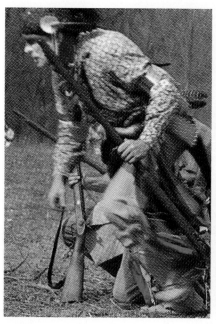 

Fort Wayne under **siege.** When a place is held under siege, no food or other supplies can reach it. A siege is a way of trying to force surrender. In September of 1812, Harrison ordered his troops to relieve the fort and punish the Miami. The soldiers followed his orders and burned a few Miami villages around Fort Wayne.

After the villages were burned, the Miami withdrew to where the Mississinewa and Wabash rivers join near present-day Peru, Indiana. To be sure the Miami would cause no problems, Harrison demanded that they turn over their important leaders to him. The Miami refused.

In November of 1812, Harrison formed an army of 600 men to attack the Indians. The soldiers reached the first Indian village on December 17, 1812. During that day and the next, the Indian villages were burned.

The Army of the Northwest, led by Harrison, then continued into Canada to fight the English and their Indian allies. On October 5, 1813, the two armies met in the Battle of the Thames near Detroit. Tecumseh was killed and the United States forces won the battle.

From then on, the Indians could do little to stop the settlers from moving into Indiana. More and more land was given up. In one treaty, called the Treaty of St. Mary's, the Miami gave up one third of the state. Their once great nation now was home to just a few hundred Indians. The rest of the Indians went to reservations in Oklahoma and Kansas.

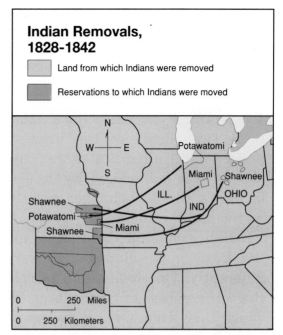

Indian Removals, 1828-1842

☐ Land from which Indians were removed

■ Reservations to which Indians were moved

MAP STUDY *Indians were sent to reservations from all over the United States. This map shows the removal of Indians who lived in the Indiana area. How many separate areas were set up for these Indians?*

Lesson Review

Comprehension

1. What two Indian leaders led the early fighting of Indians against the settlers?
2. What happened in 1793 at the council near Detroit?
3. What did Tecumseh want to protect for the Indians?

Critical Thinking

4. Why was it difficult for the United States government and the Indians to reach an agreement?
5. What, do you think, led to the eventual defeat of the Indians?

Place

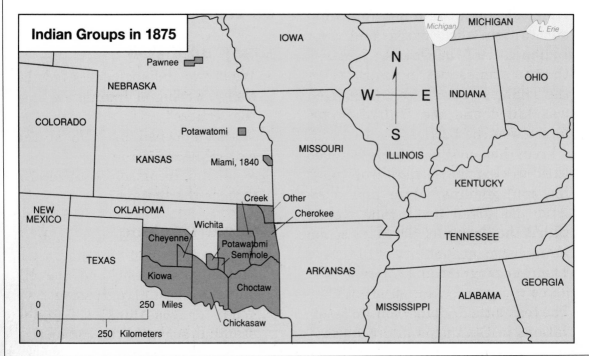

Until the late 1700's, more than two thirds of the area of present-day United States was considered to be Indian land. By the early 1900's, this had changed greatly. So too had the Indian way of life.

Indian groups of the Plains and the Eastern Woodlands lived very differently. This was due in part to the differences in the places in which they lived. Over many years, each Indian group had created a way of life that would best use its surroundings.

The map on page 70 shows where some Indian groups lived when they had their first contact with settlers. Although the map shows only approximate locations, most groups stayed in these general areas. Each of these groups had a different way of life. The Indians of Indiana lived mostly in wooded areas. They hunted for game and farmed small areas of land near rivers.

On the other hand, Plains Indians such as the Cheyenne, Kiowa, and Wichita often traveled in larger areas than the Indians of Indiana. This was because they hunted large buffalo herds. These herds roamed over a large area of flat, treeless

MAP STUDY *About how many miles apart were the two Potawatomi settlements?*

Indian Groups in 1875

(Map showing states: IOWA, MICHIGAN, L. Michigan, L. Erie, OHIO, NEBRASKA, INDIANA, COLORADO, MISSOURI, ILLINOIS, KANSAS, KENTUCKY, NEW MEXICO, OKLAHOMA, TENNESSEE, TEXAS, ARKANSAS, GEORGIA, MISSISSIPPI, ALABAMA. Indian group labels: Pawnee, Potawatomi, Miami, 1840, Creek, Other, Cherokee, Wichita, Cheyenne, Potawatomi, Seminole, Kiowa, Choctaw, Chickasaw. Scale: 0 — 250 Miles; 0 — 250 Kilometers. Compass rose: N, S, E, W.)

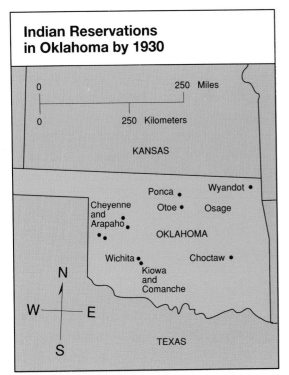

Indian Reservations in Oklahoma by 1930

0 — 250 Miles

0 — 250 Kilometers

KANSAS

Ponca •   Wyandot •

Cheyenne and Arapaho •   Otoe •   Osage •

OKLAHOMA

Wichita •   Choctaw •

Kiowa and Comanche

N W E S

TEXAS

MAP STUDY *Oklahoma became a state in 1907. How important were Indians to the state 23 years later?*

land. The Indians would move their villages as they followed the buffalo.

By 1875, Indian groups no longer lived in the woodlands of Indiana and Ohio. They also no longer were allowed to roam the Central Plains area freely. They had been moved by the United States government to special areas of land west of the 95° W line of longitude.

The map (left) shows where some of the Indian groups were sent to live. Small areas of land in Kansas and Nebraska were set aside for groups such as the Pawnee, the Miami, and some of the Potawatomi. However, most of the Eastern and Central Plains Indians were sent to live in the area known today as the state of Oklahoma. This region was called the Indian Territory.

This change was very hard for all the Indians. The Indian Territory was different from where the Woodland Indians used to live. They had once relied upon the forests for their basic needs. Their new home was now a dry, treeless plain where the winds seemed to blow forever. The Plains Indians were kept in one area, no matter where the buffalo went. They had to learn to farm in order to feed themselves.

Over the next 55 years, the Indian Territory changed as settlement of the United States spread west. By 1930, the Indians were limited to even smaller areas. *Indian land* no longer meant "land as far as the eye could see."

Comprehension

1. What parts of the country were set aside for the Potawatomi?
2. How was the Indian Territory different from the places the Indians had lived before?

Critical Thinking

3. In what ways, other than getting food, might the move west have affected the Indians?
4. Many Indian groups seemed to have disappeared after they were moved to the Indian Territory. Why might this have happened?

CHAPTER 5 REVIEW

Words to Know

Write a complete sentence to answer each question.

1. What does an *ordinance* do?
2. What is a *township*?
3. What is the job of a *legislature*?
4. Who is a *delegate*, and what does he or she do?
5. What is a *council*?
6. Why do people sign *treaties*?
7. In a war, what does an *ally* do?
8. What is a *siege*?

Main Ideas

1. Why did the United States government need to divide the Northwest Territory?
2. What were three problems people faced in settling the Northwest Territory?
3. Why was the grid system created for the Northwest Territory?
4. What law set up a government in the Northwest Territory?
5. Who was the first governor of the Northwest Territory?
6. In 1800, Ohio left the Northwest Territory. What was the remaining part called?
7. Where was the new territorial capital after 1800?
8. Who were the two powerful chiefs of the Miami and Shawnee who fought the settlers?
9. Where did the Indians defeat Arthur St. Clair?
10. Which general finally defeated the Miami and Shawnee in Ohio? What was the name of this famous battle?
11. Who was the young Shawnee who dreamed of uniting Indians?
12. Where did Harrison defeat the Shawnee Indians?
13. On which side did the Indian federation fight during the War of 1812?

Critical Thinking

1. After the War for Independence, many Americans wanted to own their own land or to possess more land than they already had. The territory newly won from the English was about as large as the whole country had been before the war. Many Americans looked to this new area for the land they wanted. Some simply went into the new area and set up new lives for themselves. What do you think might have happened if the government had not made new laws for these lands? What problems might have occurred?
2. Several Indian leaders tried to form a united group of Indians to fight the settlers who were moving onto their land. Two of these groups succeeded in winning some important battles. Why, do you think, did the alliance that was defeated by Harrison fail?

Writing for Understanding

1. Imagine that you are a settler on the new lands of the Northwest Territory. You have some ideas of your own about how the new lands should be used. How should law and order be kept? How can land be divided fairly? Write your ideas in a letter to the President. Your letter should include what problems the settlers face and how you think the government should solve these problems. Tell the President why you think your ideas are good and why they would work.

2. Use what you have learned to write a short play about the meeting of Tecumseh and William Henry Harrison at Vincennes. Try to use the words you think each man would have said. Be sure the words fit with what you know about each man's position. Try to make the men, the setting (Grouseland), and the conversation seem realistic.

Applying Skills

Use the maps below to answer the questions.

1. Compare the scales of the two maps. How do they differ?
2. How many miles is it from Gary to Fort Wayne on each map?
3. How did you find your answer to question 2?
4. Why should your answer to question 2 be the same no matter what map of Indiana you are using?

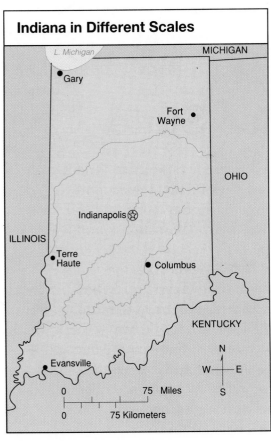

Indiana in Different Scales

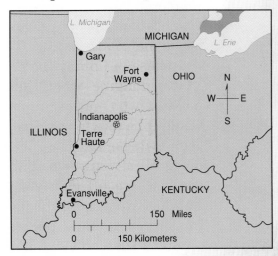

CHAPTER 6

The Hoosier State

Have you ever looked around your community and wondered how it began? You know that farms, towns, and cities cannot appear magically overnight. Someone had to build the roads, set up the shops, start the schools and churches, and plant the crops.

Now imagine what life must have been like for the pioneers who made their way into Indiana Territory. What would it be like to move into the frontier and have to build your own house, grow your own food, and find ways to make all of your own fun? Most pioneers had come from areas where all of these things were readily available. Think of everything the pioneers had to do without on the frontier. Yet, many people were willing to come to the territory that, in time, would become Indiana.

LESSON 1 The Push for Statehood

United States leaders knew that somehow frontier areas could become states. What did Indiana citizens have to do before their area could become a state?

KEY WORDS

representative   (rep'ri zent'ət iv)
constitution   (kon'stə tü'shən)
slavery   (slāv'ərē)

Many people came to Indiana to start new lives. They liked the area and all of the opportunities that the land had to offer. While most of these people were happy with their territory, they also wanted to be a part of the United States. They thought being citizens of a state would help them sell their crops to the cities in the East. As more and more people came into the territory, Hoosiers knew that they would not have to wait long for statehood.

The Birth of Indiana

Because the population of Indiana grew so quickly, the people soon were able to apply for statehood. In 1800, 5,641 Americans lived in Indiana Territory. By 1810, this number had jumped to 24,520. In 1811, Hoosiers began pressing the United States government for statehood.

War in the Way Two problems stood in Indiana's way. First, the Ordinance of 1787 said that an area needed 60,000 residents before it could become a state. Second, the new United States was about to go to war with England again. That war is known as the War of 1812. For a time, Americans set aside adding states to their country while they fought the English.

The War of 1812 finally ended on December 24, 1814. On that day, the Treaty of Ghent was signed. Peace was declared among the English, Americans, and Indians.

The Treaty of Ghent was signed in Ghent, Belgium. John Quincy Adams, who later became the sixth President, was there.

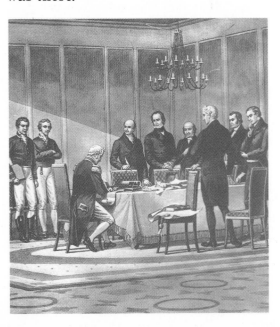

After the War After the War of 1812, the population of Indiana jumped again. By 1815, 63,897 people lived in the area. At last, Indiana had enough residents to become a state, and Hoosiers asked again.

A New Constitution

Jonathan Jennings was the territory's **representative** in Washington, D.C. A representative is someone who is chosen to speak for others. Jennings asked the United States government to allow the people of Indiana to write a **constitution**, which is a document setting up laws for a government.

The United States government agreed and on June 10, 1816, 43 men met at the territorial capitol of Corydon. These delegates elected Jennings president of the convention.

Strong Debate Jennings and the other delegates faced some problems. Many of the people living in Indiana had come from Southern states. **Slavery** was legal in the South but had been outlawed in the Northwest Territory. Slavery occurs when people are owned by others and have no freedom. Many people in the South owned black people as slaves. The slaves worked for no pay on the large Southern farms. Some Southerners who came to Indiana did not want to give up their slaves.

Other people came from Northern states. Most of these people thought slavery was wrong. They wanted to make it illegal in Indiana.

Corydon was the state's first capital. Today the city—along Route 64 in southern Indiana—has about 3,000 residents.

The capitol at Corydon was small. Since the weather was hot that summer, the delegates sometimes met under a huge elm tree. Difficult decisions about the state constitution were made under the elm. Because of those meetings, that tree came to be called the Constitutional Elm.

A large elm provided shade for the 43 delegates who wrote the Indiana constitution. What was the most debated issue they considered?

Jennings spoke forcefully against slavery. Some people living in the southern part of the territory and along the Wabash River insisted slavery should be legal. Finally, the delegates decided that slavery would be illegal in Indiana.

New Rights for Hoosiers The delegates spent much time studying the constitutions of Ohio and Kentucky, Indiana's two neighboring states. They put together what they thought were the best features of these documents.

First the delegates guaranteed that Hoosiers would have rights of freedom of speech, press, and worship. The constitution also said that white and black children would have free schools all the way through college. The document, however, did say that black children would have to go to separate schools.

When the delegates finished the constitution, they sent it to the United States government for approval. On December 11, 1816, Indiana finally was admitted as the nineteenth state. Jonathan Jennings was elected as the state's first government leader.

Jennings had a hard time living up to the promises in the constitution. For one thing, the state had almost no money. How could free schools be built? How could roads be made through the wilderness to carry harvested crops to market? These were challenges that the people of Indiana would face together.

Jonathan Jennings was the first person to sign the new state constitution. Why was it appropriate for him to sign first?

Lesson Review

Comprehension

1. What two problems stood in the way of Indiana's statehood?
2. What issue created the most debate at the constitutional convention in Corydon? How was this issue solved?
3. What roles did Jonathan Jennings play in Indiana's early government?
4. What did the Indiana constitution guarantee its citizens?

Critical Thinking

5. What steps were followed as Indiana became a state?
6. Why might Indiana's problems as a young state be common to all new states?

Reading Line Graphs

As you learned in the Hand-book (page 12), graphs can be helpful in presenting information. Line graphs are best for showing how something changes over time. By comparing two line graphs, you can make conclusions about how two subjects are similar or different.

The first graph below shows the value of goods from other countries over a certain period of time. The second graph shows the rural population of the United States during the same period of time. Study the graphs to answer the questions.

1. Did the rural population of the United States rise or fall between 1800 and 1820?

2. Look at the first graph carefully. How can you tell that the amount of goods coming to the United States from Europe was affected by the War of 1812? Why, do you think, was this so?

Project

Use the information in the table below to make two graphs. Your line graphs will show the number of students in Taft Elementary School and Martin Luther King Elementary School over a three-year period.

	1989	1990	1991
Taft	250	275	320
King	300	310	290

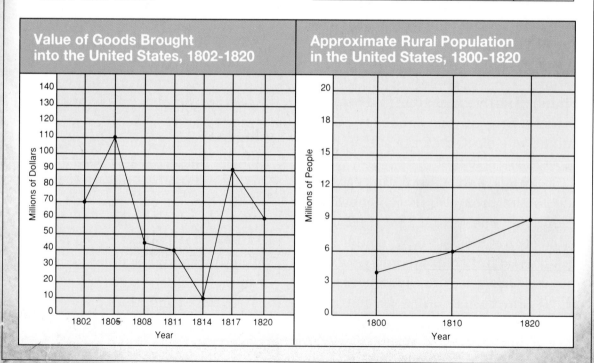

Value of Goods Brought into the United States, 1802-1820

Approximate Rural Population in the United States, 1800-1820

LESSON 2   Pioneer Life

The pioneers who came to the frontier had few belongings. What were the most important things they needed to have on the frontier?

KEY WORDS
flatboat   (flat'bōt)
keelboat   (kēl'bōt)
lean-to   (lēn'tü)
pewter   (pyüt'ėr)
preserve   (pri zėrv')
flax   (flaks')
mill   (mil')

Indiana's residents had worked hard to make their territory a state and to make the laws that would help everyone live together. However, much work still was left to be done. Before long, hard-working pioneers slowly began to build communities throughout Indiana.

A Population Boom
By 1820, the population of Indiana had soared to 147,178 people. Many of these people were pioneers who moved to the frontier to build homes and farms. The story told below about one famous pioneer family is not much different from that of any other family.

The Lincoln Family In 1816, a man named Thomas Lincoln was living in Kentucky. He had heard stories about the fertile Indiana soil. He knew there were many rivers and streams that could make farming in Indiana more profitable, or worth more money. In 1816, the year Indiana became a state, Thomas Lincoln moved his family, including a young son named Abraham, to a stream called Little Pigeon Creek in southern Indiana. Abraham Lincoln would grow up to be President of the United States.

Like the Lincolns, many pioneers came from the South. Some pioneers came from as far away as the Carolinas. Most of them walked all the way to Indiana.

CHART STUDY *About how many people moved to Indiana between 1800 and 1820?*

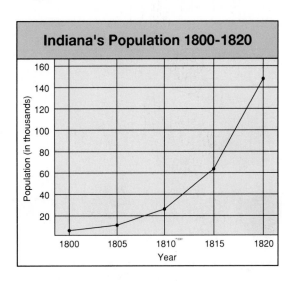

Indiana's Population 1800-1820

125

River Travel Other pioneers came from the North and the East. These people usually traveled on roads that led to Pittsburgh, Pennsylvania. Then they boarded **flatboats**, which were wide boats with flat bottoms, that simply floated down the Ohio River.

Traveling upstream was more difficult than floating down a river. For example, if families wanted to settle on the western Wabash River, they used a **keelboat**, a wide boat that they pushed upriver with a long pole. Since the keelboat had to be pushed against the river current, traveling was very slow.

Starting a New Life

Like most pioneers, Thomas Lincoln's first job on his new land was to build a shelter. The first shelter Lincoln built was a three-sided **lean-to**, which was made from poles covered with bark. On the open side, the Lincolns kept a fire blazing to warm the small shelter.

The First Farm Lincoln's next job was to start clearing the land. At that time, most of Indiana was still thick forest. In order to plant crops, pioneers had to cut down trees.

The first cabin of Abraham Lincoln's family was simple both inside and outside. What materials were used to build the cabin?

Each pioneer family usually chopped down trees on about two acres during the first year on the frontier. Pioneers quickly planted a crop such as corn so the family would have some food by winter.

A New House Many of the trees the pioneers cut down then were used to build log cabins. The cabin the Lincoln family lived in was much like other pioneer homes. An average cabin had just one room about 20 feet (6 meters) long by 15 feet (4.5 meters) wide. To make a log cabin, pioneers notched the ends of logs so they would hold together. Then the logs were laid on top of one another to form a wall.

The spaces between the logs were filled in with mud, dirt, and chips of wood. This same material was used to line the inside of the cabin's log chimney to keep it from burning up.

At first, the cabins usually did not have furniture. The pioneers later made furniture from the wood on their land. Even then, furniture was very simple. For example, tables were made of boards laid across thin, wobbly legs tied together. Stools were used instead of chairs. Pioneers often slept on padding on the floor rather than on beds.

A Simple Life To cook, most pioneer families used three pans they brought with them—a three-legged spider skillet, a big iron pot, and a Dutch oven. All the cooking was done over the fire. Sometimes

Pioneers used simple tools—like these pitchforks—made of readily available materials. They usually brought their cooking pans and other metal objects with them.

families did not even have forks and spoons. Instead, they ate with knives. If the pioneers had plates and drinking cups, they usually were made of **pewter**, a soft, silver-colored metal.

The food the pioneers cooked was simple. Every meal included corn. The corn was baked into cornbread, fried into mush, or eaten off the cob.

For the first year on the frontier, the men hunted for their family's meat. A deer was a welcome sight to a hunter, but most men could find small animals more easily.

Wild berries were often a part of a pioneer's diet. Mulberries, raspberries, blackberries, and grapes grew in the forest. Sometimes the pioneers could find a paw paw or persimmon tree loaded with fruit.

The people who settled the Indiana frontier had to know how to do many different things. They had to be carpenters, farmers, and hunters. They caught fish, built and kept up the cabin, prepared new kinds of food, and made all their own clothing.

More Land, Bigger Farms

Life slowly became better for the pioneers. When their work was done, pioneers were able to enjoy themselves. Sometimes several families got together and had a log rolling party. Dead trees were cut down and rolled into a big pile. Then, when night came, the pioneers burned the trees to make a big fire.

After they had built shelters and planted their first crops, the new farmers usually began to raise some animals. First, they would buy hogs and a milk cow. The pioneers salted and dried the pork from the hogs. After the meat was treated in this way, it would last for a whole winter.

Daily Work If you visited a pioneer cabin, you would find a small garden. The pioneers planted vegetables such as peppers, cucumbers, cabbage, and turnips. They also grew spices in small plots nearby.

Like the pork, the vegetables had to be **preserved**, or saved, so the families could use them throughout the winter. Potatoes and turnips were buried. Cucumbers and cabbage were pickled to make pickles and sauerkraut. Fruit was made into jellies and preserves. Spices added to meats and vegetables helped the foods stay preserved for a long time.

The pioneers had to use available materials to make their clothing. At first, most clothing was made of deerskin. Later, when a crop of **flax** was in, the women spun the plant into fibers which could be made into cloth for comfortable clothes.

Frontier Danger You can see that pioneer life was full of hard work. The life also was full of danger. For example, something as simple as letting the cows graze in the forest could be deadly to the pioneers. The cows sometimes ate a poisonous weed called snakeroot. The cows would live, but their milk would

Snakeroot plants have pretty flowers and leaves.

contain the poison. Whole families could be killed by milk sickness. This is how Abraham Lincoln's mother died.

Diseases were dangerous to the pioneers as well. Serious diseases such as scarlet fever, typhoid, pneumonia, and tuberculosis were common. When disease or accident struck, the pioneers had to do the best they could to care for the sick. Few doctors lived in the frontier.

Mills and Villages Many pioneers were able to survive in the frontier, and, before long, small villages began to spring up in Indiana. Usually a village was built around a **mill**. This was a place where farmers brought their corn or other grains to be ground into flour.

Because the mills needed water to work, they were located on small streams. A large wheel with paddles was built so that it dipped into the stream. As the stream flowed, it turned the wheel. The wheel turned other gears inside the mill. The gears turned large circular stones that ground the grain.

The mills became gathering places for the farmers. They would come to the mills to have their grains ground into flour. Before long, merchants built stores nearby where farmers could buy supplies. Eventually other people would join together to build a church in the area. Perhaps a school would be built next. In this way, the mill became a natural place to begin a village.

Old mills like Beck's Mill (above) still can be found in Indiana. Where would you look to find an old mill?

Lesson Review

Comprehension

1. How did the pioneers travel to Indiana?
2. What did pioneers have to do in order to start farms?
3. What did the pioneers eat?
4. What dangers did pioneers face?
5. Why did villages usually develop around mills?

Critical Thinking

6. Name five things the pioneers needed on the frontier.
7. Why was the ability to make things by hand important to pioneers?

Elihu Stout's *Indiana Gazette*

Imagine that you are living in the hills or forests of Indiana in the early 1800's. How would you find out news about your neighbors? How would you know what was happening in the rest of the world?

These are questions that Elihu Stout might have asked himself in the early 1800's. He knew how important news could be to the settlers of Indiana. Mr. Stout had a plan for getting information to the settlers.

Mr. Stout's life was just like the lives of many other Hoosiers in the 1800's. He was born in Newark, New Jersey, on April 16, 1782. His family moved to Lexington, Kentucky, when Elihu Stout was just a boy. When he turned sixteen, he got a job as an apprentice in a print shop. In time, printing became his trade.

In 1800, the Indiana Territory was formed. A new capital was established at Vincennes. Many people from Kentucky became pioneers and moved to the territory. Mr. Stout's plan was to move to Vincennes and start his own paper so the new settlers could stay informed.

Starting this paper was very difficult, however. For one thing, there were no printing presses in the territory. Mr. Stout would have to bring one all the way from Kentucky. Unfortunately, at that time, no good roads or railroads had been built.

The printing press Elihu Stout brought from Kentucky to the Indiana Territory was very large and heavy. Why did he have to bring the press with him?

In 1803, Mr. Stout went to Indiana to see what he could do. He walked through the forest trying to find a way to Vincennes. At that time, there was not a good way to travel by land. When Mr. Stout finally arrived in Vincennes, he told General Harrison, the territorial governor, about his plan for a paper. General Harrison agreed that it was a good idea.

Mr. Stout returned to Kentucky to buy the materials he needed to start the paper. Because Mr. Stout decided to travel by water, he loaded the materials on a small boat. Then he floated down the Kentucky River, into the Ohio River, and up the Wabash River. It was a difficult and dangerous journey, but Mr. Stout finally arrived in Vincennes.

On July 4, 1804, the first issue of the *Indiana Gazette* was published. Just three years later, in January of 1807, a fire destroyed Mr. Stout's building and his press. He did not give up his newspaper, however. He returned to Kentucky and bought another press. By then, some of the forests had been cleared so he used pack horses to carry the press across the countryside to Vincennes.

Because of Mr. Stout's efforts, Hoosiers had a way to find out news about their territory. When they wanted to know how the plans for statehood were going, for example, they turned to Mr. Stout's paper.

Mr. Stout won the respect of many people for his honesty. People often asked him to run for public office, but he always refused. He did not think it was right for someone who owned a paper to run for office.

Elihu Stout published his paper in Indiana for 41 years. For many years, his was the only paper published in the area.

From the time Mr. Stout moved to the Indiana Territory, he stayed in Vincennes and served his fellow Hoosiers. He felt it was important to help his town grow and prosper. The people of Vincennes always remembered Elihu Stout for what he had done for them.

Citizenship and You

1. Why might Mr. Stout's newspaper have been important to Indiana's early growth?
2. Why are newspapers important to Indiana communities today?
3. What news could you and your friends contribute to your community newspaper?

LESSON 3 A Growing Indiana

You have seen how many people came to Indiana to start farms. What other reasons besides farming might someone have had for coming to the new state?

KEY WORDS
utopia (yü tō′pē ə)
symbolize (sim′bə līz)
canal (kə nal′)
bankrupt (ban′krəpt)
immigrant (im′i grənt)

While most towns in Indiana grew up around the mills and the farming communities, some were started away from farms. Farmers were not the only people to see opportunities in the new state of Indiana. Other people came to the area for many different reasons.

A few hundred families came from Germany to settle in Pennsylvania with George Rapp.

A New Town for New Beliefs
Some religious groups thought they also could have a new start in Indiana. One such group was called the Rappites. These people followed the teachings of George Rapp. He thought people should work hard together instead of each person working for himself or herself. Rapp also thought the property and products of a community should be owned by all members.

Harmonie The Rappites had come from Germany in the early 1800's and settled first in Pennsylvania. Then they came to Indiana in 1814. They founded a village called Harmonie in Posey County along the Wabash River.

The Rappites worked hard. Within just a few years, they had built one of the most successful and beautiful communities in Indiana. George Rapp became an important man. He was one of the delegates to the state constitutional convention in Corydon.

In fact, some people in Indiana thought the Rappites were too successful. Some nearby farmers were suspicious of the Rappites and their beliefs. After ten years, George Rapp sold Harmonie to Robert Owen, and the Rappites all moved away.

Robert Owen (inset) believed that a person's surroundings were very important. While living in Great Britain, he worked to improve the living conditions of the mill workers. In New Harmony (above), he built one of the first kindergartens.

Utopian Society Robert Owen was living in England when he wanted to start a new type of community that was **utopian**. In a utopian community, the residents live apart from the rest of society, believing that an ideal life will be possible if they stay within their own community. Owen called his community New Harmony.

To start his village, Owen asked some of the smartest people he could find to move to New Harmony. At first, teachers, scientists, and writers came to the community. These people started the first free public school, kindergarten, theater groups, and newspapers in Indiana. After only two years, however, the residents of New Harmony had had enough of the wilderness. Most of them left the utopian community.

Even Robert Owen left New Harmony and went back to England. His sons stayed in Indiana and became important citizens. One son, Robert Dale, became a government leader in Washington, D.C. The other son, Richard, became the first president of Purdue University.

The New Capital

Remember that the first capital of Indiana was Vincennes on the Wabash River, and then later Corydon was made the capital. Corydon is in the far south of Indiana near the Ohio River. As more people began to settle in the middle and northern parts of Indiana, Hoosiers realized that Corydon was too far away from most people. Traveling still was difficult.

The site chosen for Indianapolis was in the wilderness. Why are Indians shown in this drawing?

A Wilderness Spot After some debate, a new site was chosen in 1821. The new city would be built near a little village called Fall Creek in Marion County, at about the middle of the state. This city is another example of a community that was built for reasons other than farming.

At first, Hoosiers could not decide what to call their new city. Some people wanted the city named after Tecumseh. Other people wanted the name to **symbolize**, or stand for, the state. Finally everyone agreed to name the new capital Indianapolis. This name means "city of Indiana" in Greek.

A Planned City Indianapolis could not be built all at once, of course. At first, the new capital looked like any other wilderness area. Yet, a plan had been made. A land surveyor named Alexander Ralston was chosen to map out how the city would look. Ralston based his design on the city of Washington, D.C., which he had helped to plan.

Ralston's city plan (see page 58) looked very much like a grid. The state capitol building was in the middle. Four wide roads came into the center from the outside four corners of the city. This plan made the site of the capitol building important.

Roads, Canals, Railroads

Soon after Indianapolis was made the new capital city, the people of Indiana realized something. Although the new city was close to many Hoosiers, no roads had been built to help people travel there. Indiana also needed good roads to help people settle the north and move their farm products to other parts of the United States.

Many farmers relied on rivers for transportation. Most roads were either dirt trails cut through the forest or corduroy roads, which were wide trails on which logs had been laid. They were called corduroy roads because they looked like corduroy fabric. Try to imagine how bumpy a road like that would be. A few roads were covered with crushed rock. These roads were smoother and easier to use, but there were not very many of them.

The National Road Hoosiers wanted the federal government to help them make a better transportation system. In 1815, the United States had started building a road that would cross the nation, starting in Cumberland, Maryland. Indiana leaders wanted this road to go through their state.

One reason corduroy roads were a good idea was because trees were plentiful in Indiana. However, many accidents occurred along corduroy roads. Later, the trees used to build the roads were cut into planks so the roads would not be so bumpy. Unfortunately, the planks did not last long in wet weather. The National Road was made with a long-lasting material—crushed stone.

By 1830, the National Road had come to Indiana. By 1834, the road connected Richmond, Centerville, Indianapolis, and Terre Haute. Finally goods could be transported from western and central Indiana to the Wabash. Today Interstates 40 and 70 follow this route.

Artificial Rivers Not only were new roads being built, but the 1830's in Indiana were a time of **canal** building. Canals are waterways that are built to allow the passage of boats or ships. Flat barges were pulled up and down the canals by teams of mules walking along the banks. This kind of transportation was cheaper and faster than hauling products over roads.

In 1832, the Wabash and Erie Canal was begun. The canal started at Toledo, Ohio. In time, it connected Toledo with Evansville on the Ohio River. That route made the canal the longest canal built up to that time in the United States.

New Immigrants Two other large canals were started but never finished for several reasons. For one, the state government went **bankrupt**, which means it could not pay its bills. Another reason was the arrival of the railroads in Indiana. Trains moved goods faster and more cheaply than canal boats could. Trains did not need herds of mules. Plus, trains did not need to be fixed as often as canals did.

Still, the canals were important for more than just transportation. Many Irish and German **immigrants** had come to Indiana to help build the canals. Immigrants are people who have come from other countries. Many of them stayed in the state to become farmers or to work in the early factories. These people played an important role in the early development of Indiana.

Early Education

As Indiana grew, its people had more need for education. Pioneers had not needed many schools in the days of the frontier.

Public Schools With railroads and canals, however, Indiana farmers began to do more trading with other states. They needed to know more about reading, writing, and arithmetic. The state constitution said all Hoosiers had a right to free public schools, but the young towns did not have enough money to support schools. The state government— still short on money—could not help pay for Indiana's educational needs.

Some religious groups stepped in to help. The first school classes usually were held in churches or seminaries where young men learned about the ministry.

Building canals was difficult work. Still, many immigrants were happy to have the jobs canal work offered. Why, do you think, was canal work very difficult?

A re-creation of the first Notre Dame building—a log chapel— is on the campus today. The huge campus has its own radio and television stations, post office, power plant, and a hotel.

Sometimes a school was started by a group of families. These groups would build a school, set up a school board, and hire a teacher. Going to these schools was expensive. Students were charged 50 to 70 dollars for three months, which was quite a bit of money in those days.

Colleges Religious groups also started the first colleges in Indiana. During the 1830's, the Presbyterians founded Hanover College, Wabash College, and Indiana College—later called Indiana University. The University of Notre Dame was begun in 1842 by French priests. Northwestern Christian University was started in 1855 in Indianapolis by the Disciples of Christ.

Lesson Review

Comprehension

1. What did the Rappites believe?
2. Who founded New Harmony?
3. Why was Corydon not successful as the capital?
4. How was Indianapolis designed?
5. Why were roads and canals important to Indiana?
6. Why were immigrants important to Indiana?

Critical Thinking

7. Name two reasons—besides farming—why people moved to Indiana.
8. Why did education become more important to Hoosiers as Indiana was developed?

CHAPTER 6 REVIEW

Words to Know

Write the word that fills in the blank to complete each comparison.

constitution   pewter   flax
lean-to   mill

1. A *castle* is to a *king* as a ____ is to a pioneer.
2. *Gold* is to *coin* as ____ is to *drinking cup*.
3. *Rule book* is to *baseball* as ____ is to *government*.
4. *Auto factory* is to *cars* as ____ is to *flour*.
5. *Leather* is to *shoes* as ____ is to *clothing*.

Main Ideas

1. According to the Ordinance of 1787, how many residents did a territory need before it could become a state?
2. After what war did Indiana have enough people to become a state?
3. Who was the territory's first representative to the United States government?
4. What issue was debated strongly during the constitutional meeting at Corydon?
5. On what month, day, and year was Indiana admitted to the United States?
6. Why did the early settlers believe that farming in Indiana would be very profitable?

7. In what two ways did pioneers travel to Indiana?
8. What was the first thing farm families did to the land?
9. Of what materials were the first pioneers' houses made in the Northwest Territory?
10. Name five foods the pioneers ate.
11. How did the pioneers preserve vegetables and meat?
12. Name two dangers often faced by the pioneers.
13. How did a village start?
14. Where did George Rapp start his utopian community?
15. After Corydon, where was the capital located next?
16. In what city did the National Road begin?

Critical Thinking

1. Almost all the settlers who moved into the Northwest Territory after the War for Independence wanted the territory to become a state. Why, do you think, did the settlers want statehood?
2. In the early and middle 1800's, several groups of people tried to set up utopian communities in the new territories. Some of these groups came from Europe and others came from the eastern part of the United States. Why, do you think, did these people decide to move in order to build their communities?

Writing for Understanding

1. Imagine that you are a settler who came to Indiana from Kentucky. Write a letter to your relatives who live in a town in Kentucky. Tell them what the journey to Indiana was like.

2. Write a plan for your own utopian community in the present day. Begin by writing a list of things your community would believe. Then explain in two or three paragraphs why you are establishing this new utopia and who could join. Answer questions like these: Where would you live? What would you do? How would you make a living? For example, you might start a utopian community based on peaches. All citizens would have to like to eat peaches. The group might support itself by making and selling peaches to supermarkets. You might locate the community near packing plants or truck routes.

Applying Skills

Use the line graphs below to answer the questions.

1. What does each line graph show?
2. How many miles of canals were built between 1830 and 1850?
3. How many miles of railroad track were built between the years 1840 and 1860?
4. Based on these two graphs, what can you say about the effect of railroads on canals?

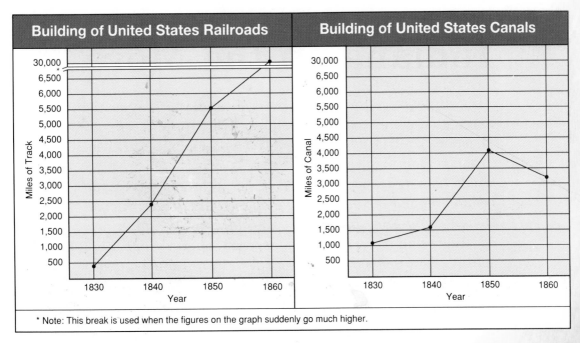

* Note: This break is used when the figures on the graph suddenly go much higher.

CHAPTER 7
Indiana on the Move

Big changes happened to Indiana and the rest of the country during the mid-1800's. The Indiana writer Theodore Dreiser described what was happening to cities in the region.

Great industries were moving in. . . . Streetcar lines had been extended far out into the open country in anticipation of rapid growth. The city had laid miles and miles of streets and sewers through regions where. . .one solitary house stood alone. . . .There were regions open to the sweeping wind and rain, which were lighted throughout the night with long, blinking lines of gaslamps fluttering in the wind.

LESSON 1 Indiana and the Civil War

When a country goes to war, many unfortunate things happen. Lives are lost and property is damaged. Besides these things, what else might happen as a result of war?

KEY WORDS
civil war (siv′əl wôr′)
Underground Railroad
        (un′dėr ground rāəl′rōd)
amendment (ə mend′mənt)
sharecropper (sher′krop ėr)
reaper (rē′pər)

From 1861 to 1865, the United States fought a war. In this war, Americans did not fight against another country; they fought against one another. This war was the **Civil War**. A civil war is fought between citizens of the same country.

Americans from the North fought Americans of the South over several problems. Some Southern states wanted to stop being a part of the country. They felt they were not treated fairly by the government. One of the issues that caused much disagreement was slavery.

Slavery and War in Indiana

As you know, slavery was not allowed in Indiana after the first state constitution was signed. Southern states, however, did allow slavery. Slaves worked on the large farms of the South.

Even though slavery was illegal in Indiana, black people were not always treated well. In fact, when the new state constitution was written in 1851, Article 13 said that no black people could move into the state of Indiana.

A Secret Escape Some Hoosiers, however, worked hard to help black people. A few risked their lives on the famous **Underground Railroad**. This was not a real railroad. It was a

Stops on the Underground Railroad— known as stations—were the homes of people who wanted to help slaves.

Quakers such as Levi and Catharine Coffin (above) were among the first people to speak out against slavery.

system of secret routes slaves used to escape from the Southern states. Some people in the North hid the escaped slaves in houses along the way. Several such stations were located in Indiana.

Levi and Catharine Coffin were important people on the Underground Railroad. The Coffins lived in Newport—now called Fountain City. They helped thousands of black people escape slavery. The Coffins felt their help was a religious duty. They were Quakers, members of the Religous

Society of Friends. One Quaker belief is that all people should be able to live in peace and freedom.

Hoosier Volunteers As the nation went to war, many Hoosiers played an important role. On April 15, 1861, President Abraham Lincoln sent out a call for volunteers to fight for the Union, or Northern, army. More than 10,000 Hoosiers agreed to join the army to fight.

In all, Indiana had 129 regiments, or groups of soldiers, that were formed during the Civil War. This included most of the 28th Regiment, a group of black soldiers fighting against the states from which they had fled.

Morgan's Raid Some soldiers were kept at home to protect the state. They were called on to defend Indiana twice. The first time was in June of 1863. Confederate soldiers from the army of the South entered Indiana by crossing the Ohio River from Kentucky into Cannelton. They raided several farms, looking for horses, before they escaped.

The biggest attack came the next month from a group of soldiers led by Confederate General John Hunt Morgan. These soldiers, called Morgan's Raiders, attacked the old capital of Corydon. Then they headed north to Salem. They burned parts of the town and destroyed bridges behind them so Indiana's home guard could not follow.

Morgan's Raiders rode north and east toward Ohio through the towns

Morgan's Raiders began surprise attacks behind Northern lines in May of 1862. They were very successful until the time of their surrender on July 26, 1863, in Lisbon, Ohio.

of Vernon and Dupont. Indiana Governor Oliver Morton was furious. He ordered thousands of men to track down Morgan and his band, but by the time an army could be raised, Morgan had escaped into Ohio. There, surrounded by Ohio troops, Morgan's Raiders surrendered.

Camp Morton Indiana was the home of a large prisoner-of-war camp. After the Union won an important victory in Tennessee, captured Confederate soldiers were sent north to Indianapolis. A camp, named after Governor Morton, was built there.

Richard Owen, the son of Robert Owen, commanded the camp. He was known as a kind commander who treated his prisoners fairly. In fact, a group of former Confederate prisoners erected a statue of Richard Owen in Indianapolis in 1916.

The Civil War was hard on the United States, especially the South. Much of the South was destroyed in the war. Indiana was much less affected. Only Morgan's Raiders had caused any damage. Still, some hard times came to parts of Indiana right after the war.

War Recovery

Although Indiana was part of the victorious North, the state suffered some difficulties because of the war. Before the Civil War, towns in southern Indiana, especially along the Ohio and Wabash rivers, sent many farm products to Southern cities. After the war, this changed.

In sharecropping, the landowner supplies what is needed to farm the land. The sharecropper then receives only a portion of the money earned.

Loss of Markets Most farmers in the South grew cotton rather than food, so Indiana's food products had sold well in Southern markets. Before the war, Hoosier towns like New Albany, Cannelton, and Evansville grew into important port cities. Indiana's farmers did well.

With much of the South destroyed, however, the farmers made less money. Southerners had no money to buy Indiana's products. Towns in the south of Indiana fell on hard times. They decreased in importance as people began to look at the growing northern Indiana towns.

Freedom for Black People Other changes happened in Indiana because of the war. Article 13 of the state Constitution was overruled by the Fourteenth **Amendment** to the United States Constitution. An amendment is a change in the Con-

stitution. This Amendment, passed in 1868, said no state could make any laws denying rights to people just because of their color. Finally black people could move to Indiana.

Many of the black people who lived in Indiana or who moved to the state after the Civil War worked on Indiana farms. Some black people were **sharecroppers**, which means they rented part of someone's farm in exchange for part of the harvest. Most sharecroppers had very little money.

The KKK When more black people began to arrive in Indiana, a disturbing group was formed. This secret group, called the Ku Klux Klan (KKK), was formed by Hoosiers who did not want free blacks to come to Indiana. For many years after the war, the KKK terrorized black citizens, sometimes using violence.

New Tools, More Food While war recovery went slowly for the state's black people, in time, things did begin to improve on Indiana farms. With the war over, better roads and more railroads were built, and farm products were sent more easily to other parts of the country. In the 1880's, a new kind of fence, called barbed wire, let farmers fence in more of their land. Farmers also could raise more animals since it was easier to keep them all in one place.

In 1831, a man named Cyrus McCormick invented a new machine called the **reaper**. A reaper has rakes that sweep plants against a sharp edge. The plants are cut and

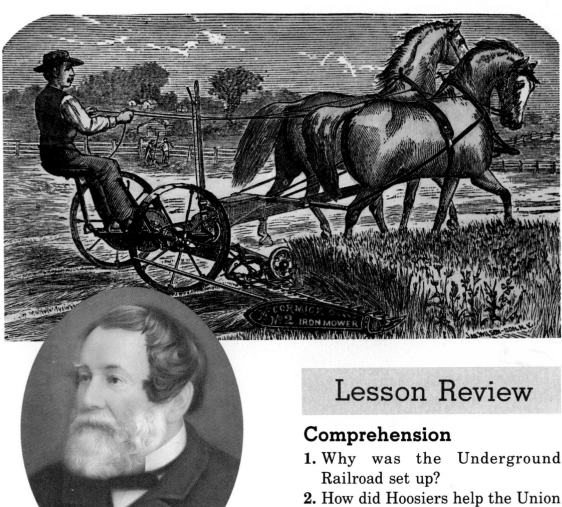

Before Cyrus McCormick's reaper was in use, crops had to be cut down by hand. Why would a machine such as the reaper help farmers to grow more crops than before?

left alongside the machine. Reapers made harvesting crops easier. After the Civil War, many farmers bought reapers. The reaper was only one of the many machines that helped farmers to grow more crops on the same amount of land.

Lesson Review

Comprehension

1. Why was the Underground Railroad set up?
2. How did Hoosiers help the Union side during the Civil War?
3. How did the Fourteenth Amendment affect Indiana?
4. Name two inventions that helped Hoosier farmers after the war.

Critical Thinking

5. Although Indiana did not suffer too much property damage or loss of life in the Civil War, Hoosiers did experience hard times because of the war. How did the war cause this?
6. Why could it be said that the Civil War contributed to the growth of northern Indiana towns?

Using a Route Map

You have learned that there are many different kinds of maps. One kind is a route map. This type of map gives you information about a course of travel. The route map on this page shows the routes of the Underground Railroad that slaves from the South followed to escape to the North. Along each route were secret *stations* where the slaves were hidden.

As you can see on the map, the routes led slaves across both land and water. Some of the most heavily traveled routes were through Ohio, Indiana, and Pennsylvania.

However, escaped slaves were not always safe in the North. Those who were caught in some areas faced the threat of being sent back to their owners in the South. Therefore, many slaves continued on to Canada where freedom was guaranteed.

Use the route map to answer the following questions.

1. What were the two main Indiana crossing points on the Ohio River?
2. After looking at the map, explain why Middle Western routes may have been so heavily traveled.
3. What two Canadian cities were final destinations for many slaves?

Project

Pretend that you have a friend from another town who is visiting and you want him or her to meet you at your school. Draw a route map from your home to your school to show your friend the way. Be sure to include details on your map.

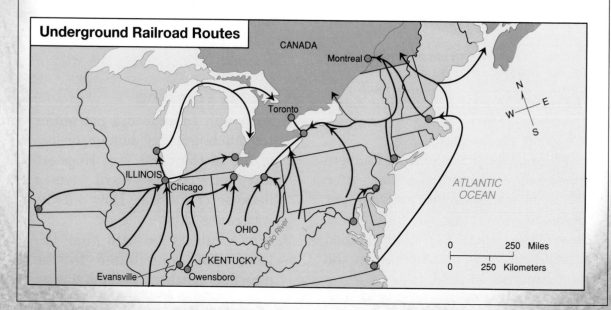

Underground Railroad Routes

CANADA

Montreal

Toronto

ILLINOIS

Chicago

OHIO

Ohio River

KENTUCKY

Evansville   Owensboro

ATLANTIC OCEAN

N
W   E
S

0   250 Miles
0   250 Kilometers

LESSON 2 Industrial Indiana

*After the Civil War, many factories were built in Indiana.
What raw materials found in Indiana, do you think,
helped the development of businesses in the state?*

KEY WORDS
industrial   (in dus′trē əl)
refinery   (ri fīn′ə rē)

After the Civil War, many Indiana farmers bought new, improved machinery. Because Indiana was mostly a farm state at that time, some farm equipment companies decided to run their businesses near the farmers they served.

Henry Studebaker (right) was the oldest of the Studebaker brothers. Clement (left) moved to South Bend in 1850 to start a blacksmith business. In 1852, Henry joined him and they formed H. & C. Studebaker in South Bend. Their first products were sturdy wagons (below).

A New Indiana in South Bend

South Bend soon became home to a new kind of Indiana. Instead of just being a farming village, South Bend turned into an **industrial** center, which means that many factories were built to make new products.

Wagons Some leaders of South Bend's changes were the Studebaker brothers. Henry and Clement Studebaker had come to Indiana from Pennsylvania. They wanted to

farm. To make more money, they also ran a blacksmith shop where they built wagons.

Studebaker wagons became popular. Farmers thought they were made well. When another Studebaker, John, came back from California with money he had made mining gold, the Studebakers expanded their wagon business. Just before the Civil War, the brothers received an order for 100 wagons from the U.S. Army. By the end of the war, the Studebakers had 200 employees.

Plows Another South Bend industry was started by a Scottish man named James Oliver. He wanted to make it easier for farmers to plow their fields. After many experiments, he developed a new plow called a chilled steel plow which made turning the soil much easier.

Growing Towns

Other creative businesspeople lived in towns such as Kokomo, Anderson, and Muncie. In these towns, as in South Bend, many businesses were started after the Civil War.

Unclean and Unsafe At first, Indiana towns were unprepared for growth. Streets still were made of dirt. No sewer or water systems had been built. People simply used their own pumps or a neighborhood water pump. Garbage often was thrown into the streets, and disease became common as a result of these unhealthy conditions.

Police and fire protection also were scarce. Most towns relied on a sheriff or marshall to keep law and order. Fire departments were made up of volunteers, or unpaid workers.

People could travel through Indiana cities on horsedrawn streetcars in the 1870's. Why, do you think, were rails installed for the streetcars?

Improvements Soon, however, towns began to change. For example, public hospitals were built. The first one opened in Indianapolis in 1866. In the 1870's, several Indiana towns installed horsedrawn streetcars that used rails sunk into the street. The streets themselves were paved with asphalt or bricks. A few towns began to create their own waterworks that provided citizens with a better water supply.

Gas made from coal had been invented in the 1850's. After the war, some cities used gas street lights. Electric street lights first were used in Wabash on March 31, 1880. The citizens were excited by this improvement. Newspaper stories said Wabash was the first town in the world with electric street lights.

In the 1870's, the telephone came to Indiana. At first, only a few people had telephones, but the new machine quickly caught on. Soon the telephone lines and electric wires filled the sky above towns.

The Gas Boom

In the 1880's, an event happened that further changed the state. A huge field of natural gas was found in central Ohio. This gas was used for power to light cities and to fuel new industries. Indiana then found its own natural gas, and the state's industries soon were able to make more and more things.

New Industries Glass companies moved into Indiana because they could use the gas to fuel their furnaces. Soon dozens of Indiana glassmakers employing hundreds of people were producing glass. One of the most successful of these new companies was Ball Brothers Glass in Muncie. At first, the company made plate glass for things like windows, but then they began to make jars used to preserve foods. In a few years, almost every home had these jars in its pantry.

Tinplate makers also came into Indiana. These companies made cans for food. One Indianapolis grocer

Why would such a tangle of wires be unwanted?

named Gilbert Van Camp began canning food. The company he started eventually became one of the largest canneries in the world.

Pharmaceutical (fär′ mə süt′ i kəl) companies, or producers of medicine, also found success in Indiana. In 1876, Eli Lilly from Indianapolis began to make medicines. His company became one of the largest pharmaceutical firms in the world.

With all of the new successful businesses in the state, banks were soon needed. As a result, Indianapolis became a banking center.

Gifts from Earth Along with natural gas, other useful natural resources were available in Indiana. As more buildings were needed, the stone quarries near Bloomington became successful. As more fuels were needed for heat and for the new electrical plants, coal from the region around Terre Haute was mined.

Elbert Gary was trained as a lawyer. He became a judge in the 1880's.

Unfortunately, the gas boom did not last. People often wasted this valuable resource because they thought it never would run out. They would burn the fuel from gas wells just to see the flames. Still, the gas boom changed Indiana from a farming state to a state with both farms and industry.

Oil, Steel, and Cars

In 1889, the Standard Oil Company built a huge oil **refinery**, a place where oil is changed into fuels, in Whiting, Indiana. The company liked Whiting's location in the northwest corner of the state. Standard Oil could ship oil across the Great Lakes or in rail cars from stations in Chicago. A steel mill followed the oil company to Whiting in 1902.

Gary Steel Then, in 1906, the United States Steel Company bought 9,000 acres outside of Whiting. The chairman of the company, Judge Elbert Gary, thought he could build a planned city for steelworkers. The new mill would be located between iron mines in Minnesota and the coalfields of southern Indiana. The lakes and the railroads could be used for shipping. A giant mill was built in the town that was named Gary after the man who had planned it.

The Car While Gary was being built, yet another new industry started in Indiana. Elwood Haynes built the second working automobile in America in his Kokomo workshop.

Ray Harroun won the first Indianapolis 500. His car was a Marmon Wasp. His average speed was about 75 miles per hour. Today's winners average more than 170 miles per hour.

At first, automobile manufacturers simply put engines into wagons to make early cars. The Studebakers, for instance, turned their wagons into gasoline-powered autos. In the years between 1900 and 1920, more than a dozen automakers were in Indiana. Some failed after a few years. Other automakers' cars became famous—DeSoto and Auburn in Auburn, the Lambert in Anderson, and the Maxwell in New Castle. The Studebaker was the most successful of the Indiana cars. Studebakers were built until the 1950's.

The Hoosier love of cars led to the founding of the Indianapolis Speedway in 1909. In 1911, a 500-mile (800-kilometer) race was held in May. Today the Indianapolis 500 is the most famous auto race in the world.

Lesson Review

Comprehension

1. Why did South Bend develop as an industrial center?
2. Name three ways that Indiana towns improved after 1850.
3. How did the discovery of natural gas in Indiana affect the growth of industries in the state?
4. Why was the Indianapolis Speedway founded?

Critical Thinking

5. Name three raw materials found in Indiana that made companies want to locate their factories in the state.
6. How did the location of some cities in Indiana help their growth?

LESSON 3 Problems to Be Solved

In many ways, growth in a city is good. What might happen, however, if a city grows too quickly?

KEY WORDS
slum (slum′)
union (yün′yən)
strike (strīk′)
reform (ri fôrm′)
grass roots (gras′rüts′)

All of the changes and new growth of Indiana's cities caused some problems. More and more Hoosiers left their farms to find work and what they hoped would be a better life in the city. In 1850, only 5 percent of Hoosiers lived in towns. By 1920, 51 percent lived in cities. As Hoosiers moved from farms to cities, their movement was from the southern part of the state to the north.

A Hard Life

Many of these new city residents were immigrants from other countries. Many people from Ireland and Germany had come to Indiana before the Civil War to help build canals. As industries grew, more Irish and Germans arrived as did people from Italy, Czechoslovakia, Yugoslavia, and Poland. Most of these new immigrants moved to cities in northern Indiana, such as Gary.

Uncomfortable Conditions Cities like Gary became crowded. Although the new immigrants worked hard, they were often poor. They could not afford houses or good apartments. Factory workers often felt they could not complain about living conditions or the small amount of money they earned. The areas these people lived in became known as **slums**, which are poorer, mostly rundown sections of a city.

Although workers were pleased to have jobs, they often had terrible conditions at home. Especially in winter, these Gary workers suffered in the slums they called home.

In 1910, some workers in the steel mills of Gary earned 17 cents an hour. Women worked for as little as 10 cents an hour. The working conditions were often terrible. Sometimes children younger than ten years old worked in factories. Many of these workers could not take time to go to school.

Workers and Unions Miners in the coalfields worked in very dangerous conditions for little pay. They were the first to join together to fight to change their living and working conditions. They formed a **union**, which is an organization of workers. The leaders of the union spoke for the miners. Next the railway workers unionized under the leadership of

Child labor was common in many industries in the early 1900's. Young children could be seen doing many jobs—from working in a vegetable cannery (above) to sorting coal in a mine (below).

Besides leading his union, Eugene Debs also was active in politics. He ran unsuccessfully for President of the United States five times.

Eugene Debs. Debs, from Terre Haute, became an important leader of the union.

Sometimes workers went on **strike,** which means they stopped working in the factories to try to force owners to give in to demands. Such strikes could lead to violence. In 1919, the federal government had to send troops to Gary to break up the Gary Steel strike.

A Voice for Farmers For a time, life was hard on some of Indiana's farms too. Prices for farm products began to drop in the 1890's. Some farmers blamed the government. They joined a new political party called Populist. The Populists did not win the presidential election

they entered, but they did convince a larger party, the Democrats, to agree with some of their ideas.

Help from Progressives Later a group of people called Progressives joined together to help city residents. These Progressives wanted to help poor people and improve the lives of factory workers. They fought for new laws to protect children and for clean food supplies.

One famous Progressive was Indiana Senator Albert Beveridge. He became a powerful leader in the United States government and fought for laws making child labor illegal. The senator also encouraged conservation of the nation's natural resources and the improvement of public education.

Beveridge knew most people wanted these **reforms,** or changes for the better. In 1912, he worked for a new progressive party called the Bull Moose party. He said, "This party comes from the **grass roots.** It has grown from the soil of the people's hard necessities." Now when someone says something has grass roots support, he or she means that it has grown from local support.

Changes in Cities The work of Albert Beveridge and other reformers helped ease the pain of poverty. Settlement houses, places where poor people could go for help, were started throughout Indiana. New laws stating how buildings should be built helped prevent new slums.

Before he became a senator, Albert Beveridge practiced law in Indianapolis.

Food laws helped assure that people would not receive unsafe meat. New public works improved cleanliness, and health regulations helped stop the spread of disease.

Better Education Education also improved for Hoosiers, but the improvements came slowly. Beginning in 1867, public schools were built and Hoosiers began to see the importance of education. In 1913, a law was passed that required children to attend school until age sixteen.

New universities and colleges also developed in Indiana. These new colleges sometimes received money from wealthy people. The Ball brothers, whose companies made glass jars, started Ball State in Muncie. DePauw University in Greencastle was named for a wealthy industrialist named Washington C. DePauw.

Unfortunately, the new educational system was not open to all Hoosiers. Many black people could not attend school until 1877. After that, black children were educated in separate schools that were often poor. In some places, this condition lasted until after 1945.

War and Progress in a New Century

All the reforms were not complete when a new catastrophe struck. Another war, World War I, had broken out in Europe. At first, the United States did not get involved. Most Americans preferred to stay out of European problems. However, in 1917, President Woodrow Wilson sent American forces to Europe.

Many Hoosiers fought in the war and many died. Most of the deaths were from wounds and disease. Many of the soldiers sent by the United States trained at Fort Benjamin Harrison, near Indianapolis.

Good Times and Bad After the war, good times were mixed with bad times in Indiana. Like people living in the rest of the United States, most Hoosiers were successful in the 1920's. As businesses boomed, people had more money than ever before to spend. They also had lots of time for fun activities.

Americans became very interested in books, movies, cars, and sports. Hoosiers joined the nationwide football fever as the Notre Dame college team became the most successful team of the 1920's.

Then came the Great Depression, a severe economic crisis, of the 1930's. As was true all over America,

The Great Depression left many people out of work and hungry. The photograph (above) shows the kind of place some people called home and how they tried to earn money.

Indiana banks and businesses lost money. Many Hoosiers lost their jobs. Some people even lost their homes and other possessions.

Just as Indiana and the rest of the country began to recover from the depression, Hoosiers again went to fight for their country. In 1941, the United States entered World War II. Many Hoosiers joined the war effort both at home and in battle.

A Modern Transportation Hub
After World War II ended in 1945, things again improved for Indiana. More people began moving west. That meant Indiana's position as a crossroads of transportation became even more important. The new interstate highways crisscrossed the state in all directions. Soon Indiana was truly a hub of the United States.

Lesson Review

Comprehension
1. What brought European immigrants to Indiana?
2. Why were unions formed?
3. What did the Progressives want to do?
4. How did education improve in Indiana after 1867?
5. How did life improve for Hoosiers in the 1920's?

Critical Thinking
6. As the new Indiana cities grew rapidly in the 1900's, what problems had to be solved?
7. Why did the government eventually have to pass laws to improve conditions in cities?

CHAPTER 7 REVIEW

Words to Know

Answer the following questions with a sentence.

1. Why do workers *strike*?
2. What is a *civil war*?
3. How does *sharecropping* work?
4. What does a *reaper* do?
5. What does a *refinery* produce?
6. What is a *slum*?
7. Why do people join a *union*?

Main Ideas

1. What war was fought in the United States between the years 1861 and 1865?
2. By what secret system were slaves able to escape from the South?
3. How many regiments did the state of Indiana contribute to the Union war effort?
4. Who was General John Hunt Morgan, and what did he do?
5. What was Camp Morton used for?
6. What changes came to Indiana as a result of the Civil War?
7. What was Article 13 of the Indiana state constitution, and how was it abolished?
8. Name two inventions that helped Indiana farmers after the war.
9. Who were Henry and Clement Studebaker?
10. How did James Oliver's plow help farmers?
11. Name three things that improved life in Indiana towns.
12. Identify Judge Elbert Gary and Elwood Haynes.
13. Name three makes of automobiles that were manufactured in Indiana between 1900 and 1920.
14. Who were the Populists and the Progressives?
15. Who was Albert Beveridge, and what did he do?
16. What war did the United States enter in 1917?
17. What happened in the United States during the 1930's?
18. What war did the United States enter in 1941?
19. Why did Indiana become a hub of transportation after 1945?

Critical Thinking

1. The gas and coal booms had a big effect on Indiana. For example, newer and bigger industries could use these energy sources to make a wide variety of products like glass and steel. What were some of the effects these new industries had on Indiana? Include ways they affected business, education, and the lives of people.
2. The lives of people in Indiana changed after the Civil War. Many Hoosiers left the farms and went to cities. New immigrants came from Europe to work in the cities. However, many of these people were poor. Their children often worked long hours in dangerous

factories. Factory workers made very little money. Living conditions were often unsanitary. Keeping these facts in mind, explain some reasons why unions developed as industries grew.

Writing for Understanding

1. Pretend that you are living in Indianapolis during the years 1870 to 1900. Write several diary entries and date them each a few years apart. Describe how your life has changed during those years. Include details about how the town looked in 1870 and how it looks with each new entry. What are some things you can do that are different from one year to the next? How do you feel about the changes?

2. Use what you have learned about Indiana's past to write your own small history of the state. Include the most important events from the time Indiana became a state. When you write, be sure to try to express the feelings of the people. Do not simply write a sentence that tells a date and says what happened. Instead, explain why these events were important and how they changed Indiana.

Applying Skills

Use the route map (right) to answer the questions.

1. At what town in Indiana did Morgan's Raiders cross the Ohio River from Kentucky?
2. Where did Morgan's Raiders go after their first town?
3. In what direction did Morgan's Raiders go during their first raids? In what direction did they go after Salem?

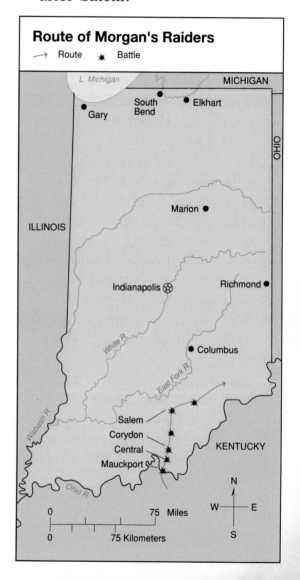

Route of Morgan's Raiders
→ Route   ✱ Battle

UNIT 2 REVIEW AND STUDY GUIDE

Key People/Places	Key Terms	Key Ideas	
New Laws for New Lands (pages 102-119) Jefferson, Washington, Little Turtle, St. Clair, Harrison, Clark, Wayne, Tecumseh ___ Northwest Territory, Vincennes, Fort Wayne, Prophetstown	Northwest Territory, ordinance, township, legislature, delegate, council, treaty, ally, siege	■ American leaders faced problems in governing the Northwest Territory. After struggles between Indians and settlers, Indians lost most of their land.	1750 ■ **1787** Government set up for Northwest Territory 1800 ■ **1816** Indiana made 19th state ■ **1830** National Road reaches Indiana
The Hoosier State (pages 120-139) Jennings, Lincoln, Rapp, Owen ___ Corydon, Harmonie, Indianapolis, *Rivers*—Ohio, Wabash	representative, constitution, slavery, flatbed, keelboat, lean-to, pewter, preserve, flax, mill	■ After the War of 1812, people of the Indiana Territory took official steps to become a state. ■ People flocked to Indiana, cities grew, and improvements were made.	
Indiana on the Move (pages 140-158) Coffins, Lincoln, Morgan's Raiders, Owen, Studebakers, Gary, Haynes, Beveridge, Debs, De Pauw, Wilson ___ Corydon, Camp Morton, Indianapolis, Bloomington, Terre Haute, Whiting, Gary	civil war, Underground Railroad, amendment, sharecropper, reaper, industrial, refinery, slum, union, strike, reform, grass roots, depression	■ After the Civil War, some Indiana towns suffered, but a slow recovery was achieved. Indiana, rich in raw materials, served as the home for many prosperous industries. Growth of Indiana cities caused problems requiring reforms.	1900 ■ **1906** Steel Company starts building Gary ■ **1920** 51 percent of Hoosiers live in cities

UNIT 3

Indiana: Local, State, and National Government

▲ Stump Speaking by George Caleb Bingham

Indiana State Capitol: House of Representative.

IN THIS UNIT

This unit is about the different levels of government—national, state, and local—how they work and how they affect every Hoosier. In this unit, you will find out how laws are made and you will meet some Hoosiers who have made important contributions to all levels of government. You also will find out that those people who work for the government really work for every citizen. In addition, you will see how you can be a responsible citizen of Indiana and the United States.

Forming the United States Government

KEY WORDS

confederation   (kon fed′ə rā′shən)
democracy   (di mok′rə sē)
compromise   (kom′prə mīz)
blueprint   (blü′print)

After the War for Independence, the leaders of the new country began a difficult job. They needed to establish a new system of government for the nation.

This job was difficult, but it also was interesting and rewarding. After all, the leaders could decide upon any type of government they wanted. They could avoid creating many of the problems they saw in other systems. Their main goal—to be as fair as possible to the new citizens of the United States—actually could be reached if they worked carefully together.

Early Solutions

Creating a system of government was a difficult task for our nation's founders. At first, they tried a system called a **confederation**. They drafted a plan of government known as the Articles of Confederation.

In a confederation, the national government is not very strong. Under such a system, the separate states were able to do almost whatever they wished to do. There were few laws that led to unity among the states. Often the states disagreed among themselves. This made it hard for the national government to raise money, to support an army, or to enforce laws.

In 1787, our nation's founders met in Philadelphia to create a new system of government. Some of the most famous delegates included (left to right) George Washington, James Madison, Benjamin Franklin, and Alexander Hamilton.

An Important Fear Why did the leaders choose a confederation? Remember that the War for Independence had been fought in part because the colonists feared a large, powerful government they could not control. A confederation calmed their fears because it left most of the government's power in the hands of the states.

Still, after a few years, most leading Americans felt that the confederation was not working. They wanted to make adjustments or changes in the rules. However, this was difficult since all the states needed to agree.

A New Government Delegates met at Philadelphia to make these changes. As they started their work, however, they began to see that they would have to start all over with a new form of government. They decided to make a strong **democracy**, a government that is made and ruled by the people.

The delegates had no models of this type of government to follow. The United States was the first modern democracy in the world. Only the writings of some great thinkers and the wisdom of the other participants guided each delegate. They used these ideas to help them. They also had the experience they had gained from using the Articles of Confederation. They knew what had gone wrong, and they knew what they wanted to fix.

At the Convention

Imagine for a moment that you are at the convention in Philadelphia.

The Constitutional Convention lasted four months. The meetings were secret. The delegates did not want to be influenced by other people. Because cameras were not yet invented, the only visual records of what happened are paintings and drawings. However, a complete written record was kept by James Madison.

Your actions could affect the citizens of your country for many years to come. You might feel nervous. You certainly want to be very careful in making decisions. You will be very serious about your job.

The Goal The delegates at the convention probably had these same feelings. They discussed the issues for a very long time. They wanted to make the new government strong, but they also wanted it to include the people as much as possible.

Sometimes the discussion among the delegates looked like a battle. Delegates with strong opinions wanted to make sure their wishes became laws. Sometimes other delegates disagreed. Often the two sides would **compromise**, or each agree to some things that they did not like in order to win on other issues.

The Document By the end of the meeting, the delegates had come up with a strong document called the Constitution of the United States of America. Its first words told the story of the new government.

"We the people of the United States," begins the document, "in order to form a more perfect union. . ." With these words, the delegates were telling the people of the United States that they needed to agree and that all the people had a voice in the government.

At the time, all people did not have the rights described in the document. As time went on, however, the true meaning of the Constitution's words were fulfilled. The founders of our nation probably would be pleased to know that today people in the United States still have the right to be heard.

Fifty-five men from 12 states were part of the Constitutional Convention. On September 17, 1787, 39 of these representatives signed the finished document. The last ten days were spent polishing the wording of the Constitution. Why were so many people and so much time used to write the document?

In 1976, throughout the United States, the 200th birthday of the nation was celebrated. In 1987, the Constitution also turned 200 years old.

The Importance of Written Law

The Constitution is important to every American citizen. It is like a **blueprint**, or set of plans, for the government. Because the Constitution is in writing, it can be referred to constantly. The words of the document never change.

The Constitution is the most important tool of government in the United States. No law can be made that goes against what it says.

A Plan for Indiana Indiana has a constitution as well. Like the United States Constitution, the state's constitution is a plan for the government. The Indiana constitution is special to the laws of the state. However, nothing in the Indiana constitution goes against what is stated in the United States Constitution.

A Lasting Success The government set up by the United States Constitution has lasted more than 200 years. The document has remained unchanged longer than any other set of laws in the world. Except for some additions, the laws you read today are the same ones written more than 200 years ago.

One reason the Constitution has lasted is because it gives most of the power to run the government to the people themselves. As you can see, the work the delegates did some 200 years ago was good work indeed.

Focus Review

Define
confederation, democracy, compromise, blueprint

Comprehension
1. What problems did the United States experience when it was governed as a confederation?
2. Why did the early leaders of the nation choose a confederation?
3. What guided the delegates in creating a democracy?
4. What did the opening words of the Constitution tell the citizens?

Critical Thinking
5. Why is it important that state constitutions do not go against the United States Constitution?

CHAPTER 8

Making Indiana Work

"Daddy," Cathy asked, "What do you and the other people do in the capitol building? Why do you have to work so much? Will you talk to me about your job?"

Mr. Gregson, an Indiana senator, laughed for a second before answering. "Well, Cathy," he said, "just imagine that the state is a business set up to serve all the people living in Indiana. You and your classmates and all the other people of Indiana are the bosses. The job of government leaders is to serve all these people.

"We make many decisions. We decide how much money the state needs and how best to spend it. For example, we make sure the state has enough money to provide necessary items like roads and schools. We also make new laws or change old ones if we think a problem can be solved."

Mr. Gregson thought for a few minutes before continuing, "Remember, Cathy, Indiana has changed through the years. Indiana citizens are still pioneers, but of a different kind than the early settlers. Today Hoosiers are learning how to move forward with new ideas."

LESSON 1 State Government

The Indiana state government is like a large business. How many different parts does the government have, and what does each part do?

KEY WORDS

legislative   (lej′ə slāt′iv)
executive   (ig zek′yət iv)
judicial   (jù dish′əl)
General Assembly   (jen′rəl
    ə sem′blē)
House of Representatives
    (hous′ əv rep′ri zent′ət ivz)
Senate   (sen′ət)
district   (dis′trikt)
bill   (bil′)
governor   (guv′ə nėr)
term   (tėrm′)
veto   (vēt′ō)
justice   (jus′təs)
case   (kās′)
appeal   (ə pēl′)

Farmers and industry workers have different life-styles. Their needs are just some of the many that the government of Indiana must consider.

Indiana is not a large state. Yet the various areas of the state are unique, or different from one another. Each area's geography, the ways its people choose to make a living, and the backgrounds and life-styles of its citizens give the area its own special qualities and concerns.

People living in and around the city of Gary, for example, are concerned about different things than the people of Bloomington are. To the people of Gary, the steel industry and the laws affecting it are important. Their jobs and life-styles are centered on this industry and around big city life.

To the people of Bloomington, farming is more important. The area around Bloomington is more rural than the area of Gary, and the people's life-styles center on raising crops and taking care of the land.

This variety among people and places makes an area interesting. However, it also means many different needs have to be met.

Many People Working Together

The government of Indiana tries to meet the many different needs of its citizens. The state government is made up of men and women from all parts of the state.

In all, nearly 100,000 people work for the government of Indiana. You might know some of them. The men and women you see building a new road work for Indiana. The state highway patrol officer you pass in a car works for Indiana. Government leaders in your town and county work for Indiana.

You will read about government jobs in this chapter. As you read, remember that the government of Indiana really is made up of every single Hoosier. The government leaders work for each Indiana citizen.

Branches of Indiana State Government

Government leaders in Indiana work in three branches, or parts, of state government. These three branches are the **legislative**, the **executive**, and the **judicial**.

The members of the legislative branch work to write the laws for Indiana. These people are elected by the citizens of Indiana.

The people in the executive branch work to administer the laws of the state. For example, they make sure that the roads are kept up, that the schools are run properly, and that the state has enough money.

People in the judicial branch are the members of the state court system. Judges, lawyers, clerks, and others work to make difficult decisions about how best to apply Indiana's laws.

The Legislative Branch People who make up the legislative branch of Indiana state government work in the General Assembly. The General Assembly has two parts—the **House of Representatives** and the **Senate**. These two bodies are made up of elected representatives from all the different parts of Indiana.

The House of Representatives has 100 members, all elected by people from the different **districts,** or voting areas, of the state. The chart on page 169 shows the qualifications a person must meet to run for the House of Representatives.

The capitol building was built in 1878. Located in the middle of Indianapolis, it is surrounded by nine acres of land.

Qualifications to Run for Indiana General Assembly or Governor

	House of Representatives	Senate	Governor
Age	Twenty-one	Twenty-five	Thirty
Citizenship	United States	United States	United States
Residency	District for one year	District for one year	State for five years
Number of terms	Unlimited	Unlimited	No more than two terms in a row

CHART STUDY *Which government leader has the longest residency requirement?*

After being elected, a representative serves for two years. If the representative wants to continue serving after two years, he or she must run for re-election.

The Indiana Senate has 50 members. The qualifications for running for the Senate are listed on the chart on this page. State senators serve four years before having to run for re-election.

The representatives and senators from all over Indiana gather each year at the capitol in Indianapolis on the second Monday of January. Their legislative session, or meeting, lasts until March 15 or April 30, depending on the year.

During the session, the General Assembly may decide on as many as 1,500 **bills**, or possible laws. The bills cover many areas of Hoosiers' daily lives. For example, the General Assembly might work on bills involving highway safety, school improvements, or tax changes. If the General Assembly makes a law requiring schools to change their lunch menus, you probably will find yourself eating new foods in the school cafeteria.

On rare occasions, the General Assembly also considers changes to the state constitution. Changing the Indiana state constitution is more difficult than passing an Indiana law. A change in the constitution must be approved by the General Assembly two years in a row. Then the people of Indiana must agree — by voting "yes" in an election.

The Executive Branch The highest government leader in the state, the **governor**, heads the executive branch of Indiana government. Many people work in the executive branch to help the governor manage the laws of the state.

The chart on this page shows the qualifications a person must have to run for governor of Indiana. The governor's **term**, or time in office, is four years. A governor cannot serve more than two terms in a row.

The executive branch has many responsibilities. One big job for this branch is deciding how the state

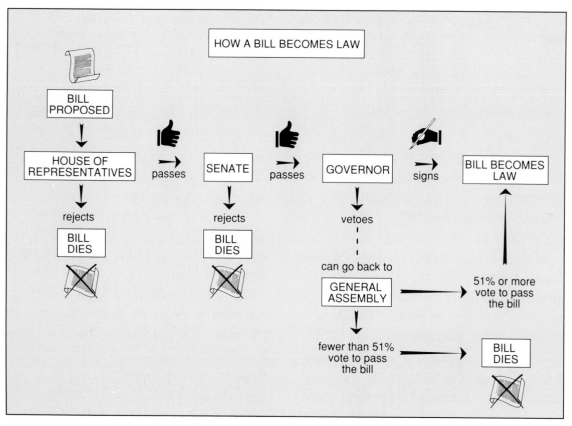

HOW A BILL BECOMES LAW

BILL PROPOSED → HOUSE OF REPRESENTATIVES → *passes* → SENATE → *passes* → GOVERNOR → *signs* → BILL BECOMES LAW

HOUSE OF REPRESENTATIVES → *rejects* → BILL DIES

SENATE → *rejects* → BILL DIES

GOVERNOR → *vetoes* → can go back to → GENERAL ASSEMBLY

GENERAL ASSEMBLY → 51% or more vote to pass the bill → BILL BECOMES LAW

GENERAL ASSEMBLY → fewer than 51% vote to pass the bill → BILL DIES

DIAGRAM STUDY *What happens if fewer than 51 percent of the General Assembly vote to pass a bill?*

should make and spend money. The branch makes the decision and then presents a plan to the General Assembly for approval.

The executive branch also proposes new laws and reviews all the bills passed through the legislative branch. After reviewing each bill from a legislative session, the governor makes a decision about it.

Let's look at an example—the bill about lunch menus in schools. The chart on this page can help you follow the process.

If this bill passes through the legislative branch, it goes to the governor. He or she can approve the bill

and make it a law. The governor also might **veto**, or reject, the bill.

As the governor decides, he or she has help. Other members of the executive branch gather facts to help the governor make the best decision about the bill. For the lunch menu bill, they might do research about healthy meals or costs of different foods. Then they will report all of their findings to the governor.

Let us pretend the governor studies all the facts about the lunch menu bill and decides to veto it. What happens next?

In some states, governors are very powerful. If they veto a bill passed by the legislative body, the bill can become law only if two thirds of the legislators vote to pass the bill again. In Indiana, however, the governor does not have quite as much power over these decisions.

The Indiana state constitution says that a regular majority (51 percent) of the General Assembly can override, or defeat, the governor's veto. This means that even though the governor has vetoed the bill on lunch menus, it still could become law. The bill can go back to the General Assembly and be passed with a 51 percent vote. Usually the Indiana General Assembly and the governor try to agree on a new law so that both can accept it.

The Judicial Branch Indiana's court system makes up the judicial branch of state government. This branch has the job of deciding exactly what the state laws mean and if they are being followed.

The state courts have three levels: the circuit courts, the Court of Appeals, and the Indiana Supreme Court. The chart on this page shows how a person can become a judge for the judicial branch of Indiana.

DIAGRAM STUDY *What career do state judges have before they become judges?*

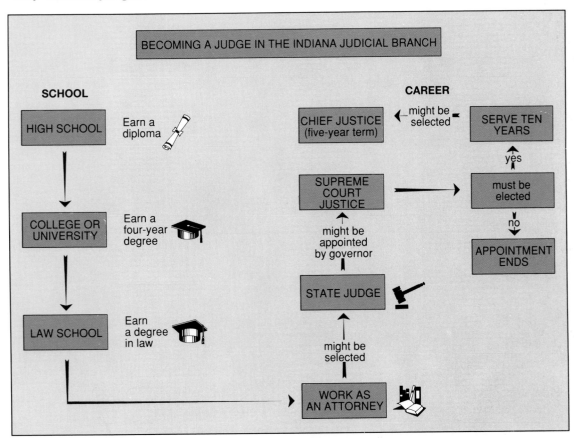

BECOMING A JUDGE IN THE INDIANA JUDICIAL BRANCH

SCHOOL

HIGH SCHOOL — Earn a diploma

COLLEGE OR UNIVERSITY — Earn a four-year degree

LAW SCHOOL — Earn a degree in law

CAREER

WORK AS AN ATTORNEY

might be selected

STATE JUDGE

might be appointed by governor

SUPREME COURT JUSTICE

must be elected

yes — SERVE TEN YEARS

no — APPOINTMENT ENDS

might be selected

CHIEF JUSTICE (five-year term)

Notice how many more steps are required to become a state Supreme Court judge. These judges are called **justices**. Every five years, one of the justices is named the chief justice. The chief justice has more responsibilities than the other justices. He or she decides which **cases** will be reviewed in the Indiana Supreme Court. A case is a matter for a law court to decide. The chief justice also decides which justice will work on each case.

Each Indiana state court conducts trials, or reviews of how the laws are being applied. Each time a trial is held, a specific case is decided. Most trials start in the circuit courts. Some of these trials may be **appealed**, or argued again, in the Court of Appeals. A few trials may go to the Indiana Supreme Court for review.

Let us see how the judicial branch works. The chart on page 173 shows how a case moves through the different levels of Indiana courts.

Indiana government buildings, including the Capitol building (below), are all very beautiful. Why, do you think, are these buildings visited and admired by Hoosiers?

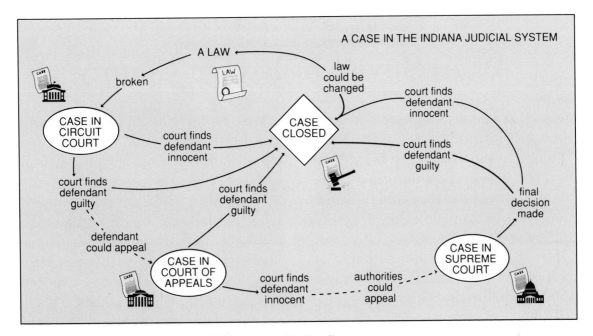

A CASE IN THE INDIANA JUDICIAL SYSTEM

A LAW

broken

LAW

law could be changed

CASE IN CIRCUIT COURT

court finds defendant innocent

court finds defendant guilty

CASE CLOSED

court finds defendant innocent

court finds defendant guilty

court finds defendant guilty

defendant could appeal

CASE IN COURT OF APPEALS

final decision made

CASE IN SUPREME COURT

court finds defendant innocent

authorities could appeal

DIAGRAM STUDY *What could happen if the Supreme Court found a defendant innocent?*

Suppose there is a law saying people can ride their bicycles only during the daylight hours. Now suppose a man is given a ticket for riding his bike just as the sun is setting.

When the man appears in a circuit court to have his case decided, he says that he was not wrong. He says he received the ticket during daylight hours. If after reviewing the law and the facts of the case the circuit court decides the man was in the wrong, he still can try to win again. He can take the case to the Court of Appeals. If the man wins in the Court of Appeals, the authorities then could take the case to the Indiana Supreme Court. There, the authorities would try to convince the court that the law was applied correctly. The Supreme Court would make the final decision on the case.

Lesson Review

Comprehension

1. Why are the different areas of Indiana unique?
2. Name the two parts of the Indiana General Assembly.
3. Name three duties of the Indiana executive branch.
4. How is the power of the Indiana governor limited?
5. What are the three levels of Indiana state courts?

Critical Thinking

6. How does each branch of the Indiana state government help protect the rights of Hoosiers?
7. Why does each branch of Indiana government contain different levels within it?

An Archivist in Brown County

You easily can read a history book to learn about the past. Have you ever wondered where historians find the information that they write about? Sometimes they find information because of people like Dorothy Bailey of Brown County.

Mrs. Bailey is a grandmother. She is also the archivist for The Brown County Historical Society. An archivist is a person who collects all sorts of papers and documents and then files them in a special room, called an archive, where the items will be protected for years. When a historian wants to learn about Brown County, he or she can use the archive set up by Mrs. Bailey.

Mrs. Bailey started her archive in 1972. She saw a need to collect and save documents from the past as well as items from the present.

First Mrs. Bailey had to learn what an archive should be like. She went to the University of Notre Dame to learn how to be an archivist. Then she used money donated by interested people to build a place for the historical items.

Mrs. Bailey is not paid for her work. She is a volunteer. She works hard because she thinks saving the past is important. Mrs. Bailey also works to save the present so people in the future will know what Brown County is like today.

The Brown County Historical Society is located in Nashville, Indiana. The society also operates the Brown County Museum, a collection of reconstructed buildings from the 1800's.

Through her hard work, Dorothy Bailey has kept alive Brown County's past.

"The present and future people can remember the past and who made it and what it was like to live then," says Mrs. Bailey. "There is no other way people will know. An archive is a great big window on the past."

Part of Mrs. Bailey's job is talking. She talks to the oldest residents of Brown County and records their conversations. These recordings are called oral histories. They tell about life in the past in the words of the people who lived through those years. In all, Mrs. Bailey has taken more than 80 oral histories. She also has published a book called *Brown County Remembers*.

Schoolchildren in Brown County also have taken oral histories. Some eighth-graders recorded their talks with older people. Then the students wrote about their talks for their local newspapers. Mrs. Bailey thinks projects like this are important. She says they help teach young people about the past in a way that helps them enjoy learning about it.

Mrs. Bailey works very hard at her job. However, she believes the work is worth the trouble. After all, she says, "I'm proud of where I live."

Long-time residents of Brown County enjoy getting together and sharing their memories. Often Dorothy Bailey is there to record what they say.

Citizenship and You

1. Make a list of people in your community whom you could interview to find out interesting historical facts about the area.
2. Many families pass down their memories through oral histories. Talk to a family member to learn an interesting family story that has been remembered in this way. Record the story to share with other family members.

LESSON 2 State Government Leaders

Many government leaders help the state run smoothly. What does each type of leader do?

KEY WORDS
committee (kə mit′ē)
lieutenant governor (lü ten′ənt guv′ə nėr)

You can see how important all three branches of state government are. The way they work together is also important. Equally important is how each individual leader helps the state government run smoothly.

Branches Working Together

The executive and legislative branches must work together to propose new laws. Both branches must help decide whether or not each law is in the best interest of Indiana and its citizens.

The judicial branch also looks at the laws. This branch lets the other two branches know if a law goes against the state constitution and should be repealed. The state constitution—Indiana's second—has been in effect since 1851. Going against this constitution is illegal in the state of Indiana. The judicial branch also helps the other branches see when a law needs to be made more clear or exact in its wording.

All of the people who work for the government of Indiana work for you. Some of these people are elected by Hoosiers. Others are appointed to

Many people work for the Indiana state government. For example, people help keep the state clean, serve in the General Assembly, and direct the daily operations of cities and towns.

Indiana legislators are busy at work even when they are not in the capitol building. This legislator, interested in education, is visiting an elementary school to get firsthand information.

their positions. Either way, they all work very hard. They are in their jobs because they believe they can help make Indiana a better place.

Government Leaders' Jobs

Indiana's state leaders work hard to help the state. Let us find out more about the job of each type of Indiana leader.

A Legislator While serving as Indiana representatives, your district's legislators travel from your district each year to the legislative session in Indianapolis. After the session is over, they return to your district. However, their jobs as legislators do not really end. They continue to represent you and all the people in your district.

For example, the legislators and their secretaries must answer mail from the people of your district. They also must stay informed about all state business, especially the issues that affect the people in your district. In addition, the representatives must prepare themselves for the next legislative session. Even when the legislature is not in session, the legislators attend meetings away from home.

Do you know who your district's legislators are? See if you can find out more information about them.

The Governor The governor of Indiana is more than a political leader. He or she is the top executive of the biggest business in Indiana—the state government. The governor must be sure the many departments of the state government, like those in charge of highways, education, and agriculture, are working properly. He or she runs many meetings of **committees** set up to make the state run more smoothly. A committee is a group of people specially chosen to review, take action on, or make a report about an issue or group of issues. The governor also travels fairly often to represent Indiana throughout the world.

Whenever the governor is out of the state, the **lieutenant governor** takes care of the governor's duties. The lieutenant governor also serves as the president of the senate. That means he or she can preside over debates and, in case the senate has a tie vote, can break the tie by voting.

You might want to write to the governor or lieutenant governor. Even the most important leader likes to hear from fellow Hoosiers.

The Supreme Court Justice For a five-year term, the chief justice has a great deal of responsibility. You have read about several of the chief justice's jobs. You can imagine how much studying and reading the chief justice must do to keep informed about Indiana laws. The chief justice also spends much time directing the actions of the other justices.

Indiana governors like Governor Evan Bayh (right) enjoy giving awards to deserving Hoosiers. Here Bayh presents the state's highest honor—Sagamores of the Wabash—to Landon Turner (seated). Turner, a former Indiana University basketball star, was crippled at the height of his career in an automobile accident.

Do not worry, though. The chief justice always will take time to read a letter of appreciation. You might even write to the chief justice about a law that concerns you.

Lesson Review

Comprehension

1. Why do the three branches of Indiana government work together?
2. How do committees help the governor?

Critical Thinking

3. Name two specific jobs that each of these government leaders does: legislator, governor, lieutenant governor, chief justice.

Reading a Table

Tables and graphs show information in different ways. Exact figures are best shown in a table. For this reason, population information often is presented in a table.

The table below shows how many state legislators worked in the governments of several states in 1987. It also shows the population of these states in 1987. Use the table and graphs to answer the questions.

State Legislators in 1987

State	Population	Total Legislators
New York	17,560,000	211
Indiana	5,500,000	150
Ohio	10,800,000	132
California	23,700,000	120
Alaska	405,000	60

1. Which state has the most legislators? Which has the fewest?
2. Which state has the most people? Which has the fewest?
3. How many legislators does Indiana have?
4. Together the two bar graphs (right) show the same information that the table shows. Tell why the table is a better choice for showing the information.

Project

Make a table with three columns. In the first column, write the name of the tests you take for one month. In the second column, write how many minutes you spent studying for each test. In the third column, write the grade you received.

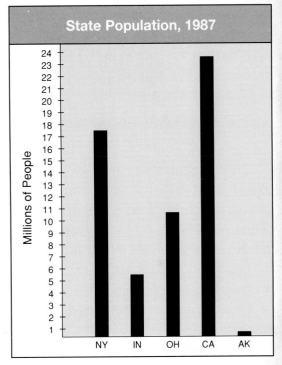

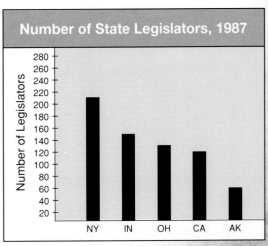

LESSON 3 Local Government

Every morning when you go to school, you walk or drive along streets. Who is responsible for making sure the streets are clean and the lights are working?

KEY WORDS

trustee   (trus'tē')
commissioner   (kə mish'ə nėr)
mayor   (mā'ėr)
city manager   (sit'ē man'ij ėr)
mayor-council system
   (mā'ėr koun'sel sis'təm)

There is another level of government that affects you even more directly than state government. That level is your local government. This is the level of government used to manage your township, county, and city. Each of these local systems has an organized government. But it is important that all three systems work closely together.

Township Government

Indiana was divided into townships by the Ordinance of 1787. Today, these townships are administered, or managed, by township **trustees** who take care of the business of the township. The responsibilities of the trustees include some fire protection and the maintenance of roads and the local cemetery.

The township trustee is elected by the people living in the township and works very closely with them. If, for example, people in the Madison Township in Tipton County thought the local cemetery needed to be cleaned up and more regularly maintained, they might approach the township trustee directly. The trustee then would have to take care of the problem.

Who is responsible for maintaining this rural Indiana road?

BREAKFAST
24 HRS. 1½ Mi

County Government

The government leaders of most Indiana counties are elected. These elected leaders then appoint staff members to help them in their jobs. Depending on the size of the county, the government leaders' jobs can be full-time or part-time. Let's look at the Tippecanoe County government system as a typical example for Indiana counties.

In Tippecanoe County, the county government is made up of a board of **commissioners**. These commissioners are elected by voters from the various districts within the county. The board of commissioners sets county policies on issues such as providing court space for county courts and keeping up with garbage disposal. The board also is responsible for deciding what types of buildings should be built in different areas of the county, inspecting the buildings, and maintaining some schools. To decide on these issues, the board meets regularly in the Tippecanoe County Courthouse.

In Tippecanoe County, the commissioners also must work closely with the two towns within the county, Lafayette and West Lafayette. These towns have their own governments.

City Government

Indiana cities use several forms of government. The size of a city or town often determines how it is governed. A small town might be governed simply by a board of its citizens. Some cities appoint or elect

All over Indiana, in courthouses like the Tippecanoe County Courthouse (above), county government leaders make important decisions. They decide how to handle major county issues such as county road maintenance, enforcement of the law in rural areas, and elections.

a **mayor**, a chief executive who has assistants to help manage city affairs. Other cities have a **city manager**, often appointed, who deals with the day-to-day business of city government. Since the 1930's, however, most Indiana cities have used a system of government in which a group makes decisions.

How One System Works Under the **mayor-council system** of city government, voters in the city elect a council of men and women to make decisions about city policies. These decisions are administered by the mayor, or sometimes by a city manager. The mayor or city manager often has influence on the council and may run council meetings.

Responsibilities Indiana city governments are responsible for removing liquid waste, collecting trash, providing police protection, keeping up the streets and city schools, and handling other important areas of daily life. Sometimes large cities set up separate governing bodies for big issues such as health and education.

Imagine for a moment how your city or town would look after one week if trash was not collected, the sewers were backed up, and the street lights were out. This gives you an idea of how important city government can be!

Combining Systems of Local Government

One Indiana county has combined its government with the government of its largest city. Since Indianapolis takes up most of Marion County, the two governments decided to combine and form one government called UNIGOV. Now UNIGOV administers both the city and the county. Much money has been saved by combining the efforts of the leaders.

Other areas of Indiana are watching UNIGOV to see how it works. People outside the state are interested too. If UNIGOV is a success, other people might try using a similar system.

The UNIGOV system has worked well and has saved money. These headquarters for UNIGOV are in Indianapolis.

Lesson Review

Comprehension

1. Who administers a township?
2. How are the members of a board of commissioners chosen?
3. Describe the mayor-council system of city government.
4. What is UNIGOV?

Critical Thinking

5. Explain how local government can affect your daily life.
6. How does the UNIGOV system save money?

LESSON 4 How New Laws Are Made

Hundreds of laws are passed each year in Indiana. How does an idea become a law?

KEY WORDS

Speaker of the House (spē′kėr əv thə hous′)
conference committee (kon′fə rəns kə mit′ē)

Marilee suggested her idea for a law in a letter to her state representative.

Many people believe they have little to do with the government. They might say that government is too complicated to understand. They might say that they never would be heard even if they tried to speak out on issues. These people should remember that all levels of government in the United States have been created only to serve the citizens. Each citizen, including you, should know the importance of taking part in government whenever possible.

Later, when you reach eighteen years of age, you can vote. Now you can write letters to leaders and try to learn about government issues. If you wanted to, you even could help make a new law. Let's look at an example of how that could happen.

The First Step: An Idea

One day Marilee was playing with her best friend, her pet spaniel Max. Marilee loved dogs, especially Max.

He even slept at the end of her bed. Max was a beautiful American cocker spaniel.

As Marilee watched Max chase after the ball she threw to him, she had an idea. She thought it would be wonderful for Indiana to have a state dog. After all, Indiana had the cardinal for the state bird. Since Max was an American breed, Marilee thought, why not have the American cocker spaniel as the state dog?

Marilee was very excited about her idea. She decided to write to her representative and tell him the idea. Marilee worked very hard on the letter. She wanted to explain her idea clearly and make the representative excited about it too.

Marilee was really surprised when she went to her mailbox a few weeks later. The representative had written back! He said he liked her idea!

The Next Step: The House

In his letter, the representative warned Marilee that her idea might not actually become law. However, he told her he was going to introduce the idea as a bill in the House of Representatives.

The First Read The representative wrote a bill and read it to the

Legislative committee members generally are chosen because they are interested in or knowledgeable about an issue. Why do you think is this a good way to choose committees?

House of Representatives. That day, the **Speaker of the House**, the representative who runs the house sessions, assigned the bill to a committee. This group of representatives would explore what the bill meant and how it would work.

When the committee met, it decided to add a few items to the bill. For example, the committee members wanted to be sure that people who owned other types of dogs would not feel left out. The committee therefore wrote an amendment, or change, saying that the state did not favor one breed over another.

The Second Read Later the committee reported the bill back to the House of Representatives. A committe member read the bill, and all the representatives discussed it. Some representatives did not like the idea of naming an official state dog. Other members favored the idea. Some tried to add more amendments to the bill.

After this second reading, the bill was reprinted with all the changes. The committee went over it one more time to make sure it was complete.

The Third Read Once again, the bill was read and debated in the house. Then the final vote was taken. The bill needed 51 "ayes," or yes votes, to be passed to the Senate. Marilee's bill made it!

On to the Senate

In the Senate, the bill could be

The story about Marilee and her dog is an imaginary one. However, it is believable because it tells about something that could happen. Every day ordinary citizens actually do propose state laws.

voted down, passed, or passed with more amendments. If the Senate made amendments, the bill would go to a committee called a **conference commitee**. There, selected members of the House of Representatives and the Senate would iron out any disagreements they had with each other's version of the bill.

The Senate passed the bill without any amendments. The bill then was sent to the governor.

The Final Step: The Governor

The governor received the bill and considered it carefully. The governor had to decide whether to sign the bill or veto it. In this case, the governor signed the bill. Marilee's idea had become the law of Indiana!

Although Marilee's new law is an imaginary example of what could happen, children in some states have proposed bills on such things as state animals, state rocks, and similar ideas. Sometimes their bills have been passed into law.

Lesson Review

Comprehension

1. How can a citizen your age participate in government?
2. What does the Speaker of the House do?
3. What actions might a committee take on a bill?
4. How many yes votes does a bill need to pass through the Indiana House of Representatives?
5. What is the purpose of a conference committee?

Critical Thinking

6. List the four steps that Marilee's bill went through to become a law.
7. Would Marilee's bill have died if the governor had vetoed it?

CHAPTER 8 REVIEW

Words to Know

Identify each of these words by writing a sentence.

1. legislative
2. executive
3. judicial
4. district
5. bill
6. term
7. veto
8. justice
9. case
10. appeal
11. committee
12. trustee
13. city manager
14. commissioner

Main Ideas

1. Name three reasons the different areas of Indiana are unique.
2. What are the three branches of government in Indiana?
3. Identify the two parts of Indiana's legislature.
4. What is the main job of the legislative branch?
5. Name two jobs of the executive branch of Indiana government.
6. How can a bill that has been vetoed still become a law?
7. Name the three levels of Indiana state courts.
8. What does the chief justice of the Indiana Supreme Court do?
9. What are three duties a legislator must perform?
10. What are three duties the governor must perform?
11. What is the role of the lieutenant governor?
12. What is the body that governs Tippecanoe County?
13. How does the mayor-council system of government work?
14. What jobs do Indiana city governments do?
15. Why was UNIGOV created?
16. Why is a bill read more than once in the Indiana House of Representatives?
17. What is the purpose of a conference committee?

Critical Thinking

1. Making good decisions for Indiana can be a difficult job. It takes all three branches of the state government working together. If one part of the government does not get along with another part, the business of the state could slow down or even stop. You have read about some qualifications people must have to be in state government. What other qualities should a state government leader have—for example, good speaking abilities or an interest in current affairs?
2. Three kinds of city government exist in Indiana. Each kind of government has advantages and disadvantages. Make a chart of the three types. Write the three kinds of city government across the top of a page. Below each heading, write one advantage and one disadvantage of that type of city government.

186

Writing for Understanding

1. Write a letter to your state representative suggesting a new law to be considered by the legislature. Try to convince your legislator that your proposed law would be good for all Hoosiers. Start by introducing yourself and explaining your idea for the new law. Tell the legislator why the law should be passed. How will it benefit Hoosiers? Be clear in your descriptions and reasoning. You also may want to think about some reasons why someone might not like your law. Then you should address each of these concerns in your letter.

2. Pretend that you are a reporter for a newspaper and that you are writing about the trial of a person accused of crossing a street against the light. Write an article about the case. Be sure to identify the accused, what the person is accused of having done, where the alleged crime happened, and what happens during the actual trial. Describe the people involved in the trial. Include the words they might say. For example, what did the judge and the lawyers say?

3. Pretend that Indiana government jobs are filled by hiring rather than through election or appointment. Write an advertisement that could be used to encourage people to apply for one of these positions—legislator, governor, or justice. Tell the qualifications a person applying for the job should have. Also make the job sound as appealing as possible.

Applying Skills

Use the table below to answer the questions.

1. How many states are included on the chart?
2. How many laws were passed in Indiana in 1988?
3. Which state included on the table passed the most laws?
4. Which state included on the table has the largest population?

Bills Passed by Some State Legislatures, 1988

State	Population	Number of Bills Introduced	Number of Bills Passed
Arizona	3,650,231	1,134	311
California	25,432,661	4,260	1,466
Indiana	5,550,000	1,072	136
Vermont	550,000	793	137

CHAPTER 9

Indiana in the United States

United States Congresswoman Simms smiled as she shook the hand of Mr. Frederick, an Indiana farmer. She was in the area of Bloomington for two days, talking to farmers about some problems they were having.

Based on what the farmers told her, Congresswoman Simms was preparing a bill to present in Washington, D.C. The farmers had been having hard times this year. They needed help from the government. If the bill passed, selling corn to foreign countries would become easier.

This would mean the farmers would have more places to sell their products. They would find it easier to make money. Congresswoman Simms felt sure the bill would pass because it would help farmers all over the country.

Even though Simms was tired from her travels, she was excited about her job. She knew she could help the farmers in her state. She knew that Hoosiers were counting on her to represent them well. She smiled as another farmer shook her hand. She was eager to talk to as many people as she could. Their ideas and concerns were important.

LESSON 1   National Government

The United States is a very big country with a large government. How is this huge government organized?

KEY WORDS
national government   (nash′ə nəl guv′ėrn mənt)
Congress   (kon′grəs)
checks and balances   (cheks′ ənd bal′əns əz)

States, counties, and cities in the United States all have governments. The United States also has another level of government that affects your life. This government is for the whole country. It is called the **national government**.

A Familiar Structure

The organization of Indiana's government follows the design of the national government. As you learn about the national government, you will recognize the three branches— legislative, executive, and judicial. Differences do exist between the national and state governments, however, as you will see.

Legislative   The legislative branch at the national level is **Congress**. Members of Congress are sent from each of the 50 states. They work to make laws for the country. Congress is made up of two parts, the House of Representatives and the United States Senate. Facts about each part of Congress are found in the chart on page 190.

Each year Congress gathers in Washington, D.C., on the third day of January. Their session must last at least until July 31st. However, sessions often run into November or December because of the large amount of work Congress does. Much of their work is on bills about taxes, making and spending money, dealing with other countries, assisting Americans who need help, and encouraging trade and business.

All of these issues affect Hoosiers. For example, if there was a terrible

The Capitol building in Washington, D.C., is where Congress meets when it is in session.

tornado in Muncie and much damage was done, Congress would find a way to provide money and aid to the area.

Bills are passed through Congress much as they are through the Indiana General Assembly. (See the chart on page 170.) Because Congress receives thousands of bills every session, committees are important. Committees are formed of members who have knowledge about a bill's subject. Each committee can give its full attention to a bill.

The committees decide whether bills should go to a general session of Congress. Many bills never get approved by committees. We say these bills have died. Bills that do make it through committees still have to be passed by both houses of Congress. If they pass, they then go to the executive branch.

Executive Whereas the governor is the chief executive of the state, the President is the chief executive of the nation. Obviously, the President has many more responsibilities than a governor has. The President manages all the different parts of government that run the United States. The President also manages the national government's relationships with other countries.

The executive branch also includes a Vice President and many departments, or parts of government, set up to help the President. The actions of each department affect Hoosiers. For example, the Department of Agriculture watches Indiana farms to make sure they are doing well. If farmers in Indiana have hard times, the department will let Congress know that the state needs help. If Indiana farmers are doing well, the department figures out why. It uses this knowledge to help farmers in other areas of the nation.

Judicial The national judicial branch includes 94 circuit courts, 12 district courts, and one Supreme Court made up of nine justices. The circuit courts, found throughout the

CHART STUDY *Each state has two senators. However, the number of representatives depends on the population. How might this help some states more than others?*

Middle Western Members of Congress in 1989

State	Population	Senators	Representatives
Illinois	11,559,000	2	22
Indiana	5,542,000	2	10
Minnesota	4,298,000	2	8
Nebraska	1,590,000	2	3
North Dakota	664,000	2	1
Ohio	10,787,000	2	21

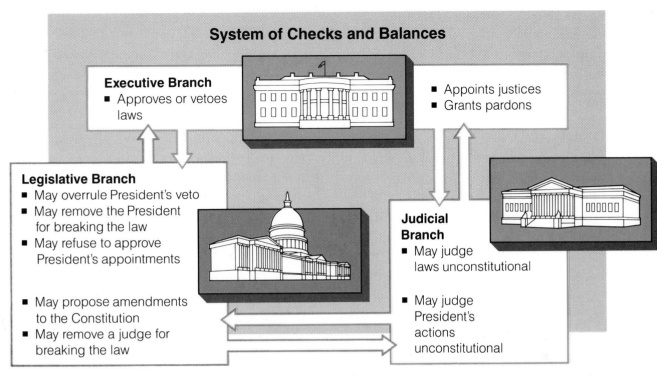

System of Checks and Balances

Executive Branch
- Approves or vetoes laws
- Appoints justices
- Grants pardons

Legislative Branch
- May overrule President's veto
- May remove the President for breaking the law
- May refuse to approve President's appointments
- May propose amendments to the Constitution
- May remove a judge for breaking the law

Judicial Branch
- May judge laws unconstitutional
- May judge President's actions unconstitutional

DIAGRAM STUDY *How does the judicial branch of the United States government check the President's power?*

United States, are where most national trials are heard. The district courts are where cases go for appeal, or the chance to be heard again.

The Supreme Court looks at laws and rules to make sure that citizens have been treated fairly. Most importantly, the Supreme Court ensures that the United States Constitution is followed.

A System of Checks and Balances

The branches of United States government were set up carefully so that no one branch would have too much power. Each branch can check the other two branches to make sure the balance of power is working. This is known as the system of **checks and balances**.

Lesson Review

Comprehension
1. What kinds of work does Congress do during a session?
2. Where does Congress meet?
3. Why are committees so important to Congress?
4. How do actions of the departments of the executive branch affect Hoosiers?

Critical Thinking
5. The United States government is set up on a system of checks and balances. How might this system protect all United States citizens?
6. How might the actions of the judicial branch of the national government affect Hoosiers?

191

Movement

As the United States grew, the government believed it was important that all regions of the country be connected. Communities would then be able to exchange goods and ideas. In the 1830's, many states improved transportation by building canals between rivers. At the same time, the government was building the National Road, also called the Cumberland Road.

The map on this page shows the canal systems and the National Road. Before canals were built, river travelers could bring with them only those things they could carry themselves. They often had to portage, or carry, their boats and goods between rivers.

Canals and the new National Road opened up Indiana to trade with other parts of the United States. Improved access to the Great Lakes opened up eastern cities to Indiana markets. The Wabash River opened up much of the South. As you can see, even in the 1800's when Indiana was considered the far west, it was a hub of transportation.

Imagine that you lived in the 1840's and made textiles, or fabrics, in Evansville, Indiana. Suppose you wanted to sell your textiles to customers in Columbus, Ohio. How would you transport your goods there?

First you would load your textiles onto a boat in Evansville. They would be shipped northeast up the

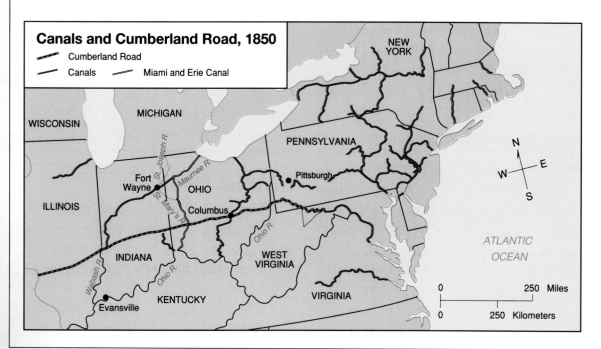

Canals and Cumberland Road, 1850

- Cumberland Road
- Canals
- Miami and Erie Canal

NEW YORK

WISCONSIN

MICHIGAN

PENNSYLVANIA

Pittsburgh

Fort Wayne

St. Joseph R.

Maumee R.

St. Mary's R.

OHIO

Columbus

ILLINOIS

INDIANA

Ohio R.

Wabash R.

Ohio R.

WEST VIRGINIA

ATLANTIC OCEAN

KENTUCKY

Evansville

VIRGINIA

N
S
E
W

0   250 Miles
0   250 Kilometers

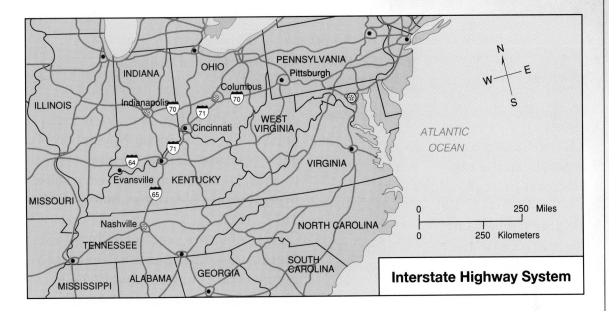

Interstate Highway System

Ohio River. Then your goods would be shipped up the Miami and Erie Canal to where it intersects the National Road. At this point, your goods would be loaded onto horse-drawn wagons for the trip over the National Road to Columbus.

Today, as you can see on the road map above, you could send your textiles by truck. The driver would get onto Interstate 64 near Evansville and drive your textiles straight to Interstate 71 at Louisville, Kentucky. The driver would then follow Interstate 71 all the way to Columbus. The whole trip would take about six hours. The same trip in the 1840's took about a week.

Notice the highway that runs east and west through Columbus, Ohio, and Indianapolis. This is Interstate Highway 70. It follows some of the original route of the National Road. As you can see, other modern highways also connect Indianapolis with many cities in the East, Middle West, and the South.

How are interstate highways possible? Over the years, state and federal tax dollars have been used to build and maintain the highways. Without these highways, trucks, for example, could not transport goods easily from city to city.

Comprehension

1. Before canals, what did river travelers do when they crossed land between two rivers?

Critical Thinking

2. Use the map on page 192 to plan a route for transporting goods between Pittsburgh, Pennsylvania, and Evansville, Indiana.

3. Plan the route you would travel to get from Nashville, Tennessee, to Indianapolis today.

LESSON 2 Indiana's Role

Indiana is just one of the 50 states. How can Indiana influence the whole government of the United States?

KEY WORDS
federal   (fed′ə rəl)
electoral college   (i lek′tə rəl kol′ij)
eligible   (el′ə jə bəl)
register   (rej′ə stėr)
polls   (pōls′)
tax   (taks′)

Indiana is an important part of the United States. Indiana business and farm products help the whole country. The state is a transportation center for the nation. Indiana also plays an important part in the nation's politics.

The state and people of Indiana have a voice in United States government. This is because the country has a **federal** government. In a federal government, powers are divided between the national government and the states.

Indiana's Voice in the Electoral College

Members of the **electoral college** are chosen by United States citizens when they vote for President and Vice President. The electoral college is the group of people who formally elect the President and Vice President. This is done in November of each year that can be divided evenly by four. In which of these years were presidential elections held—1960, 1977, 1982?

The electoral college has 538 members—one person for each member of Congress plus three people who represent the District of Columbia. Indiana's 12 electoral votes mean that the state has a voice in national politics. Presidential candidates who want those votes listen to what Indiana has to say.

Presidents live in the White House. To reach the White House, candidates need votes from all over the United States—including Indiana.

James Danforth Quayle was only forty-one years old when he was elected Vice President.

Voices in Government

Many individuals from Indiana have had important voices in United States government. They have worked for the state and for the country at the national level of government.

Leaders in Congress Indiana has had some famous members of Congress. For example, in 1809, Jonathan Jennings was elected to Congress. Indiana was still a territory at that time. Jennings worked very hard for Indiana's statehood. In 1816, when Indiana became a state, Jennings was elected the first governor of Indiana.

Other Hoosiers in Congress were part of decision-making that affects you today. In the 1970's, Senator Birch Bayh served Indiana in Congress. He was known for taking a strong stand on issues. In 1976, James Danforth Quayle of Huntington was elected to the House of Representatives. He served two terms. In 1980, Quayle defeated Birch Bayh to become a senator. In the Senate, Quayle served on three committees: the Armed Services Committee, the Budget Committee, and the Labor and Human Services Committee. He went on to be elected Vice President in 1988.

Who serves your district and state in Congress today? You can find out how they represent the state of Indiana at the national level.

Executive Leaders Two Hoosiers have run for President. In 1888, Benjamin Harrison was elected the twenty-third President. He followed in the footsteps of his grandfather, William Henry Harrison, who was the ninth President.

As President, Benjamin Harrison worked to improve foreign affairs.

Benjamin Harrison was born in Ohio but lived most of his life in Indianapolis. During the Civil War, Harrison was a hero of the 70th Indiana Regiment. After the war, he became well known throughout the country as a speaker, an attorney, and a United States senator.

When Harrison was chosen to run for President in 1888, he directed his campaign from his front porch in Indianapolis. More than 300,000 people came from all over the country to hear him speak from his porch.

Harrison won the election and entered office exactly 100 years after George Washington had been sworn in. He served one term as President and then returned to his home in Indianapolis. Harrison is remembered for his honesty, fairness, and wisdom while serving as President of the United States.

Wendell Willkie, a lawyer from Elwood, ran for President in 1940. Willkie was a successful lawyer and businessman. He was chosen to run for President because many people believed his ideas would improve the nation's economy. Willkie's campaign was full of energy, but he lost the election to Franklin D. Roosevelt. After the election, Willkie continued to be involved in politics. He worked for international peace after World War II.

Five Hoosiers have served as Vice President, including Dan Quayle. Other Indiana politicians have served in important government posts. For example, John Hay served

Wendell Willkie ran for President a second time in 1944. However, early defeats caused him to withdraw.

as a secretary to Abraham Lincoln and became Secretary of State under Theodore Roosevelt years later.

Voices of Voters

You have seen how important Indiana's government leaders can be. Everyone from the township trustee to the state's two senators works to benefit the people of Indiana. Every citizen of Indiana also can have a voice in helping Indiana.

A Precious Right The right to vote is one of the most precious rights given to citizens. Voting allows every **eligible** person to have a say in the government. A person becomes eligible to vote in the United States when he or she is a legal citizen at least eighteen years old. To be eligible, a person also must **register**, or sign up to vote.

Voting should be seen as a responsibility as well as a right. When people do not vote, they are not helping the government make decisions. In fact, people who do not vote are not taking responsibility for helping themselves.

Hoosiers can vote on local, state, and federal issues and leaders. All of these ideas and people can help the state of Indiana. Helping the state of Indiana means helping each and every citizen as well.

The Act of Voting When an election is held, voters go to the **polls**. Polls, or voting places, could be in a school, a church, or even a neighbor's garage. Volunteers, or unpaid workers, make sure the voting runs smoothly. They check to be sure all the people who come to vote have registered properly.

No matter where polls are, all voting is done in secret. With this method, nobody can pressure a voter to vote in a particular way.

Staying Informed Careful voters stay informed about politics. They listen to what government leaders say. They think about what they believe in and whether or not people and issues under discussion match their beliefs. Careful voters read newspapers and magazines so they can better understand the issues and make wise choices at the polls. After

When a person reaches the age of eighteen, he or she gains the right to vote. Why is it so important that a person use this right?

all, the people and issues voters decide upon can have a big impact on all Hoosiers.

Even though you are not yet old enough to vote, you can stay informed about politics. Remember that every person is important to a democracy, a government made and ruled by the people. You have your own voice as a citizen of Indiana and the United States. An informed citizen is an effective citizen. The more you learn now about government and politics, the better prepared you will be when you turn eighteen and can vote.

Indiana and National Issues

Many national issues, or matters of political concern, are important to Indiana because of their effects on the state. Most of these issues have to do with money and how it is raised and spent.

Indiana raises much of the money for the state through different types of **taxes**. A tax is money collected by a government to pay for its services.

Sales and Income Taxes If you buy some paper to use in school, you will be charged 5 percent extra when you pay. This extra money, or sales tax, goes to the state. People who work also pay income tax, which is a certain percentage of what they earn. These taxes also go to the state.

Federal Taxes State taxes are not enough to pay for all the things Indiana needs. Hoosiers also pay federal taxes to the national government. Remember that the word *federal* means "for the state and for the nation." Some of the federal tax money, then, comes back to Indiana to help the state.

For example, the great interstate highways that link Indiana with the rest of the country were built mostly with money collected through federal taxes. The highways help Indiana, but they also help other states.

Federal Spending Other federal payments to Indiana help individual Hoosiers who are needy. For example, Hoosiers who are out of work or

This boy is being charged Indiana sales tax. What other tax will he pay when he is old enough to work?

Tax processing centers require thousands of workers and advanced computer systems. Why is tax processing such a huge job?

who suffer from disabilities may receive money from the United States government to help them pay for their living expenses.

In all, Indiana receives approximately $15 billion per year in federal payments. This money is used for many purposes besides those about which you read. For example, federal money is used to fight crime and to rebuild damaged areas. The money also is used to help farmers. In fact, every Hoosier benefits from federal spending in Indiana. That is why having Indiana representatives in Congress is so important. They speak with a voice that is heard across the nation. They are your voice in Washington, D.C.

Lesson Review

Comprehension

1. Name three Hoosiers who have been important in United States government.
2. Who is eligible to vote in the United States?
3. How can voters stay informed about politics?
4. Why are taxes necessary?

Critical Thinking

5. How can Hoosiers have a say in the United States government?
6. How does the United States government help Hoosiers?

Using a Diagram

You have seen many diagrams in this unit. Often, diagrams can help you understand complicated processes and systems. Diagrams can show you what the parts of a system or process are, what they do, and how they relate to one another.

The electoral college is one such system that often is explained by using a diagram. The diagram (right) shows how the electoral college is used to elect the President and Vice President of the United States. The diagram also shows Indiana's role in the electoral college.

Use the diagram to answer the following questions.

1. What is the first step in the electoral college system?
2. Why does the diagram include an arrow from the top left box to the center box?
3. Where do Indiana's electors go to cast their votes for President and Vice President?
4. Who reads the votes from the electoral college members of all the states?
5. When are the new President and Vice President announced?
6. How many electoral votes does Indiana have?
7. Why is a diagram useful in explaining the electoral college system?

8. How would you need to change this diagram in order for people in other states to use it?

Project

Make a diagram showing a system for dividing household chores. Make separate boxes for each activity. Under each box, list who might help with these duties.

The Electoral College System

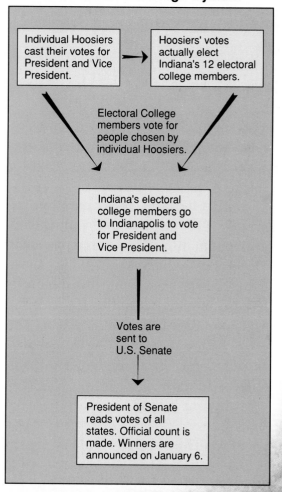

Individual Hoosiers cast their votes for President and Vice President.

Hoosiers' votes actually elect Indiana's 12 electoral college members.

Electoral College members vote for people chosen by individual Hoosiers.

Indiana's electoral college members go to Indianapolis to vote for President and Vice President.

Votes are sent to U.S. Senate

President of Senate reads votes of all states. Official count is made. Winners are announced on January 6.

CHAPTER 9 REVIEW

Words to Know

Number your paper from 1 to 4. Use each word to complete one of the comparisons.

Congress   register
President   polls

1. People can go to a school to learn and to vote at the _____
2. The Indiana state legislature votes on laws for Indiana whereas _____ votes on laws for the whole United States.
3. People enter a contest but they _____ to vote.
4. The governor is the chief executive of Indiana whereas the _____ is the chief executive of the United States.

Main Ideas

1. What are the two houses of Congress called?
2. What group decides whether or not a bill should go before the whole Congress?
3. What is the role of the electoral college in Presidential elections?
4. Name one department in the executive branch and tell what it does.
5. What judicial body is the highest court in the United States?
6. How many electoral votes does Indiana have?
7. What are the two qualifications for voting?

8. What does a careful voter do?
9. Which officials are Indiana's voice in Washington, D.C.?

Critical Thinking

1. When the framers of the Constitution were deciding how the new government should be set up, they had a difficult time figuring out how many legislators each state should be allowed to have. The big states wanted the number of Congress members to be tied to the population of the states. The small states felt this would not be fair. They feared the big states would be able to overrule anything the small states wanted, since the big states would have so many more members of Congress. The framers finally decided to base the number of representatives on the population of each state, but to have two senators for each state no matter what size the state is. From what you have learned, how can this equal number of senators for each state ensure that big states cannot rule over small states?
2. People often forget that public officials work for everybody. The government is supposed to be ruled by all the people. This means the people have to take part. What are two ways citizens can take part in government?

Writing for Understanding

1. Write a fictional newspaper story about a senator. Tell who the senator is, where the senator goes to work, what he or she does during the day, and why each job is important. Try to add some excitement to your story by having your senator work on an important bill that would affect Indiana.

2. Write a letter to the member of Congress from your district. Tell your opinion on any issue you have thought about. For example, you might believe that farmers need more help or that cars should be made safer. Choose one issue and write the letter to find out more about it. Ask the member how he or she feels about the issue.

Applying Skills

This diagram shows that the division of state government is like that of the national government. Use the diagram to answer these questions.

1. Which two branches make decisions about money?
2. In what area do all three branches of state government have a say?

The Three Branches of State Government

Executive Governor	**Legislative** Legislature	**Judicial** State Courts
■ Carries out the laws ■ Decides how to spend money ■ Commands the National Guard	■ Makes the laws for the state ■ Decides how to raise money	■ Settles arguments about the law ■ Judges the accused based on the law

UNIT 3 REVIEW AND STUDY GUIDE

Key People/Places	Key Terms	Key Ideas	
Making Indiana Work (pages 166-187) Gary, Bloomington, Indianapolis, Tippecanoe County, Lafayette, West Lafayette, Indianapolis, Marion County	legislative, executive, judicial, General Assembly, House of Representatives, Senate, district, bill, governor, term, veto, justice, case, appeal, committee, lieutenant governor, trustee, commissioner, mayor, city manager, mayor-council system, Speaker of the House, conference committee	■ Indiana government has different branches that each perform certain duties. ■ Government leaders perform different tasks. ■ Jobs performed by local government greatly affect our daily lives. ■ There are specific steps taken to make an idea become law.	1800 **1816** Jonathon Jennings elected first Indiana Governor **1888** Benjamin Harrison elected President 1900
Indiana in the United States (pages 188-202) Jennings, Bayh, Quayle, Benjamin and William Henry Harrison, Willkie, Hay ——— Washington, D.C.	national government, Congress, checks and balances, federal, electoral college, eligible, register, polls, tax	■ The national government inspired Indiana's state government and has a system of checks and balances. ■ Indiana plays a role in national government through its state leaders, well-informed voters, and taxpayers.	**1940** Wendell Willkie runs unsuccessfully for President **1988** J. Danforth Quayle elected Vice President

UNIT 4
Living in Indiana

▲ *Monument Circle*

German dancer

IN THIS UNIT

In this unit, you will learn about the most important part of Indiana—the people who live in the state. You will learn where Hoosiers came from and how they keep alive their heritage. You will read about what Hoosiers do for fun—and how they make a living. You also will learn how Indiana and its citizens keep up with many changes that occur in the state, the nation, and even throughout the world.

A Changing World

KEY WORD
adapt   (ə dapt')

One thing always can be said about the world around us—it changes every day. In this unit, you will read about some of the changes Indiana has seen in recent years.

Change All Over
You know that at one time Indiana was mainly a farming state. What happened to turn Indiana into a manufacturing and transportation center? How did the state and its people **adapt**, or change, to meet the challenges brought by rapid growth and development?

An Old Way The first European and American settlers owned small pieces of land and grew corn and animals. They traded with other states for different kinds of foods and for manufactured goods.

This way of life was not very complicated. Most Hoosiers never thought of working with a business in another country. Many citizens of Indiana never left the state at all.

New Products, New Ways By the end of the 1800's, inventions like

Rural areas in Indiana were slow to develop. This 5¢ & 10¢ store—the first in Elkhart—was opened in 1899.

large railroad systems and better ocean-going ships seemed to make the world a smaller place. As it became easier to ship goods, new products from other countries began to come into Indiana. In turn, Indiana's products went to other countries.

A New Challenge
Since the turn of the century, change has come very fast. The United States fought in World War I in Europe. It became a leader in world affairs. Then, after World War II, the United States became the most powerful country in the world.

Americans—including many Hoosiers —began going to other countries to work and live.

A New World Indiana began looking far beyond its own borders. During the war, many farms around the world were destroyed. Other countries desperately needed American food. Indiana's farmers sold much of their crops to these other countries.

The world also needed to rebuild cities and factories. It needed steel and parts. Indiana's factories helped supply these things to the rest of the world. Hoosiers helped the world recover. Businesses boomed. Many people left the farms and moved to the growing cities.

New Competition Once the world had recovered from the war, other nations began to compete for the business that Americans had controlled. Germany and Japan built strong economies. European nations united to form a group called the Common Market. These changes meant that the United States faced some difficult times. The world's most powerful nation needed to adapt to remain strong.

Today the Middle West is a trading center for the world. The inside of the Chicago Board of Trade building is extremely busy as deals are made for products (below). On the top of the building, the famous "Goddess of Grain" statue overlooks the huge city of Chicago (inset).

A Smaller World One other big change was the growing use of computers and other electronics. These machines make communication with other places almost instantaneous. In other words, you can pick up a phone and—in an instant—call almost any other country around the globe. International business is done in the flash of an eye by computer.

Keeping up with these changes has been a challenge for the United States and Indiana. Hoosiers have had to adapt to a new way of thinking. Now, instead of thinking just about their towns and farms, Hoosiers also must think about other countries like Japan and those in Europe and South America. Hoosiers must be able to keep up with the rapid pace of change.

This modern communication device—commonly known as a fax machine—can send a page of information or pictures to any other fax machine in the world.

State Symbols

Fortunately, Indiana is able to keep alive many of its traditions in the midst of much change. In this way, Indiana remembers its past as it heads into the future. One way Indiana remembers its past is with state symbols.

The peony, Indiana's state flower, has lovely blossoms of red, pink, or white.

Birds, Flowers, and Rivers The state flower—the peony—and the state bird—the cardinal—remind Hoosiers that Indiana was once a wild country. These symbols stand for the beauty of nature.

The state song—*On the Banks of the Wabash*—reminds Hoosiers of the important part that river played in the state's history. The song also tells of the river's beauty.

A Famous Image Of course, there is the well-known state nickname— "Hoosier." Nobody knows exactly where this nickname developed or even exactly what it means. Some say it came from a French word. Others say it came from an Indian word. No matter where the nickname came from, however, people from Indiana are very proud to be called Hoosiers.

The state motto—"Crossroads of America"—helps Hoosiers recall that the state has been a meeting place for all Americans from other parts of the country. Today the motto describes the important role Indiana plays in the nation's transportation system.

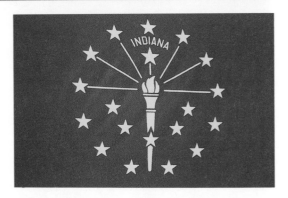

The Indiana state flag is simple but meaningful. What does the torch on the flag represent?

The Indiana state seal shows Indiana during pioneer times. It is placed by the governor on all important papers.

The state flag is also symbolic. It features a large torch representing knowledge and liberty. This torch is surrounded by a field of 13 small stars that stand for the original 13 American colonies. Closer to the torch's flame is a field of six more stars. All the stars together indicate that Indiana was the nineteenth state admitted to the United States.

Hoosier Celebrations In addition to state symbols, Hoosiers remember their past with festivals, games, art, and special occasions. They celebrate their unique place in the United

States. Different groups of people also celebrate their heritage with festivals that they brought to the state from other lands. In these ways, Hoosiers carry some of their traditions into the changing world.

Focus Review

Define
adapt

Comprehension
1. How did Indiana help other areas of the world after the war?
2. How have improved communication equipment and computers made the world seem smaller?
3. Name three ways that Hoosiers remember their traditions.

Critical Thinking
4. To what new challenges, do you think, will Hoosiers need to adapt?

CHAPTER 10

Indiana's Way of Life

Kenny Foster lives in Terre Haute, Indiana. He has a pen pal named Tomás who lives in Mexico. Tomás never has been to Indiana, and Kenny wants to describe his state to him in a letter. Kenny can tell Tomás all about Indiana's history, but he also wants to tell his pen pal about some of the things that make Indiana special. Kenny wants to tell about how he and his neighbors live, work, and play.

What would you write about if you were Kenny? What special things make Indiana different from any other place? What special things does Indiana share with other places? As you read this chapter, you might find out some interesting facts you did not know before.

LESSON 1   Indiana Heritage

Heritage is a people's history and traditions passed from parent to child. Where can you find examples of Indiana's heritage?

KEY WORDS
culture   (kul'chėr)
landscape   (lan'skāp)

Literature, music, art, and crafts are things that give you a feeling for the time in which you live and also of times that have passed. These things make up part of your **culture**. The way of life for a group of people — including everything they believe, know, and do — is the group's culture. Indiana's culture is rich with many examples of fine art that have been produced by Hoosiers.

The Indianapolis Symphony Orchestra is paid for by interested Hoosiers. It is a part of Indiana's culture.

Hoosier Fine Arts

By studying examples of Indiana literature, art, and music, you can find out about the heritage and history of the state's people.

Literature If you read a list of famous Hoosiers, you might be surprised to see how many of the people were writers. Indiana is known for being home to many famous authors. Some of these authors wrote about life in Indiana in books such as *The Hoosiers, The Gentleman from Indiana,* and *Alice of Old Vincennes.* You can see that Indiana is an important part of these books. Indiana is a special part of the authors' heritage.

Booth Tarkington, one famous Indiana writer, was born in Indianapolis in 1869. His childhood gave him ideas for much of his work. One of his most famous books is called *Penrod.* The main character of the book, Penrod Schofield, aged 12, has many adventures that closely relate to Tarkington's boyhood.

Perhaps the most famous poet from Indiana is James Whitcomb Riley, who was born in Greenfield in 1849. He is known as the "Hoosier Poet." Riley wrote for children and about children.

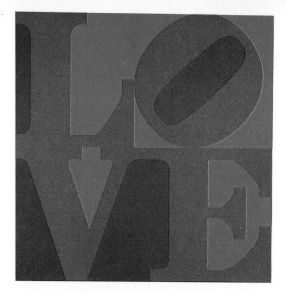

Robert Indiana's painting Love *is a type of art known as a word-image. Why is this a good name for this type of art?*

Another famous Hoosier writer is Ernie Pyle. He did not write poems or novels. Instead, Pyle was a newspaper writer who reported from the battlegrounds of World War II. His writing gave Americans a close-up view of war from the eyes of the soldiers.

Art Imagine that you are going to take a car trip through Brown County. What would you feel as you looked at the beautiful scenery? How would you show others what you felt? Many artists have found the scenery in Brown County inspiring. This means that they have been filled with ideas about how to show others what they see and feel.

Theodore Steele, an Indiana artist who was born in 1847, is especially known for his **landscapes** of the countryside around Brown County. A landscape is a painting or photograph that shows an area of land.

For another artist, Indiana was so important that he actually changed his name to match the state's name. Robert Indiana, born with the name Robert Clark, created one of the most famous symbols of the 1970's, a painting of the word "Love."

Music Some people choose to express their feelings in a way that others can hear—music. The state of Indiana has produced many musicians and songwriters.

Two Hoosier musicians became famous in the United States during the 1940's and 1950's. Cole Porter—born in Peru, Indiana—was especially known for the musicals he wrote. A musical is a play in which the story is told to music. Hoagy Carmichael, born in Bloomington, was known for his work on music for movies. Your grandparents probably remember many of these two musicians' songs.

Hoagy Carmichael (left) went to law school before becoming a songwriter. Cole Porter (right) was only eleven years old when he sold his first song.

John Mellencamp's songs—like the Farm Aid concerts he organized—usually have a message about social issues. Mellencamp is proud of his Middle Western roots.

One famous Indiana musician today is John Mellencamp. Mellencamp always has spoken well of his state. He writes songs that tell about the difficulties faced by Indiana farmers. In 1985, Mellencamp helped to put on a special musical concert called Farm Aid. All of the money made from the concert went to help American farmers. The concert was so successful that it has been held again every year since.

Unlike many musicians who leave their home states after they are successful, Mellencamp chose to stay in Indiana. He even built a recording studio in an old Indiana farmhouse.

One Indiana Craft

Crafts are another way to see a people's heritage. Usually a type of craft uses materials that are readily available in the area. The way the craft is made is passed from one generation to the next.

Jasper, Indiana If you walk down a street in Jasper, Indiana, you will see signs for many businesses— Brosmer Lumber, Decora Cabinets, Fleck Chair Manufacturing, Forest Products Manufacturing, Indiana Desk Company, Inwood Office Furniture, Jasper Cabinet Company, and Jasper Woodworking. What can you tell about the businesses in Jasper just by reading these signs?

If you guessed that woodworking is very important to the people of Jasper, you are right. You probably also guessed that Jasper is located near a forest.

You might also have thought that many people in Jasper must be able to work well with their hands. These craftspeople create beautiful and useful things out of wood.

Wood Capital Jasper is known as the "Nation's Wood Capital." The town is the home of Kimball International, Incorporated—the maker of

213

pianos and organs with wood cabinets. These musical instruments are shipped throughout the world. All of the instruments are made by the craftspeople who live in Jasper.

Let's look more closely at the craftspeople of Jasper. By reading a list of their names, you can learn something about them. Omer Sturm and John Gramelspacher are just two people that are listed. If you know anything about the German language, you can tell by their names that these men are of German heritage. Many people in Jasper share this heritage.

One People's Way of Life

Sometimes you can find examples of a people's heritage in the fine arts or crafts they produce. Other times you can learn about heritage simply by observing the way a group of people choose to live. Their way of life shows what is important about their culture to them.

The Amish One group of people who share the same heritage and customs with one another came to live in Indiana many years ago. Unlike their neighbors in Jasper, however, these people have a way of life that has not changed very much over the years.

Can you imagine what it would be like not to be able to walk into a dark room and turn on a light? What if you couldn't get into your family car to go shopping? Suppose you had to make all of your own clothing. How would you feel if you never could watch television?

If you were an Amish child, none of these things would seem strange. These children enjoy customs and

The Jasper Desk Company in Jasper, Indiana, produces desks and other pieces of office furniture. What does the factory need to take from the environment?

THE OLDEST OFFICE
FURNITURE MANUFACTURER
IN THE UNITED STATES
The Jasper Desk Company, formerly the Jasper Furniture Company, was organized in 1876 on this site.

If this Amish boy gets married when he grows up, his parents will build his wife and him a house attached to their own. In this way, the Amish community grows while remaining separate from other Hoosier neighborhoods.

practices that perhaps are different from yours. Their grandparents and great-grandparents came to Indiana many years ago. Many settled in the area around Shipshewana. Here the Amish practice a way of life that has changed little over the years.

Living Simply In the Amish religion, it is important to live as simply as possible. Because of this, many Amish do not have many modern conveniences like electricity or new farm machinery. Most Amish people do not drive cars. Instead, they drive horse-drawn carriages.

The Amish share some of their culture with other Hoosiers. They often sell products such as cheese in stores and markets. Amish architecture influences other builders in the area. Their handmade furniture is prized by collectors.

Learning about the Amish is just one way to find out about Indiana heritage. As you learn about other people in your state, and as other people learn about you, the culture of the state will continue to grow.

Lesson Review

Comprehension
1. Name one famous Indiana writer, artist, and musician.
2. Describe the Amish way of life.

Critical Thinking
3. Name four things you would research if you wanted to find out more about Indiana's heritage.
4. How can sharing between different groups of people help Indiana's culture grow?

The World's Largest Museum for Children

The Children's Museum of Indianapolis is in a very large building. If you visited the museum, you might find it hard to believe that it all began with a small exhibit in a very small house. Today children from all over the world visit the world's largest children's museum. How did it all begin?

In 1924, Mary Stewart Carey visited the Brooklyn Children's Museum in Brooklyn, New York. It was the world's first children's museum. Mrs. Carey knew at once that the children of her own city should have a special museum where they could learn about many things in a fun environment.

Mrs. Carey often was involved in doing things for others in Indianapolis. When she came home, she talked to other women in her community. Soon they shared her enthusiasm for a children's museum. Together, in 1925, they founded the Children's Museum. Its first home was in a small house.

The first items to be exhibited in the museum were donated by the children of Indianapolis. Children from all the city's neighborhoods contributed items that had belonged to their parents and grandparents. Because many of the families of the children had come to Indiana from other countries, the items represented many different cultures.

Mary Stewart Carey worked hard to found the Children's Museum of Indianapolis. The museum's first location was a small carriage house—a building where carriages pulled by horses are stored.

The Communication Center is just one of the many interesting displays in the Children's Museum.

The museum became so successful that soon the exhibit needed a larger building. In 1927, the exhibit was moved into Mrs. Carey's own home on North Meridian Street in Indianapolis. Through the years, the museum continued to grow.

During the 1940's, the museum was moved to a large mansion. For the next 30 years, workers added on to the mansion in order to house the growing collection. By 1972, many teachers wanted to bring their students to the museum. Even though thousands of students came to the museum, 18,000 students had to be turned away that year because the museum was too small.

The community knew that a new, large building would have to be built for the museum's collections. By 1976, a 203,000 square foot building was completed to exhibit more than 140,000 items. Even with such a large building, only 10 to 20 percent of the collection can be displayed at one time.

Today the museum has become very famous around the world. More than 1.5 million people each year come to see all the things the museum has to offer. It is one of the 20 most-visited museums in the country.

The Children's Museum of Indianapolis is more than an interesting place to visit. It also employs many Hoosiers. More than 150 people work for the museum, and volunteers contribute nearly 20,000 hours of their time each year.

The dream for a children's museum that began with Mrs. Carey's 1924 visit to Brooklyn has grown into one of Indiana's proudest achievements. Because of Mrs. Carey's dream, thousands of children—and adults—have a place where they can experience amazing and wondrous things.

Citizenship and You

1. What things would you like to see displayed in the museum?
2. If you were asked to contribute to the museum, what would you give?

LESSON 2 Hoosier Sports

Sports offer players the opportunity to compete.
What do sports in Indiana offer Hoosier fans?

KEY WORDS
tournament (tùr′nə mənt)
amateur (am′ə tėr)

Americans are known worldwide for their love of sports—football, baseball, basketball, soccer, track and field, water sports, golf, tennis, and many, many others. As the Crossroads of America, Indiana has become almost as much of a hub for sports as it is for transportation. Hoosiers are noted as great sports fans, participants, and supporters.

Hoosier Basketball

If you discuss sports in Indiana, chances are good that before long the discussion will center around basketball. Some people argue that Indiana has more basketball fans than any other state. Let's look at one year alone—1987—to see how important basketball is to the state.

1987—A Big Year In 1987, three events brought national attention to Indiana basketball. First, a movie came out about an Indiana high school basketball team. The movie, *Hoosiers,* was set in the 1950's.

Second, a book was written about Bob Knight, a very successful Indiana University basketball coach. *A Season on the Brink* became a national best seller.

Finally, the Indiana University Hoosiers won the National Collegiate Athletic Association (NCAA) championship for the fifth time. For

When Bob Knight led the Hoosiers to the NCAA championship in 1987, he had been coaching Indiana University basketball teams for 16 years. The 1987 championship was the Hoosiers' third under Knight.

Nearly 200,000 fans follow the women's high school basketball tournament in Indiana each year. Why might college coaches also attend the games?

weeks during 1987, Hoosier basketball in one way or another was often in the news.

High School Basketball Probably the most popular form of basketball in Indiana is at the high school level. You can see how popular the sport is by looking at the size of some high schools' gymnasiums. Eighteen of the twenty largest high school gymnasiums in the United States are in Indiana. Some small high schools with no more than 500 students have gymnasiums that can seat up to 4,000 people.

Every March the whole state seems to stop to watch the four-week high school basketball **tournament**. A tournament is a series of games that are played to determine the best team. In 1987, 940,000 fans attended the boys' series, and 190,000 followed the girls' series. Some single games had as many as 40,000 spectators.

The time during this tournament has come to be known as Hoosier hysteria. *Hysteria* means to lose control of yourself because of a strong emotion. Of course, Hoosiers do not lose control of themselves over high school basketball, but they do feel strongly about the sport.

No one knows for certain why basketball is so popular in Indiana. Basketball did not begin in Indiana, but its inventor, James Naismith of Massachusetts, said, "Basketball really had its origin [beginning] in Indiana, which remains today the center of the sport."

Perhaps the fact that Indiana once was mostly a rural state is one reason basketball became so popular. The farmers' schoolchildren could play the sport between the fall harvest and the spring planting. Basketball also could be played indoors during the winter when the weather was cold.

Larry Bird—An Important Player Probably the most admired and well-known basketball player to come from Indiana is Larry Bird. He grew up in the small rural town of French Lick, Indiana. Bird played for Indiana State University and was part of the team in 1979 when it went to the NCAA championship.

Larry Bird went on to play professional basketball for the Boston Celtics. He has led the Celtics to several championship titles. You can imagine that many Hoosiers follow Larry Bird's career with pride.

Hoosiers and Other Sports

Basketball is not the only sport that Hoosiers enjoy. For example, let's look at important things that happened in other sports during 1987—the big year for basketball.

Football Notre Dame, home of The Fighting Irish sports teams, was very proud of one of its football players in 1987. In that year, Tim Brown won the Heisman Trophy. This award honors the top college player in the country. Brown was the seventh player from Notre Dame to win the trophy. He was also the first player since 1949 to win the trophy while playing a position other than running back or quarterback.

Tim Brown played wide receiver for The Fighting Irish. He was also an important part of Notre Dame's special teams—the players who are on the field during punts or kickoffs. Tim Brown was very good at catching the kicks of other teams and running them back up the field. Sometimes he returned the kicks all the way to the other team's goal, scoring a touchdown.

Like Larry Bird, Brown is another Indiana athlete who made it to professional sports. He was chosen to play for the Los Angeles Raiders in the National Football League.

Each year the Heisman Trophy is awarded to the outstanding college football player in the United States. Tim Brown moved the ball 1,847 yards for Notre Dame in 1987— the year he won the Heisman Trophy.

In 1987, Indianapolis was host to the Tenth Pan American games, an international sporting event.

Special Olympics In August of 1987, 4,700 athletes from all 50 states and from 70 countries participated in the International Summer Special Olympics in South Bend. The participants in Special Olympics are children and adults who are mentally challenged. As a result of their conditions, some of the athletes also have physical disabilities. However, Special Olympians of all ages and abilities overcome their disabilities to compete in events such as track and field, swimming, horseback riding, tennis, and basketball.

To reach the international level of competition, Special Olympians first must win at the local, state, and national games. However, at each level, all participants are rewarded for meeting the challenge.

Pan American Games Indianapolis calls itself the **Amateur** Sports Capital of the World. People are amateurs in sports when they play without receiving money for their efforts. Indianapolis hosts many amateur sporting events every year.

In August of 1987, Indianapolis hosted the Tenth Pan American games. The Pan American games are almost as important to many amateur athletes as the Olympics. The games are held every four years, one year before the Olympics. Athletes from countries throughout the Western Hemisphere compete in events such as swimming, track and field, and gymnastics.

Indianapolis was only the second city in the United States to host the games since Chicago hosted them in 1959. The Pan American games were held in the world-class sports facilities of Indianapolis.

Lesson Review

Comprehension

1. Name three events that dealt with Indiana basketball in 1987.
2. What is Hoosier hysteria?
3. Name two Indiana athletes who made it to professional sports.
4. Why does Indianapolis call itself the Amateur Sports Capital of the World?

Critical Thinking

5. How might Indiana benefit from the people's sports interest?
6. How can you tell that sports are important to Hoosiers?

Using a Schedule

Suppose you want to take a bus trip to the different cities and towns in Indiana that you have read about. How would you be able to take such a trip? You would need to read a bus schedule.

Schedules can be drawn in many ways. The schedule below shows when buses leave Indianapolis between 6:00 A.M. and 10:00 A.M. each weekday. The schedule tells the number of each bus, what door you go through to board the bus, and to what city or town the bus is going.

Read the schedule as you would a chart, starting on the left and moving to the right. Use the schedule to answer the questions that follow.

1. At what time does the first bus on the schedule leave?

2. Where does the first bus go?
3. How many buses go to Gary during the time shown?
4. During which hour on the schedule do the most buses leave?
5. At what time does the last bus on the schedule leave?
6. Through which door would you board the earlier of the two buses going to Evansville?
7. At which town does the bus bound for Corydon stop?

Project

Your daily activities can be put on a schedule too. Make a schedule of your daily routine for a week. Include the time you rise, eat breakfast, leave for school, have classes, and any other daily activities in which you participate.

Indianapolis Bus Schedule — Morning Departures

Time	Bus Number	Door Number	Destination
6:00	12	1	Fort Wayne
6:15	9	4	Gary
6:45	13	2	Evansville
7:00	21	3	Vincennes
7:30	1	1	Columbus
8:00	7	5	Cincinnati
8:30	14	4	Gary
9:00	11	2	Fort Wayne
9:30	10	1	French Lick-Corydon
10:00	15	3	Evansville

LESSON 3 Special Hoosier Events

People often gather together for celebrations. What are some reasons people have for celebrating?

KEY WORD
annual (an'yə wəl)

People all over the world get together to celebrate from time to time. Sometimes they honor a person, a place, a historical event or object, or even the changing of seasons. While every celebration is different, usually celebrations include things like good food and music. Sometimes these events are called festivals—days set aside for celebration.

Indiana has many, many festivals throughout the year. One reason this may be so is because of the importance of farming in the state's history. When most Hoosiers were farmers, many festivals were begun to celebrate the harvest. After months of hard work, farming families came together to enjoy themselves once the crops were in. These **annual** events, or yearly gatherings, soon became organized festivals.

Fort Wayne Festivals

Today, of course, not all festivals have something to do with farming. Some celebrations, in fact, center around a special person.

Johnny Appleseed Festival If you live in Fort Wayne, you know that every summer you and your neighbors get together for the Johnny Appleseed Festival at Johnny Appleseed Park. As is true for most

When other people were fighting to claim land for themselves, Johnny Appleseed was busy making the land better for everyone by planting apple trees. This is one reason a festival (below) is held in his honor each year.

JOHNNY APPLESEED.

festivals, special food is a big part of the event. Two things people can enjoy are apple cider and pastries called elephant ears. Some people like to dress in old-fashioned clothing that resembles what Johnny Appleseed would have worn.

Who was Johnny Appleseed and why do people honor him? His real name was John Chapman. He planted thousands of apple trees throughout the American frontier, including Indiana, during the early 1800's. Johnny Appleseed also is known for the great kindness he showed to the early pioneers.

Over the years, stories about Johnny Appleseed have been exaggerated greatly, so that some people are surprised that he really did exist. He spent about the last ten years of his life in Fort Wayne. His grave is in the park bearing his name.

Three River Festival Another summer festival in Fort Wayne uses something special in the environment—rivers. During the Three River Festival, people enjoy many events. As you probably can guess from the name of the festival, rivers play a big part in the festivities.

One highlight of the festival is the raft race. The participants enter different kinds of rafts, both serious and silly, in the race. Making it to the finish line is not the most important part of this race. Having fun, being with other people, and enjoying the outdoors are what make the race and the festival fun.

Community news was posted on the walls inside covered bridges.

Parke County Festivals

Parke County is in the western part of Indiana. Two festivals in this county are held in seasons other than summer.

Covered Bridge Festival One Parke County festival, held in the autumn, does not celebrate a person or a place, but an important object in Indiana history—covered bridges.

The covered bridges in Indiana are special to many people. The bridges were built in the 1800's. During this time, Hoosiers were busy working on their roads. Some streams and rivers in the state were difficult and even dangerous to cross. The first bridges that were built did not make travel much easier.

Later covered bridges made it easier to travel. They also provided a place for travelers to find shelter from wind, rain, and even snow. Before long, covered bridges were built all over the state.

Today workers can build modern, safe bridges that could replace the covered bridges. However, many people feel it is important to preserve the covered bridges as part of Indiana's history. During the Covered Bridge Festival, visitors can tour the 35 covered bridges that are still in Parke County.

Maple Sugar Festival Another festival in Parke County is the Maple Sugar Festival, which is held in the spring.

Sap enters a tree through its roots. It carries water and minerals that the tree needs to grow. Buckets can catch sap when it flows from trees in spring.

Many maple trees grow in Parke County. In early spring, when the days begin to become warm and the nights are still cold, maple sap flows from the trees. The sap is collected and boiled to make maple sugar. During the festival, people can sample this sweet product that comes from maple trees.

These are just some examples of the types of festivals that Hoosiers enjoy. You probably can think of many others. Next time you hear about or attend a festival, think about what it celebrates. Then join in the celebration and have fun!

In this chapter, you have read about important things that help explain Indiana's way of life. Maybe now you could help Kenny Foster to write interesting letters to Tomás, his pen pal in Mexico. Maybe you would like to have a pen pal of your own. You could share what makes Indiana special and different from any other place.

Lesson Review

Comprehension

1. What is a festival?
2. What can people enjoy at the Johnny Appleseed Festival?
3. For what is Johnny Appleseed remembered today?
4. What is the main event at the Three River Festival?
5. Why were covered bridges built?
6. Why have covered bridges not been replaced by modern bridges?
7. What sweet product comes from maple trees?

Critical Thinking

8. How have some festivals helped to preserve Indiana's heritage?
9. Which festival described in this lesson would you most like to see? Explain your answer.

CHAPTER 10 REVIEW

Words to Know

Number your paper from 1 to 5. Write the word that fills in each blank next to each number.

culture   landscape
tournament   amateur
annual

Indiana's high school basketball 1. ____ is an important part of Indiana's 2. ____ . This 3. ____ event interests many thousands of Hoosiers. Since the players are not paid, they are 4. ____ basketball players. All in all, this event is as much a part of Indiana as is the rugged Brown County 5. ____ .

Main Ideas

1. Name three famous writers who were born in Indiana.
2. What is the name of the famous painting Robert Indiana created in the 1970's?
3. What is Cole Porter known for?
4. Who is John Mellencamp and what special yearly event did he help to organize?
5. How does heritage affect industry in Jasper, Indiana?
6. What are some Amish beliefs and practices?
7. What do Larry Bird, Tim Brown, and Bob Knight have in common?
8. What sport is an Indiana favorite?
9. What makes the Special Olympics so special?
10. What great amateur sporting event did Indianapolis proudly host in 1987?
11. What was Johnny Appleseed's real name and why is he important to Indiana?
12. What is a covered bridge?
13. What are some things festivals say about life in Indiana?

Critical Thinking

1. There are many kinds of people living in Indiana. For example, the Amish have chosen to live in a way that is different from the way of life of most other people. People of German heritage have customs that might be different from people with an Irish heritage. Yet all these people are Hoosiers. With this in mind, do you think it is possible to say that Indiana has one culture? Why or why not?
2. As you know, sports are very important to Hoosiers. Most Hoosiers like to do well in sports, but most also agree that whether or not you do well is not as important as enjoying whatever sport you play. Why are sports fun? What good things do you think can come out of playing sports?

Writing for Understanding

1. Your librarian or your teacher can help you find a recording of songs by Hoagy Carmichael or Cole

Porter. Listen to these songs. After each one, write a short paragraph about what feelings the song gave you. Were they happy or sad feelings? What was it about the music that made you feel a certain way?

2. Many Hoosiers read the sports section of their newspapers every morning to find the latest news and results of games from the day before. Many readers have favorite sportswriters whose articles they look forward to reading. Read the sports section of your local newspaper. See how different sportswriters write. Then write your own story about one of the sporting events described. Do not copy what someone else wrote—just use the information and put the story in your own words. Be sure to think about your readers. Will they want to finish the whole story? How can you get them interested in your story right away?

Applying Skills

Use the schedule of events below to answer the questions.

1. The events of what festival are outlined in the schedule?
2. How many events are scheduled?
3. What is the first event and when will it take place?
4. If you wanted to compete in both the pie eating contest and the egg toss, about how much time would you have to rest or do other things between the two events?
5. How many different locations are being used for the events of the Pioneer Days festival?

1991 Pioneer Days Festival
Schedule of Events

Event	Time	Place
Egg toss	9:00 A.M.	Park
100-yard dash	9:30 A.M.	Fairgrounds
Pancake breakfast	9:30 A.M.	Park
Horse race	10:30 A.M.	Fairgrounds
Square dance	11:00 A.M.	Park
Art show	All day	Park
Pie eating contest	11:30 A.M.	Park
Log rolling	12:30 P.M.	Fairgrounds
Food and livestock show	All day	Fairgrounds

CHAPTER 11

Hoosiers at Work

Imagine that you are having breakfast in this small Indiana restaurant. Now think about how many people it took to make your breakfast possible.

Work on your breakfast started on Indiana farms. Eggs, meat, cereal, bread, milk—all these products came from the hard work of farmers. Transportation workers also were important. Trucks and railroads carried the food from farms to the stores where the products were bought.

Businesses also helped make it possible for you to eat your breakfast in the restaurant. A bank probably loaned some money to the restaurant owner to start the business. Construction workers built the restaurant. Computer companies set up the cash register and the telephone system.

Finally, people in the restaurant made the food and served it to you. They will clean the table and wash your dishes when you leave.

As you can see, Hoosiers have many different jobs. In this chapter, you will read about just some of these jobs.

LESSON 1 Indiana Farmers

Farming is valuable work. In what ways is farming in Indiana important to all the people of Indiana, the United States, and the world?

KEY WORDS
economy (i kon′ə mē)
income (in′kəm)
livestock (līv′stok)
poultry (pōl′trē)
drought (drout)

Even though farmers almost always welcome rain, too much water might harm young plants.

Probably no other workers depend on nature as much as farmers. If too little rain falls during the summer, crops do not grow well. Dangerous weather conditions such as tornados or floods can damage crops.

Other conditions besides weather sometimes make farming difficult. Farmers always must be aware of the prices at which they can sell their crops. They must make important decisions about how to take care of their soil and their animals. They have to know about machinery and how to manage money.

Farmers in Indiana know that their work is important. Through farming, they provide a living for themselves and their families. Also, the whole state of Indiana depends on the work of the farmers in many ways, especially when it comes to the state's **economy**—the sale of goods and services to make money.

Crops

How important is Indiana farming, or agriculture, to Indiana, the United States, and the world? Every year, farming adds about 4 billion dollars to the economy of the state. Many people—not just farmers—benefit from the money that is earned from farming.

Corn Most money from farming is earned through growing crops, especially grains. The most plentiful crop in Indiana is corn. This crop, which is used to feed humans and animals, brings in about 24 percent of Indiana's total farm **income**. The money that comes in to a person or a business for work is the income.

229

Much work goes into caring for a crop like corn (above). Fortunately, farmers have the help of heavy machinery (inset).

Most of the corn grown in Indiana remains in the state to feed animals or to supply industries whose products are made from corn. Some of these industries include a cereal company in Warsaw, Indiana, a Mexican food company in Jeffersonville, and a vegetable oil producer in Decatur.

Soybeans The next largest money-making crop in Indiana is soybeans. This crop brings in about 21 percent of the state's farm money.

Soybeans are full of healthy protein, and they can be used to make many different kinds of foods. For example, soybeans are found in margarine and are used as fillers for beef.

Some soybeans are stored for future use. Most crops like soybeans can be stored for up to five years.

Selling Crops Internationally Indiana, like other agricultural states, sells some crops internationally. In recent years, many crops have been sold to China and the Soviet Union. For example, if China had a year of bad weather and did not produce as many crops as it needed, Indiana crops might be bought by the Chinese to supply what they need. In this way, the amount of crops sold internationally depends on how much foreign countries can produce themselves.

Animals

Many Hoosier farmers raise animals, or **livestock**, that also contribute greatly to Indiana's farming earnings. Animals raised on a farm such as cattle and hogs are livestock.

Hogs In the pioneer days, hogs were the most popular livestock in Indiana. Hogs are butchered for their meat, known as pork. The hogs that farmers raise today, however, are not much like those the pioneers raised. The hogs the pioneers raised were somewhat wild and could look quite fierce. Today's hogs are kept in pens and are not frightening at all.

Poultry The second most popular type of animal raised in Indiana is **poultry**. Chickens, turkeys, ducks, and geese that are raised for their meat and eggs are called poultry. Indiana is the second largest poultry and egg-producing state.

Cattle The two other major animal products that Indiana farmers produce are beef and milk. Cattle are butchered for their meat, called beef. The beef is put into refrigerated railroad cars to be shipped throughout the nation.

Milk is turned into dairy products such as butter, cheese, and frozen dessert. Because dairy products cannot be stored for more than a few days, they are trucked just a short distance from the dairy. Beef and milk each account for about 10 percent of Indiana's farming income.

Ties Among Farm Products Some farm products depend on other products. For example, corn often is fed to hogs. If Indiana farmers do not produce enough corn, they will have to buy it from others at a higher price. This means hogs will be more expensive to raise, and farmers might raise fewer hogs. If this happens, when you go to the store to buy pork, you will pay more than usual for it. This is because a product costs more to buy when less of it is available.

Animals have different names depending on several things. For example, the name poultry *is used for many kinds of birds that are known as fowl. When pigs get to be a certain weight, they are then called* hogs. *Cattle* is a plural noun used both for cows (females) and bulls (males).

231

As you can see, if one part of the state's farming suffers, other parts might be affected too. In addition, people who buy farm products also will notice a difference in prices.

Challenging Work

While Indiana's farm success is good news, life on a farm can be a challenge. In the 1980's, Indiana was hit with a long **drought**. A drought is a time when little or no rain falls. Without rain, many farmers could harvest only small crops. Some farmers had to give up their farms.

Prices Farmers also can be affected by prices. The price of a product can go up and down. Many things affect the prices of farm products.

Sometimes prices are determined by how much it costs to transport products. At other times, pricing is determined by how much of a product is available. For example, if farmers have too many years of bumper, or extra, crops, the price of products might go down. When the price of their products goes down, farmers make less money. If they have **debts**, or money that is owed to someone else, farmers might have to go out of business.

Rewards In spite of the difficulties, farming can be rewarding. In the springtime, for example, many farmers welcome the sight of newborn calves. Other farmers are happy in the fall during harvest time as they bring in a successful crop.

Scientists cannot explain exactly what causes droughts. Sometimes winds that push away moist air are partly responsible. Whatever the reason behind them, droughts can destroy once healthy plants.

Lesson Review

Comprehension

1. Name three things that can make farming difficult.
2. How much money does agriculture bring to Indiana?
3. Name two important crops and two popular livestock that are raised in Indiana.
4. What are two things that can affect the prices of crops?

Critical Thinking

5. How is Indiana farming important to the state and to other areas of the country?
6. How are Indiana farmers affected by world events?

LESSON 2 Indiana Industry Workers

Many Hoosiers work in industries. What kinds of jobs do they have?

KEY WORDS
service industry (ser′vəs in′dəs trē)
customer (kus′tə mėr)

You have read about Hoosiers who many years ago began industries in which workers manufactured goods. The Studebakers manufactured wagons. Judge Gary's company made steel. Eli Lilly manufactured medicines. Today Indiana has hundreds of different industries that make many kinds of products.

Manufacturing Industries

The first manufacturers in Indiana began a long history of making automobiles and automobile parts in the state. For example, Indiana was one of the first states to begin building automobiles. Today this industry is still important to Indiana. General Motors has a large auto assembly plant at Marion, Indiana, and workers for Chrysler form engines at a plant in Indianapolis.

Engines Thousands of Hoosiers work in factories that make things related to automobiles. Columbus, Indiana, is just one town in which citizens depend on a manufacturing factory. Cummins Engine employs 7,500 people. The company makes diesel engines. These engines power most of the big trucks you see on highways. The engines also are found in mining equipment and tractors around the world.

Navistar is another important employer in Indiana. This company employs more than 2,000 people in Indianapolis. This plant, or factory,

This is an old Studebaker factory. How might today's automobile factories be different from this one?

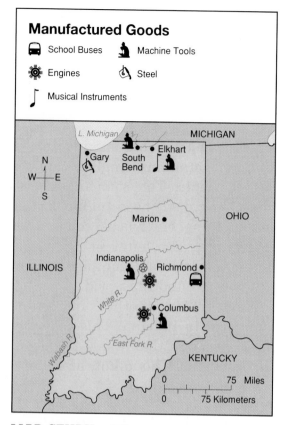

Manufactured Goods

🚌 School Buses 　🔬 Machine Tools

⚙️ Engines 　🔥 Steel

♪ Musical Instruments

MAP STUDY *What manufactured goods are produced in the northern part of Indiana?*

also makes diesel engines. Many of these engines are used in ambulances that help save people's lives.

Machine Tools Along with engine manufacturing, the making of machine tools is an important Indiana industry. It helps the auto plants by making machines that shape or drill metal parts. The cities of South Bend, Columbus, Indianapolis, and Elkhart are some important machine tool-making centers.

Steel Of course, to make an automobile or tractor, manufacturers need steel. Steel making is the largest manufacturing industry in Indiana. Almost all Indiana steel is made in the northwestern corner of the state.

The largest of the steel-making plants is the USX Gary Works. USX is the new name for United States Steel, which was founded by Judge Gary. Other large firms include LTV, Inland Steel, and Bethlehem Steel.

As you know, steel making began in Indiana because of the state's location near coalfields, railroads, and iron mines. Today these resources are still at work.

Musical Instruments Do you play a musical instrument? If you do, chances are good your instrument was made in Indiana. The manufacturing of musical instruments is one interesting industry that has found a home in Indiana.

You might remember that Elkhart is a city where hundreds of people manufacture musical instruments. It all began more than 100 years ago with Colonel C.G. Conn. He played a cornet, which is an instrument that looks like a trumpet. He accidentally injured his lip, making it difficult to play. Conn made a special mouthpiece for his instrument. Other musicians wanted mouthpieces just like Conn's and before long, the C.G. Conn Company began.

Now Elkhart is known as the "Band Instrument Capital of the World." More than 20 music-related businesses are found in the city. The instruments are sold all over the United States and the world.

Service Industries

Some industries do not manufacture goods such as steel and automobiles. Industries that do not involve manufacturing are called **service industries**. Workers in these industries provide services for people. Doctors, salespeople, teachers, and hotel and restaurant employees all provide services.

As the population of Indiana grows, and more people visit the state, service industries grow as well. This means that more and more people are employed in these industries. Let us look at Indianapolis as an example of this growth.

Travel Improvements Indiana's state motto, "Crossroads of America," was chosen in 1937. At that time, many highways led into Indianapolis, making it easy for people to come and go by car. Fifty years later, in 1987, the Indianapolis International Airport was expanded greatly. Now people easily can travel by airplanes in and out of the state. The airport handles more than 5,000,000 people each year. Another expansion was completed in 1989. As a result, new jobs were created for workers such as ticket agents, parking attendants, and baggage handlers.

Hotels and Restaurants With so many people coming into the airport, more hotels and restaurants were needed. From 1984 to January of 1989, 29 new hotels opened in the city. By the end of 1989, Indianapolis had more than 15,500 hotel rooms.

Building and improving an airport takes much time and money. Why would Indiana put so much work and money into improving the Indianapolis International Airport?

Hotels employ many different service workers. Cooks, clerks who check guests into and out of their rooms, and people who deliver room service are just three examples.

Many new restaurants were built too. For example, from 1983 to 1986, one new restaurant a month opened in Indianapolis. As you can imagine, many new jobs were created in the new hotels and restaurants.

New Office Space Not all service industries depend on visitors. Many businesses in Indiana provide services for residents. These businesses also grew in the late 1980's. For example, as the population of Indianapolis grew, the city needed space for new stores and offices.

Circle Centre will be completed by 1992. This one-billion-dollar group of buildings will have stores, offices, and meeting rooms. It will cover three and one-half blocks in downtown Indianapolis. Doctors, dentists, salespeople, and office workers will be needed to fill the buildings.

Comprehension

1. In what ways is the automobile industry important to Indiana?
2. What is one of Indiana's largest manufacturing industries?
3. Why did steel making begin in Indiana?
4. What Indiana city is known as "The Band Instrument Capital of the World"?
5. What do workers in the service industries provide?

Critical Thinking

6. Indiana has many different kinds of industries. Why might this be good for the state's economy?
7. Why will service industries probably continue to grow?

Understanding Time Zones

As people do business with one another all over the world, they must consider time zones before they communicate by telephone.

As the earth rotates, some parts are getting dark, while others are getting light. Because of this, the world is divided into time zones.

Look at the map of time zones and answer the questions that follow.

1. If it is noon in New York, what time is it in Los Angeles?
2. How many time zones does this part of the United States have?
3. How many time zones does Indiana have? What are their names?
4. If it is 9 A.M. in Indianapolis, what time is it in Denver?
5. If you lived in San Diego and wanted to call Miami at 7 A.M., what time would you call?

Project

Using the telephone is only one activity influenced by time zone changes. Consider watching a sports event on TV. If a football game is played in California at 2:00 P.M., at what time would you watch it in Indianapolis? Make up five questions that show how time zone changes influence events. Have a partner answer your questions.

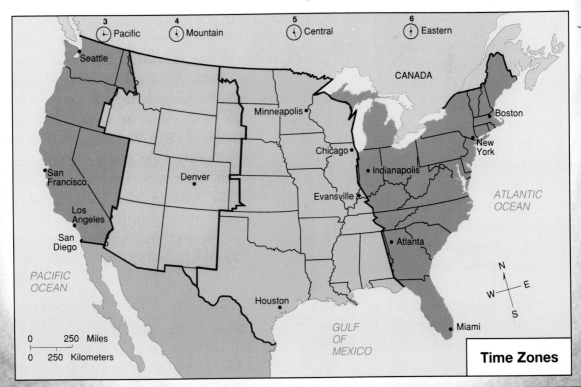

Time Zones

CHAPTER 11 REVIEW

Words to Know

Answer each of the questions with a complete sentence.

1. What is an *economy*?
2. What is *income*?
3. What animals are *livestock*?
4. If you had *poultry* for dinner, what might you be eating?
5. What happens in a *drought*?
6. What is a *service industry*?
7. Who is a *customer*?

Main Ideas

1. Name three things farmers need to know to be successful.
2. What is the most plentiful crop in Indiana?
3. Describe two ways soybeans can be used.
4. Which animals do Indiana farmers raise most?
5. Name the two food products that come from poultry.
6. What are dairy products?
7. Why are corn farmers important to hog growers?
8. How can the prices of farm products be affected?
9. Name two companies that make engines in Indiana.
10. Name three manufacturing industries in Indiana besides the automobile industry.
11. Why is it important for the state of Indiana to have both farming and industry?
12. Name three improvements that have helped Indianapolis grow.
13. Why is "Crossroads of America" a good motto for Indiana?

Critical Thinking

1. Farmers throughout Indiana use all sorts of modern machines to help them in their work. In fact, except for the Amish people, most farmers would not be able to stay in business if they did not have the use of machines like tractors, threshers, plows, heaters for barns, and milking machines for cows. With this in mind, explain how people on farms depend on people in cities and how people in cities depend on people on farms.
2. Changing from a manufacturing economy to a service economy can be hard because workers shift from making things like steel and cars to serving the needs of other people—as in advertising or banking. Recall what you have learned about industry in Indiana and about how a service industry works. Which skills might a factory worker have that a service worker might not have?

Writing for Understanding

1. Pretend that you live on a farm and are best friends with another student who lives in a city, or that

you live in a city and have a friend that lives on a farm. You decide to write your friend a letter that reads like a diary. Start with Monday morning and explain to your friend what you do that day. Continue for at least three days. Remember that you are also a student, so you need to describe school activities as well as the farm or household chores you do. Also describe the things you do for fun. Tell your friend how you feel about living on a farm or in a city.

2. Corn has been important to Hoosiers since the days of the Indians. Today it is a very important crop. Without corn, the state's economy would be hurt. Write a play that tells about how corn became so important. Have a stalk of corn be the narrator of your play. You can find most of the information you need in your book. Other characters should include Indians, pioneers, and farmers from small and big farms.

3. Imagine that you work for the Circle Centre development in downtown Indianapolis. Your job is to convince businesses to rent office space in the complex. Write an advertisement telling people about Circle Centre. Explain why Indianapolis is such a good place to rent office space. Make the advertisement sound convincing.

Applying Skills

Use the time zone map below to answer the questions.

1. What time is it in Evansville when it is 3 P.M. in New Albany? (Hint: When a time zone line is crossed, there is a difference of one hour. As you move from east to west, the difference makes the time one hour earlier.)
2. How many time zones are found in Indiana?
3. What are the names of the time zones in Indiana?

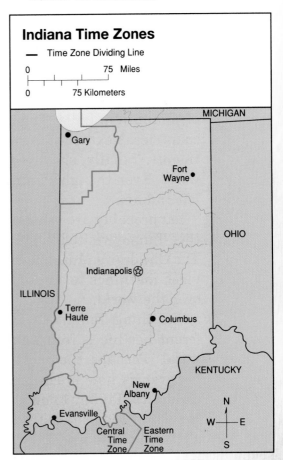

239

Indiana Keeping Up with Changes

Today Tammy experienced life in more than 70 countries. First, she felt what it would be like to ride on an elephant from India. Then, she talked to children in other countries. Next, she listened to music from all seven continents. Finally, she tried on clothing from all over the world. Even though Tammy did all these things, she never left Indiana.

You probably are wondering how Tammy managed to do this. Tammy visited the "Passport to the World" exhibit at The Children's Museum in Indianapolis. This exhibit uses video machines to simulate, or copy, experiences from all over the world.

One thing Tammy learned at the museum is how different her life is from that of other children all over the world. Perhaps the most important thing she learned, however, is how much her life is the same as the other children's. Tammy knew that she was a citizen of Indiana. However, today she learned that in many ways she is also a citizen of the world.

Changes for People and Businesses

Indiana is affected by changes that happen within the state, in the country, and throughout the world. What are some of these changes?

KEY WORD

technology   (tek nol′ə jē)

Have you ever heard anyone talk about the Three R's? When your parents and grandparents were schoolchildren, they probably spent most of their time learning about reading, writing, and arithmetic. Can you guess why these subjects were called the Three R's?

Today, of course, students still study these subjects. However, great changes have occurred in the world since your parents and grandparents were in school. These changes affect what you learn and how you learn.

Changes in computers are good examples of change. In the 1940's, a computer named ENIAC was developed. Even though ENIAC was very slow and was so large it took up a whole room, it was an exciting development. Today computers are improved. They are capable of doing much more than ENIAC. Personal computers are so small that they can sit on your desk at school.

Computers are just one way the world has changed in the past 40 or 50 years. In this lesson, you will learn about other changes that have affected Hoosiers.

Changes within the State

Indiana began as an agricultural state. People worked on farms and lived in wide, open spaces. Today most Hoosiers work for manufacturers and live in cities. How did these important changes come about?

Changes in Farm Life People began leaving Indiana farms about 1900. They went to work in new

Not only are some modern computers small enough to sit on a desk—some are small enough to take on an airplane.

The dock worker (below) depends on farmers because his job involves packing and shipping farm products. What other city workers might depend on farmers?

industries that were forming in the state. Work in the steel industry, for example, attracted many people to the northwestern part of the state.

Not everyone left the farms all at once, of course. Farming continued to be important work. Some people in the cities worked in jobs that took care of preparing the farmers' food or transporting it to other parts of the country.

Businesses Connected to Farms

Even though fewer people farm today, people in cities still depend on Indiana agriculture. For example, if no crops were grown, fewer ships would be needed on Lake Michigan. Fewer boxes would be needed to pack food for shipment. Many dock workers and other people who make boxes and crates and load them on ships would not be needed.

Cities and farms are connected in other ways too. For example, many farmers take out loans from banks to buy equipment or seed. Most of the banks that lend large amounts of money are located in cities or towns.

Small town businesses especially depend on farmers. Grocery stores, clothing stores, restaurants, movie theaters—they all need the farmers as customers. If farmers cannot earn enough money when they sell their crops or livestock, they will have less money to spend in town.

The State Today

Today agriculture employs no more than 3 percent of all Hoosier workers. Manufacturing employs about one-third, or 30 percent, of the state's workers. You might think that when the state went from being a rural state to an urban state, the people's way of life would change greatly. However, many Hoosiers believe that Indiana still has mostly rural, Middle Western characteristics. This means, in part, that people work together and help one another with change.

Changes outside Indiana

Indiana industries have to keep up with new discoveries and inventions occurring throughout the United States and the world. **Technology**—the use of tools, machinery, and scientific ideas to do a certain kind of work—is constantly changing. This means that Hoosier workers sometimes have to learn new skills, and Hoosier companies sometimes have to buy new equipment.

These adults have gone back to school to learn about technological advances. Why might continuing education be so important?

International competition is another reason industries change in Indiana. Other countries such as the Soviet Union and Japan have developed successful industries in the past few decades. These countries do not just supply goods and services to the people in their own countries, but to people all over the world.

The 7,500 people who work for Cummins Engine (see page 233) use complicated tools and machinery to do their work (below).

Foreign cars are shipped by the thousands to the United States. They are quite different from the large American cars of the 1950's.

Effects on the Automobile Industry

The Indiana automobile industry is one that has been affected by technology and competition. When the Dusenbergs made automobiles in Auburn, Indiana, most of the parts were put together by hand. Now, many years later, robots do much of the work in automobile factories. The Dusenbergs did not keep up with all the new technology. As a result, the company stopped making automobiles.

Competition also has affected the Indiana automobile industry. When the Studebakers made their cars in the late 1940's, the United States was by far the leading producer of automobiles. By the 1950's, the United States made bigger and flashier cars than any other country. Studebakers were some of the favorite models.

These large cars with the big fins and shiny chrome might look silly to you now. In fact, by the 1960's, many Americans chose not to buy these cars—including Studebakers.

United States automakers had to change their designs for many reasons. Some people were concerned about how safe the cars were. Other people felt that the cars used too much gasoline. Still other people liked the price and the size of the small cars that were coming from other countries, especially Japan. In order to continue selling many automobiles, the United States automobile industry had to change the goods that they manufacture.

Unfortunately, Studebaker did not keep up with the changes. This company, like Dusenberg, stopped making automobiles. Some companies, however, continue to help locate parts for the old Studebakers that people still drive.

Effects on Banking Not all Indiana businesses have suffered like the automobile industry from changes occurring outside the state. For example, some banking services have improved because of such changes. Hoosiers have benefited from these changes too.

A small Hoosier town in the 1940's probably had one bank that serviced the needs of the entire community. The bank had few machines, and it did not face any competition.

Today some small Indiana towns might have several banks. Some banks even might be owned by foreign companies. These banks can be connected to banks all over the state, nation, and world.

Because of new technology, banks today can provide many services to their customers. Automated teller machines provide 24-hour service. Modern computers have made it possible for money to be moved easily from one account to another.

Banking, like other businesses, certainly will face many changes in the coming years. Technology makes almost anything available to Hoosiers. With the right equipment, people throughout Indiana can do business all over the world.

Most banks provide 24-hour service for their customers. Why might people like automated teller machines so much?

Lesson Review

Comprehension

1. Why did people leave Indiana farms in the early 1900's?
2. Name three ways cities and towns depend on farmers.
3. How might changing technology affect companies and their workers?
4. List two reasons why the automobile industry had to change.
5. What helps banks provide many services to their customers?

Critical Thinking

6. How did state, national, and international changes affect Indiana in the 1900's?
7. You have read about changes in Indiana's auto-making and banking industries. Choose another Indiana industry and describe some of the changes it has experienced in the 1900's.

Reading a Mileage Chart

Imagine for a moment that you wanted to travel around the state of Indiana by car. Before you begin the trip, you want to determine how far it is from city to city. One easy way to find out this information is to use a mileage chart.

A mileage chart lists the distance in miles between cities. A mileage chart can list cities in a state, in a country, or even in the world. Using a mileage chart is easy. First find the city where you will start. Look for it along the left side of the chart. Then run your finger under the city name and across the row until you reach the column below the city you want to visit. At this point, you will find the mileage between the two cities.

For example, find the city of Gary on the left side of the chart. Run your finger across the chart to find Terre Haute. The chart tells you that the distance from Gary to Terre Haute is 162 miles.

Use the chart below to answer the following questions.

1. What is the distance between Indianapolis and Evansville?
2. What is the distance between Fort Wayne and South Bend?
3. Which two cities shown on the chart are closest together?
4. Which two cities shown on the chart are farthest apart?
5. If you were traveling from Evansville to Fort Wayne and then on to South Bend, how many miles total would you travel?

Project

Plan a trip around Indiana. Write down the sites you want to see. Use various references to find out the distances between the sites. Then make a mileage chart for your trip similar to the one below. Add up the distances between each site to determine how many total miles you will travel.

Mileage between Some Indiana Cities

	Indianapolis	Evansville	Terre Haute	Gary	South Bend	Fort Wayne
Indianapolis	—	157	78	145	140	105
Evansville	157	—	106	266	303	280
Terre Haute	78	106	—	162	115	184
Gary	145	266	162	—	58	131
South Bend	140	303	115	58	—	79
Fort Wayne	105	280	184	131	79	—

LESSON 2 Challenges for the Environment

One way that you are connected to the people of the world is through technology. How does technology affect the world's environment?

KEY WORDS
acid rain   (as'əd rān)
high technology   (hī tek nol'ə jē)
toxic waste   (tok'sik wāst)

Hoosiers often depend on the environment to make a living. Farmers use the land to grow crops. Steel companies use natural resources to make steel. Shipping companies use the waterways to transport goods. Technology links all the people of the world and makes some business activities easier than ever before.

Technology and the environment can affect each other. Unfortunately, some advances in technology have harmed the world's environment.

A Shared Environment

Sometimes damage to the environment of a place thousands of miles away can affect you and your neighbors. Likewise, events that take place in your environment might affect people in other parts of the world. You might be surprised to learn how this happens.

Think about the water in Lake Michigan. Did you know that this water can travel many miles? First the water evaporates into the air. Through air currents, the water then can come down many miles away in the form of rain. Of course, rain usually is good for the environment. Sometimes, however, even rain can be harmful. How could this be so?

Harmful Rain Steel mills near Lake Michigan use coal as fuel. When coal burns, heat and gas are released through giant smokestacks.

Unwanted smoke in the air has bothered residents of cities with heavy industry for many years. When smoke pollution was at its worst—between 1930 and 1950—the sky over some Middle Western cities was dark even at noon.

247

Acid rain is found in most states east of the Mississippi. The greatest damage is found in the state of New York (above).

Some of these gases float into the air. There, the gases mix with water. Later, when it rains, this mixture can fall as **acid rain**, a harmful blend of water and gases.

Acid rain can kill fish in lakes and damage trees in forests. Because of air currents, acid rain can fall in areas far away from the original source of pollution. United States and Canadian leaders are cooperating to find ways to correct this environmental problem.

Concern for a Forest Many people in this country are concerned about what happens to the environment far away, even in other countries. For example, some people watch what is happening to a large forest in the Amazon River region of South America. As the region's population grows and more cities and farms are developed, huge parts of the forest are cut down.

In your science class, you probably learned that living plants produce oxygen. Because the forest in South America is so large, the region provides much of the world's supply of oxygen. In this way, people all over the world, including citizens of Indiana, are connected to environmental challenges.

Harmful Substances Sometimes people put harmful substances into the environment. One example involves industries that use **high technology**, or scientific technology that involves the use of advanced devices such as computers or computer software.

Millions of plants and animals live in the huge South American forest. They could become extinct if the forest dies.

These people help keep their community clean by picking up cans. The cans then are crushed and processed so the metal in them can be used again.

Some high technology industries use dangerous chemicals in their work. These chemicals, if not disposed of properly, can leak into the ground. The chemicals then are known as **toxic waste.** This means that they are poisonous to humans and to animals.

Saving the Environment

Fortunately, technology also can be used to protect the environment. For example, factory smokestacks in Gary can be equipped with new machines that scrub out harmful gases and other air pollutants.

Government's Job The government also helps to protect the environment. Some local, state, and federal laws state that it is illegal to pollute the water or to dispose of toxic waste in an unsafe manner.

One way Indiana leaders try to prevent harm to the environment is by supervising all the possible pollutants that industries use. Special permits sometimes are needed before industries can use chemicals that could be harmful.

Your Job Keeping the environment clean is not just a job for the government or for industries. By learning about your environment and by taking responsibility for its care, you are making sure that future generations will be able to enjoy Indiana's shared environment.

Lesson Review

Comprehension
1. Name one way an event that happens in your environment can affect other people who live many miles away.
2. Why might the world be harmed if a huge forest in South America is cut down?
3. What is acid rain?
4. How can high technology industries harm the environment?
5. How does the government protect the environment?

Critical Thinking
6. Name a positive and a negative effect that technology has on the environment.
7. Why is it important for every citizen to help keep the environment clean?

Location

In the Handbook (page 9), you learned about longitude and latitude. Lines of longitude are drawn from north to south. Lines of latitude are drawn from east to west and often are called parallels because they run in the same direction at an equal distance from each other. Together the lines form a grid over the map of the world. This grid can then be used to identify the exact location of places.

These lines also have been part of disagreements. Once, for example, the United States and Great Britain could not agree on the border of Oregon. The United States wanted the border at a latitude farther north than the British thought it should be. For a time, it looked as though the two sides would fight. Finally, however, they compromised and set the border at the 49th parallel.

The city of Indianapolis sits almost directly on top of the 40th parallel. This position means the city is almost halfway between the North Pole and the equator.

In a way, Indianapolis, the capital of Indiana, is related to some cities throughout the world that are also capitals. These cities all are found along the 40th parallel. If you took an imaginary trip heading east along the 40th parallel, you would find Philadelphia, Pennsylvania—once a capital of the United States. Then, if you traveled across the Atlantic Ocean and passed through Portugal, you would find Madrid—the capital of Spain.

Continuing east on the 40th parallel, you would reach the island of Sardinia. Then you would travel through the heel on the boot of Italy, cross over Greece, and reach the Aegean Sea. Next you would come to Ankara—the capital of Turkey. Armenia, a republic of the Soviet Union, is the next place you would reach.

After passing through the Great Gobi Desert in China, you would come to Beijing—an ancient city and the capital of the People's Republic of China. The last leg of your trip would be through North Korea, Japan, and then across the Pacific Ocean to northern California. After traveling about halfway across the United States, you finally would be back to the start of your trip—Indianapolis.

All along the 40th parallel you would find a temperate climate, but some areas have different weather than Indianapolis has, due to the effects of winds, elevation, and ocean currents. For example, because Italy is next to a warm sea, winter there is not as cold as winter in Indianapolis. In the United States, two cities found

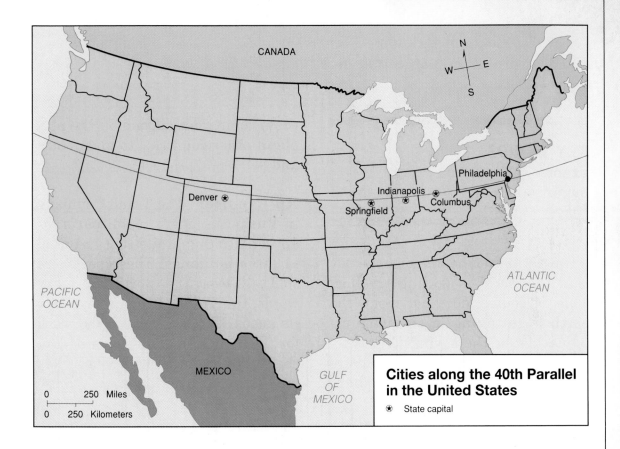

Cities along the 40th Parallel in the United States

⊛ State capital

along the 40th parallel—Denver and Philadelphia—have different weather in the winter. This is due, in part, to the fact that Denver has a higher elevation than Philadelphia.

No matter what differences you notice as you travel from place to place along the 40th parallel, you also will find many similarities. Perhaps you will meet someone who likes the same foods, music, or clothing that you like. When this happens you will realize that different people and places share things in common. Remember that geography is just one feature that ties together different areas of the world.

Comprehension

1. In which direction are latitude lines drawn? In which direction are longitude lines drawn?
2. What four state capitals are along the 40th parallel in the United States?
3. Why do some areas along the 40th parallel have different weather than Indianapolis?

Critical Thinking

4. Find the line of longitude on which your community is located. Follow this line around the world and identify all the countries and major cities along the way.

LESSON 3 Changes for Tomorrow

Trade and communications bring Indiana closer to the rest of the world. How does this affect Hoosiers?

KEY WORDS
export (ek′spōrt)
import (im′pōrt)

Have you ever heard someone say that the world is getting smaller? This, of course, does not mean the earth is shrinking in size. One explanation for the saying is that today people throughout the world are able to come together to share their experiences.

Rushville Companies

Two companies in Rushville, Indiana, provide an example of how Hoosiers work with others. Both of these companies depend on the people in other countries to make, buy, and sell their products.

An Exporter The Trane Company in Rushville makes metal parts for air conditioning units that are used in large buildings. These parts are sold all over the world. In other words, the Trane Company **exports** its goods. The 200 people who work for the Trane Company earn part of their money by selling what they make to other countries.

An Importer Another company in Rushville, Fujitsu (fü jēt′ sü) Ten, makes audio parts for car stereos. Fujitsu Ten is a Japanese company that employs Rushville citizens.

These two workers live in Rushville. The woman on the left works for the Trane Company. The man on the right tests equipment for Fujitsu Ten.

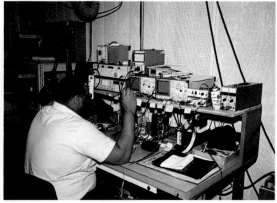

252

Many industries are affected by advances in transportation. Airplanes, for example, made it possible for packages to be delivered overnight from coast to coast. Refrigerated trucks made it possible for easily spoiled foods to be transported throughout the state. Huge ships such as this container ship can deliver very large items worldwide.

The Fujitsu Ten plant in Rushville **imports** goods. This means the plant buys materials it needs from other countries, mainly Japan. These products are used in the audio parts for the stereos. The completed car stereos then are sold throughout the United States.

Indiana in the World

Goods easily can be trucked in and out of Indiana because of well-designed roads throughout the state. For example, ten United States highways lead into Indianapolis alone. Goods also travel in and out of the state by ship. Because Indiana is a seaport state, goods easily can be exported to ports throughout the world. Because of the Indianapolis International Airport, goods also can be put on airplanes going to many countries.

A Hub Remember that once it was not so easy to reach Indiana. The pioneers' journey to the state was often difficult. Now, of course, traveling to and from Indiana is much easier because the state is a transportation center, or hub, for the country and the whole world.

You now have read many things about Indiana. You know something about its climate, landforms, history, people, and government. What do you think makes the state a special part of the world?

Let's look at Indiana as a center of activity in another way. If you throw a pebble into a pond, ripples in the water form circles that grow larger and larger as they move farther from the center. Think of events in Indiana as pebbles and the world as a pond. For people who call Indiana home, the state is like the center of the pond.

A Door to the World Over the years, the circles that surround Indiana become bigger. For the first Indians who lived in the state, the circles surrounding them were very small. They relied completely on themselves and did not need to go beyond their homes.

For you today, the circles have grown ever bigger as the rest of the world becomes easier to reach. From your home in Indiana, you can be a citizen of the world.

Lesson Review

Comprehension

1. How do companies that import or export goods depend on people in other countries?
2. Name three ways goods can be brought into and also taken out of Indiana.
3. Why is traveling to and from Indiana easy?

Critical Thinking

4. How have improvements in trade made people who live in Indiana citizens of the world?
5. Describe how easy or hard it would be for you to communicate with someone in a foreign country.
6. What other industries besides air conditioning manufacturers and car stereo manufacturers depend on imports and exports?

CHAPTER 12 REVIEW

Words to Know

Use each of these words in a complete sentence.

1. technology
2. acid rain
3. high technology
4. toxic waste
5. export
6. import

Main Ideas

1. What caused changes in Indiana farming after 1900?
2. Name three ways farms and cities are connected.
3. Are more Hoosiers today living on farms or in cities?
4. What effects does technology have on Indiana industry?
5. How has international competition forced many changes in Indiana industries?
6. Why did United States automakers have to change the designs of their automobiles?
7. Name two Indiana automakers that stopped making automobiles and tell why.
8. Name two ways banking has changed in recent years.
9. How is acid rain formed?
10. Why would Hoosiers care about what happens to a forest in South America?
11. What types of industries can produce toxic waste?
12. Who and what can help protect the environment?
13. Where do United States companies that export goods sell their products?
14. Why might an Indiana company import goods?
15. Name three ways that goods can be carried into and out of the state of Indiana.

Critical Thinking

1. Much has been written in this book about Indiana as a hub for the United States and even for the rest of the world. Now think about the hub of a bicycle wheel. Try to picture Indiana as this type of a hub. How is Indiana's job as a hub important to the rest of the United States and the world? What different things might the spokes leading out from the hub—to the rest of the world—represent?
2. Indiana faces many new problems in the changing world. For example, new industries bring new jobs to the state, but they also can bring added pollution. List some problems that might be caused by new industries. Beside each problem, suggest a way that you personally can help the situation.

Writing for Understanding

1. Oral histories are ways of remembering things from the

past and then telling those things to someone else. Oral histories give people a firsthand account of what life was like for those who are older. To see how much Indiana has changed in just a few years, write an oral history as you hear it from your grandparents, parents, or an older friend of the family. Ask questions about what the person did while growing up. Find out details about where the person lived, the clothing the person wore, what the person did for fun, and other interesting topics. When you have had your questions answered, write a brief oral history and read it to someone.

2. Research the Amazon rain forest in your library and write a short report. Your librarian will help you find books about this important forest. During your research, be sure to find out where the forest is located, what countries include the forest, what sorts of plants and animals live there, how large the forest is, and what challenges it faces. At the end of your report, suggest some solutions to its problems.

Applying Skills

Use the mileage chart below to answer the questions. The chart shows distances traveled by steamships between international ports.

1. How far do ships travel from Honolulu to Cape Town?
2. How far would a ship travel if it went from New York to London and then on to Cape Town?
3. Ships traveling between which two ports on the chart travel the fewest miles?
4. Ships traveling between which two ports travel the most miles?
5. Why, do you think, are most goods shipped from Tokyo sent to San Francisco instead of New York?
6. From which port shown on the chart might goods shipped from Indiana be exported?

Miles by Steamship between International Ports						
	Tokyo	**San Francisco**	**Honolulu**	**Cape Town**	**New York**	**London**
Tokyo	—	4,536	3,394	8,830	10,096	12,665
San Francisco	4,536	—	2,091	9,789	5,262	7,831
Honolulu	3,394	2,091	—	11,229	6,702	9,271
Cape Town	8,830	9,789	11,229	—	6,788	3,574
New York	10,096	5,262	6,702	6,788	—	3,430
London	12,665	7,831	9,271	3,574	3,430	—

UNIT 4 REVIEW AND STUDY GUIDE

Key People/Places	Key Terms	Key Ideas
Indiana's Way of Life (pages 210-227) Tarkington, Riley, Pyle, Steele, Indiana, Porter, Carmichael, Mellencamp, Knight, Naismith, Bird, Brown, Appleseed Jasper, Shipshewana, Indianapolis, Fort Wayne, Johnny Appleseed Park, Parke County	culture, landscape, tournament, amateur, annual	■ Indiana's heritage and culture can be seen in the art, crafts, and ways of life of its people. ■ Sports play a large role in the lives of Hoosiers. ■ Hoosiers gather throughout the state for celebrations and festivals related to Indiana history.
Hoosiers at Work (pages 228-239) Warsaw, Jeffersonville, Decatur, Marion, Indianapolis, Columbus, South Bend, Elkhart	economy, income, livestock, poultry, drought, service industry, customer	■ The whole state of Indiana depends on the work of farmers. ■ Hoosiers work in a wide variety of industries.
Indiana Keeping Up with Changes (pages 240-256) Soviet Union, Japan, Lake Michigan, Canada, South America, Amazon River region, Gary, Rushville	technology, acid rain, high technology, toxic waste, export, import	■ Indiana businesses have had to keep up with great changes in technology and competition. ■ Hoosiers need to take responsibility for the problem of pollution. ■ Indiana serves as a transportation and business center for the country and the whole world.

Timeline

1900

1900 Hoosiers begin moving from farms to cities

1929 Steel production becomes Indiana's leading industry

1937 Indiana state motto chosen

1963 Studebaker halts production in South Bend

1980 Drought in Indiana

1985 John Mellencamp puts on Farm Aid concert

Countries of the World

0   1000   2000   3000 Miles
0   1000   2000   3000 Kilometers

ALASKA (U.S.)

60°

CANADA

NORTH
AMERICA
UNITED STATES

40°

BERMUDA (U.K.)

ATLANTIC
OCEAN

HAWAII (U.S.)   Tropic of Cancer   20°

THE BAHAMAS
DOMINICAN REPUBLIC
PUERTO RICO (U.S. COMM.)

MEXICO   CUBA
JAMAICA HAITI   VIRGIN ISLANDS (U.S.)
BELIZE   ANTIGUA AND BARBUDA
ST. CHRISTOPHER   DOMINICA
AND NEVIS   BARBADOS
GUATEMALA   SAINT LUCIA   ST. VINCENT AND
EL SALVADOR   GRENADA   THE GRENADINES
HONDURAS   NICARAGUA   TRINIDAD AND TOBAGO
COSTA RICA   SURINAME
PANAMA   VENEZUELA GUYANA
FRENCH
COLOMBIA   GUIANA
(FR.)

PACIFIC OCEAN

Equator   0°

ECUADOR

KIRIBATI

SOUTH
AMERICA

PERU   BRAZIL

WESTERN SAMOA

TONGA
20°   BOLIVIA

Tropic of Capricorn   PARAGUAY

EUROPE

80°N   0°

20°E

40°

ATLANTIC   Arctic Circle
ICELAND   OCEAN   CHILE   URUGUAY

ARGENTINA

SWEDEN   FINLAND
NORWAY

60°N

180°   160°   140°   120°   100°   80°   60°
DENMARK   60°

UNITED
KINGDOM   POLAND

IRELAND   NETHERLANDS   SOVIET UNION
GERMANY
BELGIUM
LUXEMBOURG   CZECHOSLOVAKIA

SWITZERLAND   AUSTRIA HUNGARY
FRANCE   LIECHTENSTEIN
ROMANIA
MONACO   SAN   YUGOSLAVIA
MARINO   BULGARIA
ANDORRA   ITALY   ALBANIA
40°N   SPAIN
PORTUGAL   GREECE   TURKEY

GIBRALTAR
(U.K.)   MALTA
CYPRUS

0   500   1000   1500 Miles
0   500   1000   1500 Kilometers

Atlas

ARCTIC OCEAN

GREENLAND
(DEN.)

ICELAND

Arctic Circle

NORWAY

FINLAND

SWEDEN

SOVIET UNION

ASIA

UNITED
KINGDOM

IRELAND

DENMARK

NETH.
BEL.

GER.

POLAND

CZECH.

EUROPE

FRANCE

SWIT.

AUST. HUNG.

YUGO.

ROMANIA

BUL.

MONGOLIA

PORTUGAL

SPAIN

ITALY

ALB.

GREECE

TURKEY

PEOPLE'S REPUBLIC OF
CHINA

NORTH
KOREA

SOUTH
KOREA

JAPAN

MALTA

CYPRUS

LEBANON

ISRAEL

SYRIA

IRAQ

AFGHANISTAN

IRAN

PAKISTAN

BHUTAN

MOROCCO

TUNISIA

JORDAN

NEPAL

TAIWAN

WESTERN
SAHARA
(MOR.)

ALGERIA

LIBYA

EGYPT

KUWAIT

QATAR

BAHRAIN

SAUDI ARABIA

UNITED ARAB
EMIRATES

INDIA

BANGLADESH

BURMA

PACIFIC OCEAN

MAURITANIA

CAPE
VERDE

SENEGAL

GAMBIA

MALI

NIGER

AFRICA

CHAD

SUDAN

OMAN

YEMEN

LAOS

THAILAND

VIETNAM

CAMBODIA

MARSHALL ISLANDS

GUINEA-
BISSAU

GUINEA

BURKINA
FASO

DJIBOUTI

FEDERATED STATES
OF MICRONESIA

SIERRA
LEONE

LIBERIA

GHANA

CÔTE
D'IVOIRE

TOGO

BENIN

NIGERIA

CENTRAL AFRICAN
REPUBLIC

ETHIOPIA

SRI LANKA

PHILIPPINES

BRUNEI

EQUATORIAL GUINEA

SÃO TOMÉ AND PRINCIPE

CAMEROON

UGANDA

SOMALIA

MALDIVES

MALAYSIA

SINGAPORE

KIRIBATI

GABON

CONGO

RWANDA

KENYA

Equator

NAURU

ZAIRE

BURUNDI

INDONESIA

PAPUA
NEW
GUINEA

TUVALU

SOLOMON
ISLANDS

TANZANIA

SEYCHELLES

ANGOLA

COMOROS

INDIAN OCEAN

VANUATU

MALAWI

FIJI

ZAMBIA

MOZAMBIQUE

NAMIBIA

ZIMBABWE

MADAGASCAR

MAURITIUS

BOTSWANA

AUSTRALIA
AUSTRALIA

SWAZILAND

SOUTH
AFRICA

LESOTHO

NEW ZEALAND

20°   0°   20°   40°   60°   80°   100°   120°   140°   160°   180°

Antarctic Circle

ANTARCTICA

Strait of Juan de Fuca
Cape Flattery
Puget Sound
Seattle
Olympia
RANGE
F.D. Roosevelt Lake
Pend Oreille Lake
Clark
LEWIS RANGE
Milk R.
Fort Peck Lake
Missouri R.
Lake Sakakawea
WASHINGTON
Portland
Flathead Lake
BITTERROOT RANGE
ROCKY
Helena
MONTANA
NORTH DAKOTA
Bismarck
Columbia R.
Salem
CASCADE
OREGON
Yellowstone R.
ABSAROKA RANGE
Powder R.
G
R
E
A
T
Boise
COLUMBIA PLATEAU
IDAHO
SNAKE RIVER PLAIN
BIGHORN MOUNTAINS
Bighorn
Lake Oahe
SOUTH DAKOTA
Pierre
RANGES
Klamath
Goose Lake
Snake R.
MOUNTAINS
WYOMING
BLACK HILLS
BADLANDS
White R.
40°N
Cape Mendocino
Pit R.
Pyramid Lake
Great Salt Lake
RANGE
Cheyenne
North Platte R.
SAND HILLS
NEBRASKA
COAST
SIERRA
Lake Tahoe
Carson City
GREAT
GREAT SALT LAKE DESERT
Salt Lake City
UINTA MOUNTAINS
FRONT RANGE
South Platte R.
Sacramento R.
Sacramento
NEVADA
BASIN
WASATCH RANGE
UTAH
Green R.
M
O
U
N
T
A
I
N
S
COLORADO
Denver
Republican R.
Lincoln
San Francisco Bay
San Francisco
San Jose
VALLEY
125°W
CENTRAL
Mt. Whitney (14,494 ft / 4,418 m)
35°N
COLORADO
Lake Powell
SAN JUAN MOUNTAINS
SANGRE DE CRISTO MOUNTAINS
Smoky Hill R.
KANSAS
San Joaquin R.
NEVADA
Death Valley (-282 ft / -89 m)
Lake Mead
PLATEAU
Santa Fe
Arkansas R.
Point Conception
CALIFORNIA
MOJAVE DESERT
GRAND CANYON
PAINTED DESERT
Colorado R.
Canadian R.
OKLAHOM
Oklahoma City
CHANNEL ISLANDS
Los Angeles
Salton Sea
ARIZONA
Phoenix
NEW MEXICO
SACRAMENTO MOUNTAINS
P
L
A
I
N
S
Red R.
Lake Texoma
PACIFIC
San Diego
Gila R.
El Paso
LLANO ESTACADO
Dallas
120°W
SONORA DESERT
Rio Grande
Pecos R.
Colorado R.
TEXAS
Austin
OCEAN
Brazos R.
San Antonio

160°W
Kauai
Oahu
155°W
Honolulu
Molokai
Lanai
Maui
HAWAII
Hilo
20°N
PACIFIC OCEAN
Hawaii
0   50   100 Miles
0 50 100 Kilometers

EDWARDS PLATEAU
Rio Grande
Padre

ARCTIC OCEAN
70°N
Point Barrow
BEAUFORT SEA
Arctic Circle
BROOKS RANGE
170°E
60°N
Bering Strait
St. Lawrence
ALASKA
Yukon R.
Tanana R.
ALASKA RANGE
Mt. McKinley (20,320 ft / 6,194 m)
Anchorage
COAST MOUNTAINS
0   250   500 Miles
0   250 500 Kilometers
BERING SEA
Attu
180°
170°W
50°N
ALEUTIAN ISLANDS
PACIFIC OCEAN
260
ALASKA PENINSULA
160°W
Kodiak
Gulf of Alaska
Juneau
150°W
140°W

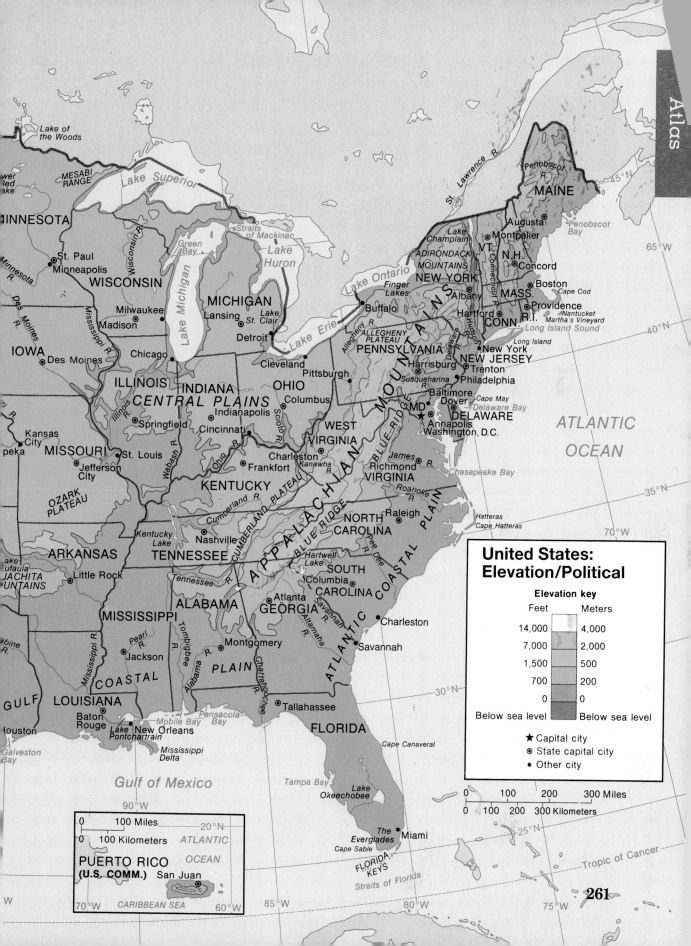

Lake of the Woods

MESABI RANGE

wer led ake

MINNESOTA

Lake Superior

St. Paul

Minneapolis

Minnesota R.

WISCONSIN

Milwaukee

Madison

IOWA

Des Moines

Des Moines R.

Mississippi R.

Wisconsin R.

Green Bay

Straits of Mackinac

Lake Huron

MICHIGAN

Lansing

Lake St. Clair

Detroit

Lake Michigan

Chicago

ILLINOIS

INDIANA

CENTRAL PLAINS

Springfield

Indianapolis

Cincinnati

Kansas City

peka

MISSOURI

Jefferson City

St. Louis

Frankfort

OHIO

Columbus

Scioto R.

Ohio R.

Wabash R.

Illinois R.

KENTUCKY

Cumberland R.

OZARK PLATEAU

Kentucky Lake

Nashville

ARKANSAS

TENNESSEE

Little Rock

ke ufaula

ACHITA NTAINS

Tennessee R.

ALABAMA

MISSISSIPPI

GEORGIA

Pearl R.

Jackson

Tombigbee R.

Alabama R.

Montgomery

PLAIN

Chattahoochee R.

COASTAL

LOUISIANA

GULF

Baton Rouge

New Orleans

Lake Pontchartrain

Mobile Bay

Pensacola Bay

Tallahassee

Houston

bine R.

Galveston Bay

Mississippi Delta

Gulf of Mexico

FLORIDA

Tampa Bay

Lake Okeechobee

Cape Canaveral

The Everglades

Cape Sable

Miami

FLORIDA KEYS

Straits of Florida

Lake Superior

Lake Ontario

Finger Lakes

Buffalo

Lake Erie

Cleveland

Pittsburgh

Allegheny R.

ALLEGHENY PLATEAU

PENNSYLVANIA

Harrisburg

WEST VIRGINIA

Charleston

Kanawha R.

Richmond

VIRGINIA

James R.

Roanoke R.

NORTH CAROLINA

Raleigh

Pee Dee R.

Hartwell Lake

SOUTH CAROLINA

Columbia

Savannah R.

Atlanta

Altamaha R.

Savannah

Charleston

ATLANTIC COASTAL PLAIN

BLUE RIDGE

CUMBERLAND PLATEAU

APPALACHIAN

MOUNTAINS

St. Lawrence R.

Penobscot R.

MAINE

Augusta

Penobscot Bay

Lake Champlain

Montpelier

VT.

N.H.

Concord

ADIRONDACK MOUNTAINS

NEW YORK

Albany

Connecticut R.

Boston

Cape Cod

MASS.

Providence

R.I.

Nantucket

Hartford

CONN.

Martha's Vineyard

Long Island Sound

Long Island

New York

NEW JERSEY

Trenton

Philadelphia

Delaware R.

Susquehanna R.

Hudson R.

Baltimore

Dover

MD.

Annapolis

Washington, D.C.

DELAWARE

Cape May

Delaware Bay

Chesapeake Bay

Hatteras

Cape Hatteras

ATLANTIC OCEAN

65° W

45° N

40° N

35° N

30° N

25° N

70° W

75° W

80° W

85° W

90° W

United States: Elevation/Political

Elevation key

Feet	Meters
14,000	4,000
7,000	2,000
1,500	500
700	200
0	0
Below sea level	Below sea level

★ Capital city

◉ State capital city

• Other city

| 0 | 100 | 200 | 300 Miles |
| 0 | 100 | 200 | 300 Kilometers |

0   100 Miles

0   100 Kilometers

20° N

ATLANTIC OCEAN

PUERTO RICO (U.S. COMM.)

San Juan

70° W

CARIBBEAN SEA

60° W

Tropic of Cancer

261

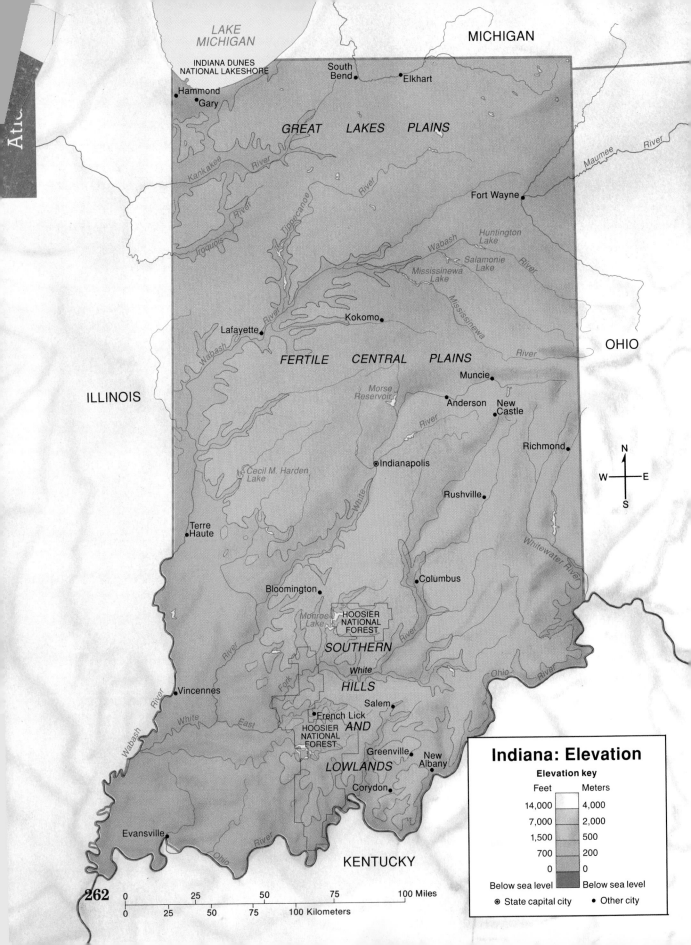

LAKE
MICHIGAN

MICHIGAN

INDIANA DUNES
NATIONAL LAKESHORE

South
Bend
•Elkhart

Hammond
•Gary

GREAT LAKES PLAINS

Kankakee River

River

Tippecanoe River

Iroquois River

Fort Wayne

Maumee River

Huntington
Lake

Wabash

Salamonie
Lake

Mississinewa
Lake

ILLINOIS

Lafayette•

Kokomo•

FERTILE CENTRAL PLAINS

Wabash River

Morse
Reservoir

Mississinewa

River

OHIO

Muncie•

Anderson• New
Castle

Cecil M. Harden
Lake

White

River

⊙Indianapolis

Richmond•

N
W   E
S

Rushville•

Terre
Haute•

Columbus•

Bloomington•

Monroe
Lake

HOOSIER
NATIONAL
FOREST

SOUTHERN

White

River

River

Vincennes•

HILLS

Fork

Salem•

White

East

•French Lick

AND

HOOSIER
NATIONAL
FOREST

Wabash River

White River

LOWLANDS

Greenville• New
Albany

Corydon•

Evansville•

Ohio   River

Whitewater River

Ohio

River

Indiana: Elevation

Elevation key

Feet	Meters
14,000	4,000
7,000	2,000
1,500	500
700	200
0	0
Below sea level	Below sea level

⊙ State capital city   • Other city

KENTUCKY

262

0	25	50	75	100 Miles
0	25	50	75	100 Kilometers

ATL.

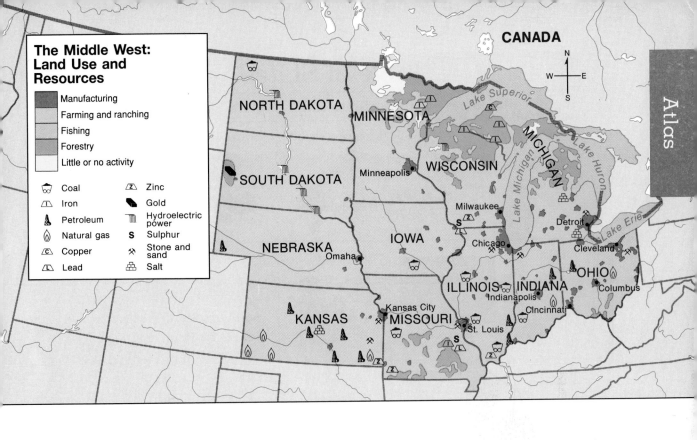

The Middle West: Land Use and Resources

Land Use:
- Manufacturing
- Farming and ranching
- Fishing
- Forestry
- Little or no activity

Resources:
- Coal
- Iron
- Petroleum
- Natural gas
- Copper
- Lead
- Zinc
- Gold
- Hydroelectric power
- S Sulphur
- Stone and sand
- Salt

CANADA

NORTH DAKOTA
MINNESOTA
Lake Superior
SOUTH DAKOTA
WISCONSIN
MICHIGAN
Minneapolis
Lake Huron
Milwaukee
Lake Michigan
IOWA
Detroit
NEBRASKA
Chicago
Cleveland
Lake Erie
Omaha
OHIO
ILLINOIS INDIANA
Columbus
Indianapolis
Kansas City
Cincinnati
KANSAS
MISSOURI
St. Louis

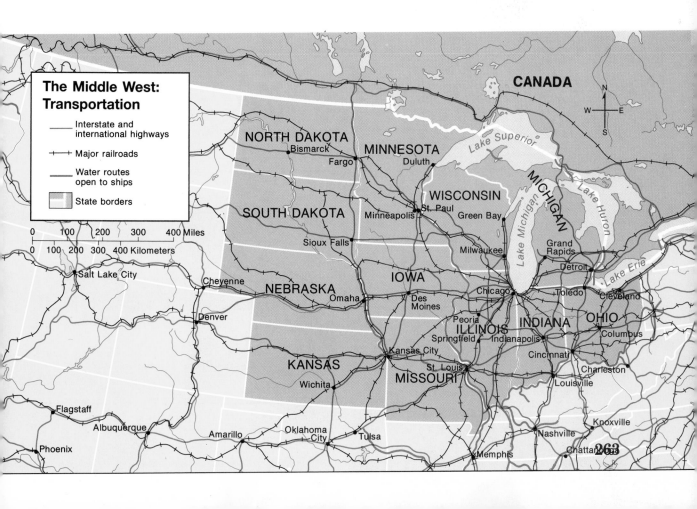

The Middle West: Transportation

- Interstate and international highways
- Major railroads
- Water routes open to ships
- State borders

Scale: 0 100 200 300 400 Miles
0 100 200 300 400 Kilometers

CANADA

NORTH DAKOTA
Bismarck
MINNESOTA
Lake Superior
Fargo
Duluth
WISCONSIN
MICHIGAN
St. Paul
SOUTH DAKOTA
Minneapolis
Green Bay
Lake Huron
Sioux Falls
Milwaukee
Grand Rapids
Lake Michigan
Detroit
Salt Lake City
Cheyenne
IOWA
Chicago
Lake Erie
NEBRASKA
Omaha
Des Moines
Toledo
Cleveland
Denver
Peoria
INDIANA
OHIO
ILLINOIS
Columbus
Springfield
Indianapolis
Kansas City
Cincinnati
KANSAS
St. Louis
Charleston
Wichita
MISSOURI
Louisville
Flagstaff
Knoxville
Albuquerque
Amarillo
Oklahoma City
Tulsa
Nashville
Phoenix
Memphis
Chattanooga

Table of States

State	State Flag	State Bird	State Flower	Population
Alabama Montgomery		Yellowhammer	Camellia	Total 4,083,000 Rank 22
Alaska Juneau		Willow Ptarmigan	Forget-Me-Not	Total 525,000 Rank 49
Arizona Phoenix		Cactus Wren	Blossom of Saguaro Cactus	Total 3,386,000 Rank 25
Arkansas Little Rock		Mockingbird	Apple Blossom	Total 2,388,000 Rank 33
California Sacramento		California Valley Quail	Golden Poppy	Total 27,663,000 Rank 1
Colorado Denver		Lark Bunting	Rocky Mountain Columbine	Total 3,296,000 Rank 26

264

State	State Flag	State Bird	State Flower	Population
Connecticut Hartford ★		American Robin	Mountain Laurel	Total 3,211,000 Rank 28
Delaware Dover ★		Blue Hen Chicken	Peach Blossom	Total 644,000 Rank 47
Florida Tallahassee		Mockingbird	Orange Blossom	Total 12,023,000 Rank 4
Georgia ★ Atlanta		Brown Thrasher	Cherokee Rose	Total 6,222,000 Rank 11
Hawaii Honolulu		Hawaiian Goose	Hibiscus	Total 1,083,000 Rank 39
Idaho ★ Boise		Mountain Bluebird	Syringa	Total 998,000 Rank 42

265

State	State Flag	State Bird	State Flower	Population
Illinois Springfield ★	ILLINOIS	Cardinal 	Native Violet 	Total 11,582,000 Rank 6
Indiana Indianapolis ★		Cardinal 	Peony 	Total 5,531,000 Rank 14
Iowa Des Moines ★	IOWA	Eastern Goldfinch 	Wild Rose 	Total 2,834,000 Rank 29
Kansas Topeka ★	KANSAS	Western Meadowlark 	Native Sunflower 	Total 2,476,000 Rank 32
Kentucky ★ Frankfort		Cardinal 	Goldenrod 	Total 3,727,000 Rank 23
Louisiana Baton Rouge ★		Eastern Brown Pelican 	Magnolia 	Total 4,461,000 Rank 20

State	State Flag	State Bird	State Flower	Population
Maine Augusta ★		Chickadee	White Pine Cone and Tassel	Total 1,174,000 Rank 38
Maryland Annapolis ★		Baltimore Oriole	Black-eyed Susan	Total 4,535,000 Rank 19
Massachusetts Boston ★		Chickadee	Mayflower	Total 5,855,000 Rank 13
Michigan Lansing ★		Robin	Apple Blossom	Total 9,200,000 Rank 8
Minnesota St. Paul ★		Common Loon	Pink and White Lady's Slippers	Total 4,246,000 Rank 21
Mississippi ★ Jackson		Mockingbird	Magnolia	Total 2,625,000 Rank 31

State	State Flag	State Bird	State Flower	Population
Missouri Jefferson City ★		Bluebird	Hawthorn	Total 5,103,000 Rank 15
Montana ★ Helena	MONTANA	Western Meadowlark	Bitterroot	Total 809,000 Rank 44
Nebraska Lincoln ★		Western Meadowlark	Goldenrod	Total 1,594,000 Rank 36
Nevada ★ Carson City		Mountain Bluebird	Sagebrush	Total 1,007,000 Rank 41
New Hampshire Concord ★		Purple Finch	Purple Lilac	Total 1,057,000 Rank 40
New Jersey Trenton ★		Eastern Goldfinch	Purple Violet	Total 7,627,000 Rank 9

State	State Flag	State Bird	State Flower	Population
New Mexico Santa Fe		Roadrunner	Yucca	Total 1,500,000 Rank 37
New York Albany		Bluebird	Rose	Total 17,825,000 Rank 2
North Carolina Raleigh		Cardinal	Dogwood	Total 6,413,000 Rank 10
North Dakota Bismark		Western Meadowlark	Wild Prairie Rose	Total 672,000 Rank 46
Ohio Columbus		Cardinal	Scarlet Carnation	Total 10,784,000 Rank 7
Oklahoma Oklahoma City		Scissor-tailed Flycatcher	Mistletoe	Total 3,272,000 Rank 27

269

State	State Flag	State Bird	State Flower	Population
Oregon ★ Salem	STATE OF OREGON 1859	Western Meadowlark	Oregon Grape	Total 2,724,000 Rank 30
Pennsylvania Harrisburg ★		Ruffed Grouse	Mountain Laurel	Total 11,936,000 Rank 5
Rhode Island Providence		Rhode Island Red	Violet	Total 986,000 Rank 43
South Carolina Columbia ★		Carolina Wren	Carolina Jessamine	Total 3,425,000 Rank 24
South Dakota Pierre ★		Ring-necked Pheasant	Pasqueflower	Total 709,000 Rank 45
Tennessee Nashville ★		Mockingbird	Iris	Total 4,855,000 Rank 16
Texas Austin ★		Mockingbird	Bluebonnet	Total 16,789,000 Rank 3

State	State Flag	State Bird	State Flower	Population
Utah Salt Lake City		Seagull	Sego Lily	Total 1,680,000 Rank 35
Vermont Montpelier		Hermit Thrush	Red Clover	Total 548,000 Rank 48
Virginia Richmond		Cardinal	Dogwood	Total 5,904,000 Rank 12
Washington Olympia		Willow Goldfinch	Western Rhododendron	Total 4,538,000 Rank 18
West Virginia Charleston		Cardinal	Big Rhododendron	Total 1,897,000 Rank 34
Wisconsin Madison		Robin	Wood Violet	Total 4,807,000 Rank 17
Wyoming Cheyenne		Meadowlark	Indian Paintbrush	Total 490,000 Rank 50

Gazetteer

Place/Description	Location	Page	Place/Description	Location	Page
Alaska, state in the United States	64°N/150°W	260	**Gary,** city in Indiana	42°N/87°W	45
Appalachian Mountains, United States	37°N/82°W	261	**Great Lakes,** North America	46°N/85°W	25
Augusta, capital of Maine	44°N/70°W	10	**Great Lakes Plains,** region of Indiana	42°N/86°W	54
Badlands, region of the United States	44°N/102°W	260	**Great Plains,** United States	40°N/101°W	25
Black Hills, mountains in the United States	44°N/103°W	260	**Gulf of Mexico,** North America	25°N/90°W	261
Boston, capital of Massachusetts	42°N/71°W	261	**Hawaii,** state in the United States	20°N/157°W	260
Canada, country in North America	50°N/100°W	258	**Houston,** city in Texas	30°N/95°W	261
Central Plains, United States	40°N/86°W	54	**Illinois,** state in the United States	40°N/91°W	261
Chicago, city in Illinois	41°N/87°W	261	**Indiana,** state in the United States	40°N/86°W	261
China, country in Asia	37°N/93°E	259	**Indianapolis,** capital city of Indiana	40°N/86°W	261
Cincinnati, city in Ohio	39°N/85°W	261	**Iowa,** state in the United States	40°N/94°W	261
Columbus, city in Indiana	39°N/86°W	119	**Japan,** island country in Asia	36°N/133°E	259
Corydon, city in Indiana	38°N/86°W	108	**Kankakee River,** United States	41°N/88°W	61
Detroit, city in Michigan	42°N/83°W	261	**Kansas,** state in the United States	38°N/99°W	260
Eel River, Indiana	41°N/86°W	61	**Kentucky,** state in the United States	37°N/87°W	261
Elkhart, city in Indiana	42°N/86°W	234	**Lake Michigan,** United States	43°N/87°W	261
Equator, line of latitude that goes around the middle of the globe	0°	258	**Lake Superior,** North America	48°N/88°W	261
Evansville, city in Indiana	38°N/88°W	45	**Lowlands,** region of Indiana	39°N/87°W	54
Flat North, region of Indiana	42°N/86°W	54	**Marion,** city in Indiana	40°N/85°W	234
Florence, city in Italy	44°N/11°E	6	**Maumee River,** United States	41°N/85°W	61
Fort Smith, city in Arkansas	35°N/94°W	8	**Michigan,** state in the United States	46°N/87°W	261
Fort Wayne, city in Indiana	41°N/85°W	45	**Middle West,** United States region	42°N/93°W	263

Place/Description	Location	Page
Minneapolis, city in Minnesota	45°N/93°W	261
Minnesota, state in the United States	46°N/90°W	261
Mississinewa River, United States	41°N/87°W	61
Mississippi River, United States	38°N/90°W	261
Missouri, state in the United States	38°N/94°W	261
Missouri River, United States	41°N/96°W	261
National Road, United States (also called Cumberland Road)	40°N/86°W	192
Nebraska, state in the United States	41°N/101°W	260
New Albany, city in Indiana	38°N/86°W	239
New Mexico, state in the United States	34°N/107°W	260
New Orleans, city in Louisiana	30°N/90°W	261
New York City, city in New York State	40°N/74°W	261
New York State, state in the United States	43°N/78°W	261
North Dakota, state in the United States	47°N/102°W	260
North Pole, northern most point on the globe	90°N	9
Ohio, state in the United States	41°N/83°W	261
Ohio River, United States	37°N/88°W	261
Oklahoma, state in the United States	36°N/98°W	260
Pennsylvania, state in the United States	41°N/78°W	261
Prime meridian, starting point for lines of longitude	0°	9

Place/Description	Location	Page
Richmond, city in Indiana	40°N/85°W	45
Rocky Mountains, United States	50°N/114°W	260
St. Joseph River, United States	42°N/86°W	61
St. Louis, city in Missouri	39°N/90°W	261
St. Mary's River, United States	41°N/85°W	61
Salem, city in Indiana	39°N/86°W	158
South Bend, city in Indiana	42°N/86°W	45
South Dakota, state in the United States	44°N/102°W	260
Southern Hills, region of Indiana	39°N/87°W	54
Soviet Union, country in Europe and Asia	60°N/64°E	259
Switzerland, country in Europe	46°N/8°E	258
Tennessee, state in the United States	36°N/88°W	261
Terre Haute, city in Indiana	39°N/87°W	45
Texarkana, city in Texas and Arkansas	33°N/94°W	8
Till Plains, region of Indiana	40°N/86°W	54
Tippecanoe River, Indiana	41°N/86°W	61
Uplands, region of Indiana	39°N/87°W	54
Vincennes, city in Indiana	38°N/87°W	108
Wabash River, United States	38°N/88°W	261
Washington, D.C., district and capital city of the United States	39°N/77°W	261
White River, Indiana	39°N/87°W	61
Wisconsin, state in the United States	44°N/91°W	261

Gazetteer

273

Bibliography

Unit One Indiana: Its Geography and Early History

The Art of the Woodland Indians, by Shirley Glubok. Macmillan, 1976. Beautiful photographs of objects created by the Woodland Indians cover the pages of this book. The works are accompanied by well-written text.

Early Settler Storybook by Bobbie Kalman. Crabtree, 1982. Take pleasure in the songs, stories, poems, artworks, story starters, and plays enjoyed by early settlers.

How the Settlers Lived by George and Ellen Laycock. David McKay Company, 1980. Take a look at the living conditions, homes, and recreation of the settlers who faced the challenges of the frontier.

Who Discovered America? Settlers and Explorers Before the Time of Columbus, by Patricia Lauber. Random, 1970. The author asks pointed questions about who really discovered America. She gives detailed information about the first explorers—the people who crossed the Bering Strait, the discovery of Vinland, and the voyages of Columbus.

Unit Two The Growth of Indiana

Abe Lincoln Grows Up, by Carl Sandburg. Harcourt, 1928. See Abe Lincoln as a boy growing up on the prairie. Adapted from Sandburg's adult biography, *The Prairie Years.*

Early Village Life by Bobbie Kalman. Crabtree, 1981. Original etchings, paintings, and drawings, as well as staged photographs fill the pages of this collection of literary sketches about life in a village.

The New Enchantment of America—Indiana by Allan Carpenter. Childrens Press, 1978. Look at the geography, history, resources, industry, key people, and culture of Indiana.

To Be a Slave by Lester Julius. Dial Books, 1968. Get a vivid picture of what it was like to be a slave. Read the lively words of people who were once slaves.

Unit Three Indiana: Local, State, and National Government

The Constitution: A New True Book by Warren Colman. Childrens Press, 1987. Gain a better understanding of the supreme law of the land and how the national government works as you read this simply told story of the United States Constitution.

Here Is Your Indiana Government. Indiana State Chamber of Commerce, 1990. Read about the government of your state. See and understand the changes that take place in Indiana's laws.

The Indiana Book of Records, Firsts, and Fascinating Facts by Fred D. Cavinder. Enjoy this fact-filled book as you learn something new about your state.

Thomas Jefferson and the Declaration of Independence by James Munves. Scribner, 1978. Learn more about this special document that marked the birth of the United States.

Unit Four Living in Indiana

Indiana by Allan Carpenter. Childrens Press, 1979. Experience the Hoosier state, including its history, its famous citizens, and its places of interest.

Indiana Through Tradition and Change: A History of the Hoosier State and Its People by James H. Madison. Indiana Historical Society, 1982. Take a closer look at Indiana's way of life. Watch Hoosiers as they work and at play. Learn about your State's heritage.

A Pictorial History of Indiana by Dwight Hoover. Indiana University Press, 1980. Enjoy the lively photographs, maps, and illustrations in this beautiful journal of the Hoosier state and its people.

Yesterday's Indiana by Byron L. Troyer. E.A Seemann Publishing, 1975. Engravings, drawings, woodcuts, and countless photographs in this pictorial history trace Indiana's past from its first settlement to the 1950's.

Glossary

Pronunciation Key

a   hat, match, carry
ā   say, late, paid, ape
ä   father, car, rock

e   let, met, very
ē   meat, free, money
ė   term, learn, worm, fur

i   if, hit, native, mirror
ī   ice, sight, buy, pirate

ō   hope, snow, soap
ô   off, all
ou   out, shout
oi   toy, joy

u   up, love, but

ü   rule, dew, youth, cool
u̇   put, foot

ə   a in above
     e in open
     i in happily
     o in gallop
     u in circus

---

acid rain (as′əd rān) Harmful rain formed when water mixes with pollutants. (p. 248)

adapt (ə dapt′) Change, as to meet new needs. (p. 206)

aerial (ar′ē əl) From the air, as in an *aerial* photograph taken from an airplane. (p. 11)

ally (al′ī) A partner, as in one who joins the same side as another in a war. (p. 114)

amateur (am′ə tėr) Person who works or plays without receiving money. (p. 221)

amendment (ə mend′mənt) A change in the United States Constitution. (p. 144)

ancestor (an′ses tėr) A person in a family who lived in the past. (p. 67)

annual (an′yə wəl) Coming or happening once each year. (p. 223)

appeal (ə pēl′) Argue a court case again in a Court of Appeals or higher court. (p. 172)

aquatic (ə kwät′ik) Dealing with plants and animals that live in water. (p. 49)

archaeologist (är kē äl′ə jist) A scientist who studies ancient peoples. (p. 67)

bankrupt (ban′krəpt) Unable to pay one's bills. (p. 132)

bill (bil′) A possible law; an idea for a law presented to the House and Senate for approval or rejection. (p. 169)

blueprint (blü′print) A set of plans. (p. 165)

canal (kə nal′) A large waterway that is built to allow the passage of boats and ships. (p. 135)

capital (kap′ə təl) A city where the government of a state or country is found. (p. 100)

case (kās′) A matter for a law court to decide. (p. 172)

checks and balances (cheks′ənd bal′əns əz) System whereby each branch of the national government can check the other two branches to make sure the balance of power among the branches is working. (p. 191)

city manager (sit′ē man′ij ėr) A person who runs a city government. (p. 181)

civil war (siv′əl wôr′) A war fought between citizens of the same country. (p. 141)

climate (klī′mət) The kind of weather a place usually has. (p. 20)

colonist (kol′ə nəst) A person who lived in one of the colonies. (p. 88)

colony (kol′ənē) A group of settlements far from the country that rules it. (p. 88)

commissioner (kə mish′ə nėr) Board member elected to set county policies. (p. 181)

committee (kə mit′ē) A group chosen to review, act on, or report on an issue. (p. 178)

communication (kə myü′nə kā′shən) The passing of information and ideas. (p. 17)

compass rose (kum′pəs rōz′) The symbol on a map that shows directions. (p. 5)

competition (kom′pə tish′ən) When two or more persons or groups are trying to do the same thing. (p. 39)

compromise (kom′prə miz) Agree to some unpopular issues in order to win on other issues. (p. 164)

confederation (kən fed′ə rā′shən) 1. A united group. (p. 85) 2. A system of government in which the national government is not very strong and most of the power lies with each state. (p. 162)

conference committee (kon′fə rəns kə mit′ē) A committee of members of the House of Representatives and Senate who iron out disagreements about a bill. (p. 184)

Congress (kon′grəs) The legislative, or lawmaking, branch of the United States government made up of the House of Representatives and the Senate. (p. 189)

constitution (kon′stə tü′shən) Document setting up laws for a government. (p. 122)

council (koun′səl) A meeting in which discussions take place. (p. 111)

culture (kul′chėr) The way of life for a group of people, including everything they believe, know, and do. (p. 211)

deciduous (di sij′ə wəs) Having the quality of losing leaves in fall. (p. 48)

delegate (del′i gət) A person who is chosen to speak for others. (p. 106)

democracy (di mok′rə sē) A government that is made and ruled by the people. (p. 163)

descent (di sent′) The family beginnings of a person. (p. 32)

district (dis′trikt) Voting areas into which a state is divided. (p. 168)

drought (drout) A long period of time when little or no rain falls. (p. 232)

economy (i kon′ə mē) The way people make money and sell goods or services. (p. 229)

electoral college (i lek′tə rəl kol′ij) The group of people who formally elect the President and Vice President. (p. 194)

elevation (el ə vā′shən) 1. Height above or depth below sea level. 2. A map that shows height above or depth below sea level. (p. 13)

eligible (el′ə jə bəl) Legally qualified, such as being *eligible* to vote. (p. 196)

equator (i kwāt′ər) The line of latitude that goes around the middle of a globe. The *equator* is numbered 0°. (p. 9)

executive (ig zek′ yət iv) The branch of government that admininsters the laws. (p. 168)

export (ek′spōrt) 1. Product sold to other countries. 2. Sell goods to other countries. (p. 252)

extinct (ik stinkt′) When a kind of plant or animal no longer exists. (p. 29)

federal (fed′ ə rəl) A government in which powers are divided between the national government and the states. (p. 194)

fertile (fėrt′əl) Having soil that is good for growing crops. (p. 56)

flatboat (flat′bōt) A wide boat with a flat bottom used on rivers. (p. 126)

flax (flaks) Plant grown for its fibers. (p. 128)

flint (flint′) A hard rock that can be chipped away until a sharp edge forms. (p. 73)

forest (fôr′əst) A tree-covered area. (p. 48)

General Assembly (jen′rəl ə sem′blē) The legislative branch of the Indiana state government; it is made up of the House of Representatives and the Senate. (p. 168)

geography (jē äg′rə fē) The study of the earth's surface and how it is used. (p. 3)

glacier (glā′shėr) Huge, slow moving river of ice. (p. 54)

globe (glōb) A model of the earth that shows where bodies of land and water are. (p. 3)

governor (guv ə′nėr) The head of the executive branch of a state government. (p. 169)

grain elevator (grān′el′ə vāt′ėr) Building for storing and unloading grain. (p. 38)

grass roots (gras′rüts′) An idea that has grown from local support. (p. 154)

grid (grid′) A set of lines that cross one another to form squares or boxes. (p. 8)

hemisphere (hem′ə sfėr) Half of a ball, such as the *hemispheres* of the earth. (p. 7)

heritage (her′ət ij) A people's history and traditions that are passed from parent to child. (p. 31)

high technology (hī tek nol′ə jē) Scientific technology that involves the use of advanced devices such as computers. (p. 248)

House of Representatives (hous′əv rep′ri zent′ət ivz) A part of the legislative branch of government. (p. 168)

immigrant (im′i grənt) A person who has come from another country. (p. 136)

import (im′pōrt) 1. Product bought from other countries. 2. Buy goods from other countries. (p. 253)

income (in′kəm) The money that comes in to a person or business for work. (p. 229)

industrial (in dus′trē əl) Having to do with industry. (p. 147)

Glossary

industry (in′dəs trē) A manufacturing or business activity. (p. 56)

interdependence (int′er di pen′dəns) When all are affected by one another. (p. 37)

judicial (jů dish′əl) The branch of government that makes difficult decisions about how best to apply the laws. (p. 168)

justice (jus′təs) A judge on the Indiana Supreme Court or the United States Supreme Court. (p. 172)

keelboat (kēl′bōt) A wide boat that was pushed up river with a long pole but floated downriver. (p. 126)

landscape (land′skāp) A painting or other artwork that shows an area of land. (p. 212)

latitude (lat′ə tüd) Lines that go around the globe from east to west used to measure how far north or south a place is. (p. 9)

legislative (lej′ə slāt′iv) The branch of government that writes the laws. (p. 168)

legislature (lej′ə slā′chėr) A group of people elected to make and pass laws. (p. 106)

lean-to (lēn′tü) A three-sided shelter made from poles covered with bark and open on the fourth side. (p. 126)

legend (lej′ənd) **1.** Key to a map that explains its symbols. (p. 5) **2.** A story. (p. 71)

lieutenant governor (lü ten′ənt guv′ə nėr) The political leader who takes care of the governor's duties when the governor is out of the state; also serves as the president of the state senate. (p. 178)

livestock (līv′stok) Any of the animals raised on a farm, such as cattle. (p. 230)

longitude (lon′jə tüd) Lines that go around the globe from pole to pole used to measure distances east to west. (p. 9)

map (map) A flat but not exact model of the earth that shows the shapes and sizes of bodies of land and water, their relative directions, and the distances between them. (p. 3)

mayor (mā′ér) A chief executive who manages city affairs. (p. 181)

mayor-council system (mā′ér koun′sel sis′təm) A form of city government in which a council of people makes decisions about city policies, which are administered by the mayor or city manager. (p. 181)

megalopolis (meg′ə läp′ə ləs) Thickly populated area including many cities. (p. 38)

mill (mil′) A place where corn or other grains are ground into flour. (p. 129)

moraine (mə rān′) A ridge or big pile of materials left by a melted glacier. (p. 55)

national government (nash′ə nəl guv′érn mənt) Government for a whole country, such as for all fifty states. (p. 189)

nationality (nash′ə nal′ət ē) The country of a person's descent. (p. 34)

natural resource (nach′ə rəl rē′sôrs) Anything useful found on or in the earth. (p. 14)

noble (nō′bəl) Person of wealth and rank; an important citizen of a country. (p. 98)

North Pole (nôrth′pōl′) The point that is farthest north on the earth or a globe. The North Pole is 90°N. (p. 9)

Northwest Territory (nōrth west′ ter′ə tōr′ē) Area surrounded by the Great Lakes and Ohio and Mississippi rivers, including Ohio, Indiana, Illinois, Wisconsin, Michigan, and parts of Minnesota. (p. 103)

ordinance (ôrd′ən ənts) Type of law. (p. 104)

pewter (pyüt′ér) A soft silver-colored metal used to make eating utensils. (p. 127)

pioneer (pī ə nir′) A person who is part of the first group to settle a region. (p. 33)

plain (plān′) Land that is mostly flat. (p. 24)

polls (pōls′) Voting places. (p. 197)

population (päp yə lā′shən) The number of people living in an area. (p. 12)

portage (pōrt′ij) Travel by carrying a boat across land between rivers. (p. 83)

poultry (pōl′trē) Any of the birds raised on a farm for their meat or eggs. (p. 231)

precipitation (pri sip′ə tā′shən) Moisture that falls as rain, snow, or sleet. (p. 47)

preserve (pri zérv′) Save, as in preparing food for future use. (p. 128)

prime meridian (prīm′mə rid′ē ən) The starting point for lines of longitude. It is numbered 0°. (p. 9)

quarry (kwôr′ē) To dig out. (p. 59)

raw material (rô′mə tir′ē əl) A material in its natural condition used to make useful products. (p. 82)

reaper (rē′pər) Harvesting machine. (p. 144)

Glossary

277

refinery (ri fīn′ə rē) Place where raw material is changed into a useful form. (p. 150)

reform (ri fôrm′) Improvement. (p. 154)

region (rē′jən) An area of the world that is different from the areas around it, but whose parts are in some way alike. (p. 20)

register (rej′ə stėr) Sign up. (p. 197)

relief (ri lēf′) Showing differences in a surface, such as a *relief* map that shows where the land rises and slopes down. (p. 12)

representative (rep′ri zent′ət iv) Someone chosen to speak for others. (p. 122)

reservation (rez′ėr vā′shən) Areas of land where Indians were sent to live. (p. 29)

scale (skāl) The part of a map that shows the relationship between distance on the map and real distance on the earth. (p. 6)

sea level (sē′lev′əl) The height of the surface of the ocean. (p. 13)

seaport (sē′pōrt) A place where oceangoing ships are loaded and unloaded. (p. 18)

Senate (sen′ət) A part of the legislative branch of government. (p. 168)

service industry (ser′vəs in′dəs trē) An industry that does not involve manufacturing, providing services for people. (p. 235)

settlement (set′əl mənt) The first small community that settlers build when they come to a new area. (p. 84)

sharecropper (sher′krop ėr) A person who rents part of someone else's farm in exchange for a share of the harvest. (p. 144)

siege (sēj) A way of forcing those on the opposite side in a war to surrender by allowing no supplies to reach them. (p. 115)

silt (silt′) Fine soil carried or deposited by water, often found along a river. (p. 74)

slavery (slāv′ə rē) When people are owned by others and have no freedom. (p. 122)

slum (slum′) A poor, mostly rundown section of a city. (p. 152)

South Pole (south′pōl′) The point that is farthest south on the earth or a globe. The *South Pole* is 90°S. (p. 9)

Speaker of the House (spē′kėr əv thə hous′) Representative who runs sessions of the House of Representatives. (p. 184)

stockyard (stäk′yärd′) Where livestock are kept before they are slaughtered. (p. 37)

strike (strīk) When workers stop working to try to have their demands met. (p. 154)

surrender (sə ren′dėr) Give up, as to an enemy in battle. (p. 91)

surveyor (sėr vā′ėr) Someone who makes exact measurements of land. (p. 86)

symbol (sim′bəl) Something that stands for a real object or idea. (p. 5)

symbolize (sim′bə līz) To stand for something else. (p. 134)

tax (taks′) Money collected by a government to pay for its services. (p. 198)

technology (tek nol′ə jē) The use of tools, machinery, and scientific ideas. (p. 243)

temperate (tem′pə rət) A climate in which temperatures change within a wide range, but without being too cold or hot. (p. 46)

term (tėrm) A time in office. (p. 169)

tornado (tôr nād′ō) A storm with whirling winds and funnel-shaped clouds. (p. 47)

tournament (tùr′nə mənt) Series of games played to determine the best team. (p. 219)

township (toun′ship′) One of the six-mile square areas of land into which the Northwest Territory was divided. (p. 104)

toxic waste (tok′sik wāst) Dangerous chemicals from industries. (p. 249)

transport (trans′pôrt) Carry. (p. 56)

transportation (trans pėr tā′shən) The moving of people and goods. (p. 17)

treaty (trēt′ē) An agreement between two or more groups. (p. 112)

tributary (trib′yə ter′ē) A river or stream that flows into another, larger river. (p. 61)

trustee (trus′tē′) A manager of a township who takes care of its business. (p. 180)

Underground Railroad (un′dėr ground rāəl′rōd) A secret route slaves used to escape from the Southern states. (p. 141)

union (yün′yən) A group of workers formed to improve working conditions. (p. 153)

utopia (yù tō′pē ə) A community in which residents live apart from the rest of society and believe an ideal life is possible. (p. 133)

veto (vēt′ō) Reject a bill. (p. 170)

Index

The letter *m* stands for *map*.
The letter *g* stands for graph, chart, table, or diagram.

Index

Acknowledgments

Charts, Graphs, Diagrams, Time Lines: 48, 87, 94, 96, 105, 124–125, 139, 160, 169, 170–171, 173, 179, 187, 190–191, 200, 204, 222, 246, 256: Book Production Systems, Inc. 12, 202: Boston Graphics. 4: George Ulrich.

Illustrations: 30, 76: Judy Nostrant. 74, 83t, 84: Stephanie Pershing.

Maps: 31, 32, 45, 54, 61, 62, 67, 70, 81, 92, 103, 107, 108–109, 115, 116–117, 119, 146, 158, 192–193, 234, 237, 239, 251: Book Production Systems. 13, 15, 24–25, 258–259, 260–261, 262, 263: Donnelley Cartographic Services. 22: Leslie Evans. 5, 6, 8, 10, 18, 20, 21: Mapping Specialists. 4, 19: George Ulrich. 16: Alan Witschonke.

PHOTOGRAPHY

Table of Contents: iii: *t,* National Park Service; *b,* Devaney Stock Photos. iv: *t,* Collection of the Denver Art Museum; *b,* The Granger Collection, New York. v: *t,* Photo Courtesy Indianapolis Motor Speedway; *b,* Indiana State Senate. vi: *t,* ©Photographic Resources; *bl,* The Children's Museum of Indianapolis; *br,* Earth Scenes ©E.R. Degginger.

Social Studies Handbook: 3: Michael Heron/Monkmeyer. 14: Philip Jon Bailey. 17: North Wind Picture Archive.

Unit One: 22: *t,* Gary Irviny/TSW/Click, Chicago. 23: Junebug Clark/Photo Researchers. 26: *b,* Gary Irving/TSW/Click, Chicago; *t,* Paul Shambroom/Photo Researchers. 27: *l & r,* Grant Heilman. 28: Courtesy Vine Deloria. 29: The Granger Collection, New York. 33: The Bettmann Archive. 34: George R. Cassidy/Third Coast Stock Source. 35: The Bettmann Archive. 37: Historical Pictures Service, Chicago. 39: *t,* Alex McClean/Landslides; *overlay,* Wide World Photos. 40: Steve Vidler/Nawrocki Stock Photos. 41: MacDonald Photography/Third Coast Stock Source. 44: IMS, Photo by Linda McQueeney ©1989. 46: *t,* ©Frank Cezus/TSW/Click, Chicago; *b,* Devaney Stock Photos. 48: *t,* Hoosier National Forest; *inset,* The Bettmann Archive. 49: National Park Service. 52: National Park Service Photo, Richard Frear. 53: Photo courtesy Christine Livingston, Gary, IN. 55: *t inset,* Kirkendall/Spring; *b,* Bob & Ira Spring. 56: *l,* John R. Hill, Publications & Education Section, Indiana Geological Survey, Indiana Department of Natural Resources; *r,* Devaney Stock Photos. 57: *t & inset,* Courtesy of Armstrong Woodwinds, A Member Company of United Musical Instruments U.S.A., Inc.; *b,* ©Peter Pearson/TSW/Click, Chicago. 58: Indiana Division, Indiana State Library. 59: Indiana Department of Commerce. 60: ©Cathlyn Melloan/TSW/Click, Chicago. 63: Devaney Stock Photos. 66: ©Frank Oberle/Photographic Resources. 68t & overlay–69t & inset: Indiana Historical Society and Glenn A. Black Laboratory of Archaeology, Indiana University. 71: Richmond Newspapers, INC. 72: *t,* Collection of the Denver Art Museum; *b,* Cranbrook Institute of Science. 73: *t & b,* The Granger Collection, New York. 75: Rare Book and Manuscript Division, The New York Public Library, Astor, Lenox and Tilden Foundations. 80: Historic New Harmony, Indiana. 81, 82, 83b: The Granger Collection, New York. 85: *t,* Culver Pictures. 85b & 86t: The Granger Collection, New York. 86: *inset,* ©Frank Oberle/Photographic Resources. 88: The Granger Collection, New York. 89: The Bettmann Archive. 90: National Park Service. 91: *t,* The Granger Collection, New York; *b,* from *A Pictorial History of Indiana,* by Dwight W. Hoover, courtesy Dwight W. Hoover.

Unit Two: 96: ©1990 Indianapolis Museum of Art, Gift of a Couple of Old Hoosiers. 97: Chicago Historical Society. 98: Independence National Historical Park Collection. 99l, 99 inset, 100: The Granger Collection, New York. 101: Auburn-Cord-Dusenberg Museum, Auburn, IN, photos by Nicky Wright. 102: *l & r,* Culver Pictures; *c,* The Granger Collection, New York. 104: Chicago Historical Society. 106: *t & b,* The Granger Collection, New York. 110: National Park Service. 111 & 112: Culver Pictures. 113: *t,* The Granger Collection, New York; *b,* Culver Pictures. 114: *l&r,* Mississinewa Battlefield Society. 120: Historical Pictures Service, Chicago. 121: Brown Brothers. 122: *t & b,* Indiana State Museum, Corydon Capitol State Historic Site. 123: Indiana Division, Indiana State Library. 126: *t,* Lincoln Living Historical Farm, Lincoln Boyhood National Memorial, National Park Service. 126b–127: The Granger Collection, New York. 128: Animals Animals ©Perry D. Slocum. 129: Genealogy Department, Allen County Public Library, Ft. Wayne, Indiana. 130–131: Lewis Historical Collections Library, Vincennes University. 132–133 inset: Historic New Harmony, Indiana. 133: *t,* Joslyn Art Museum, Omaha, Nebraska. 134: Culver Pictures. 135: The Granger Collection, New York. 136: Courtesy of Tippecanoe County Historical Association's Collections. 137: *l & r,* Photographs by Bruce Harlan. 140: Archives & Special Collections, Bracken Library, Ball State University, Muncie, Indiana. 141, 142t, 142b: Levi Coffin House State Historic Site. 143: Indiana Division, Indiana State Library. 144–145b: The Granger Collection, New York. 145b: Culver Pictures. 147t & bl: The Bettmann Archive. 147br & 148–149: Culver Pictures. 150: USX Corporation. 151: Photo Courtesy Indianapolis Motor Speedway. 152: Calumet Regional Archives, Indiana University Northwest. 153: *t & b,* The Granger Collection, New York. 154–155: The Bettmann Archive. 156: Culver Pictures.

Unit Three: 160: From the Art Collection of The Boatmen's National Bank of St. Louis. 161: ©Cathy Melloan. 162: *l,* Copyrighted by the White House Historical Association, Photograph by National Geographic Society; *cl,* Colonial Williamsburg Foundation; *cr,* The Granger Collection, New York; *r,* John Trumbull, "Alexander Hamilton," copyright Yale University Art Gallery. 163: Virginia Museum of Fine Arts, Gift of Col. and Mrs. Edgar W. Garbisch. 164: *l,* The Granger Collection, New York; *r,* Colonial Williamsburg Foundation. 165: Wide World Photos. 166: Devaney Stock Photos. 167: *t & b,* Indiana Division of Tourism. 168: ©Peter Pearson/TSW/Click, Chicago. 172: *t & b,* Mike Roeder—Indianapolis. 174: Photo Courtesy of Charlotte Reeves. 175: *l,* Courtesy of Dorothy B. Bailey; *r,* Photo courtesy George Bredewater. 176: *l,* ©Frank Siteman/Photographic Resources; *c,* Indiana State Senate; *r,* Post-Tribune, Gary, Indiana. 177: Mike Roeder—Indianapolis. 178: Courtesy of Office of the Governor. 180: ©Brian Seed/TSW/Click, Chicago. 181: ©Peter Pearson/TSW/Click, Chicago. 182: Greg Persell, Indianapolis. 183: ©James Shaffer/PhotoEdit. 184: Indiana State Senate. 185: *l,* ©James Shaffer/PhotoEdit; *r,* Animals Animals ©H. Ausloos. 188: ©D. Klumpp/TIB-West. 189: ©TSW/Click, Chicago. 194: ©Henley & Savage/TSW/Click, Chicago. 195: *t,* ©Robert Kusel/TSW/Click, Chicago, *b,* The Granger Collection, New York. 196: UPI/Bettmann Newsphotos. 197: ©Robert E. Daemmrich/Photographic Resources. 198: ©Quiwta Scott/Photographic Resources. 199: Terry Duennes, Covington, KY.

Unit Four: 204: ©Cathy Melloan. 205: ©Frank Oberle/Photographic Resources. 206: Historical Pictures Service, Chicago. 207: *inset,* ©Marc PoKempner/TSW/Click, Chicago; *b,* ©Michael Beasley/TSW/Click, Chicago. 208: *l,* Zephyr Pictures; *r,* Earth Scenes ©E.R. Degginger. 209: *l,* Indiana Department of Commerce; *r,* Indiana Division of Tourism. 210: Indiana Division of Tourism. 211: Indianapolis Symphony Orchestra. 212t: ©1990 Indianapolis Museum of Art, James E. Roberts Fund. 212 bl, 212 br, 213: Wide World Photos. 214: *b & inset,* Jasper Desk, Courtesy Jasper Chamber of Commerce. 215: ©Photographic Resources. 216–217: The Children's Museum of Indianapolis. 218: UPI/Bettmann Newsphotos. 219: *t & inset,* Dave Zeller. 220: *t,* Notre Dame, Sports Information; *b,* The picture of the Heisman trophy has been provided through the courtesy of the Downtown Athletic Club of New York City, Inc., which is the owner of the federally registered service marks consisting of the Heisman Memorial Trophy, all its likeness, and the words "Heisman Memorial Trophy", "Heisman", and "Heisman Trophy Award", which collectively are sometimes referred to as the "Heisman Service Marks". 221: Indiana Division of Tourism. 223: *b,* Historical Pictures Service, Chicago; *t,* Johnny Appleseed Festival. 224: ©James P. Rowan/TSW/Click, Chicago. 225: Devaney Stock Photos. 228: Indiana Division of Tourism. 229: ©Photographic Resources. 230: *t,* ©Frank Cezus/TSW/Click, Chicago; *inset,* ©Frank Oberle/Photographic Resources. 231: *t,* ©Guy Gillette/Photo Researchers; *c,* Devaney Stock Photos. 231b & 232: ©Frank Oberle, Jr./Photographic Resources. 233: Devaney Stock Photos. 235: *b & inset,* Courtesy, Indianapolis Airport Authority. 236: *l,* Devaney Stock Photos; *c,* ©Melanie Carr/Zephyr Pictures; *b,* ©Photographic Resources. 240: The Children's Museum of Indianapolis. 241: ©Will/Deni McIntyre/Photo Researchers. 242: *t,* ©Thomas Styczynski/TSW/Click; *b,* ©Frank Cezus/TSW/Click, Chicago. 243: *t,* ©Photographic Resources; *b,* ©Cathlyn Melloan/TSW/Click, Chicago. 244: *t,* ©Cliff Feulner/TIB-West; *b,* ©Glennon P. Donahue/Photographic Resources. 245: ©F.B. Grunzweig/Photo Researchers. 247: ©Tom Ebenhoh/Photographic Resources. 248: *t,* ©TSW/Click, Chicago; *b,* Devaney Stock Photos. 249: Courtesy of RAP Communications Inc. and Reynolds Aluminum Recycling Company. 252: *l,* Courtesy the Trane Company; *r,* Courtesy Fujitsu Ten Corp. of America. 253: *l,* ©Frank Oberle/Photographic Resources; *r,* ©Terry Farmer/TSW/Click, Chicago; *b,* ©William Clark/TSW/Click, Chicago. 254: *l,* ©Glennon P. Donahue/Photographic Resources; *inset,* ©Tony Schanuel/Photographic Resources.